Baedekers

AA

PROVENCE/CÔTE D'AZUR

THE AUTOMOBILE ASSOCIATION

Imprint

98 colour photographs
38 maps, plans and diagrams and 1 large map

Editorial work: Baedeker Stuttgart

Text: Peter M. Nahm, Ostifildern and Dr Fritz Nohr, Lahnstein

Cartography: Gert Oberländer, Munich
Georg Schiffner, Lahr
Mairs Georgraphischer Verlag GmbH & Co. Ostfildern-Kemnat (large map)

Design and layout: Creativ GmbH, Ulrich Kolb, Stuttgart

General Direction:
Dr Peter Baumgarten, Baedeker Stuttgart

English Translation: Alec Court

Source of illustrations:
Stefan Baumgärtner (7), Bruguière (1), French National Tourist Office (8),
Historia-Photo (1), Principality of Monaco (1), Peter M. Nahm (63), Ursula Pfaffinger (14),
Ullstein (2), Hotel Vistaëro (1).

Following the tradition established by Karl Baedeker in 1844, sights of particular interest and hotels and restaurants of particular quality are distinguished by one or two asterisks.

To make it easier to locate the various sights listed in the A–Z section of the guide, their coordinates on the large map of Provence are shown in red at the head of each entry.

Only a selection of hotels and restaurants can be given, no reflection is implied, therefore, on establishments not included.

In a time of rapid change it is difficult to ensure that all the information given is entirely accurate and up to date and the possibility of error can never be entirely eliminated. Although the publishers can accept no responsibility for inaccuracies and omissions they are always grateful for corrections and suggestions for improvement.

Contents

Preface

This Pocket Guide to Provence/Côte d'Azur is one of the new generation of AA/Baedeker guides.

These pocket-size regional guides, illustrated throughout in colour, are designed to meet the needs of the modern traveller. They are quick and easy to consult, with the principal sights described in alphabetical order and practical details about opening times, how to get there, etc., shown in the margin.

Each guide is divided into three parts. The first part gives a general account of the area, its history, prominent personalities and so on; in the second part the principal sights are described; and the third part contains a variety of practical information designed to help visitors to find their way about and make the most of their stay.

The new guides are abundantly illustrated and contain numbers of newly drawn plans. In a pocket at the back of the book is a large area map, and each entry in the main part of the guide gives the coordinates of the square on the map in which the particular place is situated. Users of this guide, therefore, will have no difficulty in finding what they want to see.

Facts and Figures

General

Definition of Region

The expressions "Provence" and "Côte d'Azur", however familiar they may be, are politically and historically not easy to define. The regional name "Provence" comes from the Roman Provincia Gallia Narbonensis which was founded from 125 BC onwards after the conquest of what is present-day Southern France.

Subsequently the borders of Provence were frequently altered, and today it comprises the political region Rhône-Alpes-Côte d'Azur, one of the 22 Régions of France, the Départements of Alpe-de-Haute-Provence, Hautes-Alpes, Alpes-Maritimes, Bouches-du-Rhône, Var and Vaucluse. Surrounded by this territory on the Mediterranean coast is the independent Principality of Monaco.

Even the expression "Côte d'Azur" is difficult to define. It indicates the coastal strip between Cannes and the French-Italian frontier, but is generally applied to the whole French Riviera as far west as Marseilles.

The area described in this guidebook does not completely coincide with Provence as a political region. On the one hand it takes in the chief places of interest (Gorges de l'Ardèche, Nîmes, Montpellier, etc.) on the edge of the area, on the other hand it excludes the purely winter sports areas far to the north-east.

Scenic Formation

Provence, which comprises the south-east of the French mainland, is richly blessed with beauties and cultural monuments. Its wealth of scenic forms is determined by the differing geological formations. The coastal area between Cap Couronne in the west and Capo Mortola in the east is divided into four sections, that is the Côte à Calanques (Côte Bleue), the Côte des Maures (Côte Vermeille), the Côte de l'Esterel and the Côte d'Azur in its narrowest sense.

The Côte à Calanques (Côte Bleue=Blue Coast) forms the first section. With the Rade de Marseille (Roadsteads of Marseilles) and some offshore islands it is characterised by the Calanques, torturous coastal indentations which are difficult of access (the name comes from the Provençal calanco=falling steeply). The imposing coastal formation arose as a consequence of the combination of considerable sinking of the level of the sea and a simultaneous rise in the limestone heights.

The Côte des Maures begins near Hyères and is bounded in the east by the estuary of the River Argens. With its islands this coastal area has to be included with the mountains of the Département of Var, as is illustrated by the nature of the Massif des Maures, consisting of granite, gneiss, mica-schist and phyllite. Extensive bays with, in places, excellent beaches form the line of the coast and sometimes, for example near Toulon and St-Tropez, penetrate deeply inland.

The nature of the third section of this coast, the Côte de

◀ *Pont de Langlois in Arles, made famous by Vincent van Gogh*

l'Esterel between St-Raphaël and Cannes, is determined by the reddish-brown vulcanite of the Massif d'Esterel, the porphyry of which makes a charming colourful display with the blue of the sea and its numerous islands.

The actual Côte d'Azure (Azure=blue) begins to the east of the estuary of the Siagne; this coastline is characterised by the dipping of the sub-Alpine chain and the western Alps to the south into the Ligurian Sea. To the east beyond Cannes the coast rises in terraces; the Cap d'Antibes stands out impressively, and then there follows the estuarial area of the Var, the course of the river reveals clear tectonically limited boundaries. Bays and promontories, with the backdrop of mountain slopes like an amphitheatre, give the landscape its particular attraction which, however, is more and more becoming spoiled by development.

The coastal hinterland, comprising Haute-Provence and Basse-Provence, is bordered in the extreme west by the Crau (from Latin "cravus" or "campus lapideus"=stony field), once the delta of the Durance whose smooth pebbles had been washed down from the Alps. Originally dry, about 60 per cent of the area is now irrigated and used as pasture. The territory around the Etang de Berre, a lake of about 160 sq. km (62 sq. miles) in area but only up to 10 m (33 ft) deep, serves as a relief zone for Marseilles.

To the east lies a stratified region, consisting primarily of chalk, clay and conglomerates, the highest terrace of which forms part of the basin of Aix-en-Provence. To the east and south-east of Aix the mountain chains of Provence become more prominent. Examples are the steep slopes of the Montagne Ste-Victoire, the Montagne du Cengle, the Chaine de l'Etoille and the Chaine de la Ste-Baume. But even ranges such as the Chaine de l'Estaque between the Etang de Berre and the Golfe du Lion or the Montagne du Lubéron to the east of Avignon, consisting predominantly of Jurassic and cretaceous limestone, belong to the mountain system of the Pyrenees and Provence. The depression zone around Toulon – Cuers – Le Muy, with its extensive vineyards, separates these chains from the uplands of the coast.

The deposits of bauxite in the vicinity of Brignoles bear witness to the emergence of an upland zone from the inlet of the sea which once covered an extensive area of Provence. The products of a considerable weathering of laterite became accumulated in karstic hollows forming storage places for this basic material of aluminium production.

The river systems of the Durance and of the Verdon characterise the north of the hinterland. The Lower Valley of the Durance, between Avignon and Mirabeau, is broad and follows the Pyrenees–Provence axis. It has only a few tributaries and a relatively small gradient. North of Mirabeau there is an increase in gradient and in the number of tributaries, and the Durance turns towards the north-east.

The central reaches of the Verdon which is controlled by important flood-barriers is an exception. It has cut its bed into great Jurassic limestone banks, in parts like the Dolomites. This stretch, called the "Grand Canyon of the Verdon", with the deepest gorges in Europe, is an example of an ancient breach valley. Even the tributaries of the Verdon reveal an astonishing independence from the present structure of the land. North of the Lower Verdon stretches the Plain of Valensole, a hollow filled with huge mounds of gravel. South of the Grand Canyon du Verdon extend the undulating old karstic reliefs of the Grand Plan de Canjuers and the Plain of Comps.

The east of the hinterland is mainly formed by heavily fissured fold mountains of the Alpine foothills of Grasse, to which the Montagne du Thorenc, the Montagne du Cheiron and the Montagne de l'Audiberque also belong. The rivers, however, sometimes follow the north–south direction of the Maritime Alps to the east of the Var, as is shown by the example of the Loup. The highest point of the Maritime Alps, the Cime dell'Argentera (3297 m (10,821 ft)) is actually in Italy.

The waters around the Mediterranean coast (Golfe du Lion, Ligurian Sea), are relatively warm; because of latitude, evaporation and salt content are relatively high. Even at quite great depths the temperature is rarely below 13 °C (55 °F). The surface temperature in winter ranges between 10 and 13 °C (50 and 55 °F) and in summer can reach 25 °C (77 °F).

High and low tides have a difference of only 25 cm (10 in), but the waves are frequently subject to fluctuation; quite often strong air currents cause short-lived but violent waves which can be dangerous to swimmers. Unfortunately the quality of the

France
_____ **Boundaries of Régions**
_____ **Boundaries of Départements**

Provence and the Côte d'Azur are among the most visited holiday areas of France.

Early summer in High Provence

sea-water in several places leaves much to be desired. Sewage from coastal settlements, pollution of the rivers and garbage from ships have recently necessitated regular monitoring of rivers, bacteriological control and the setting up of a warning service when excessive pollution is threatened.

The beaches vary in nature, depending on the one hand on the sea currents, and on the other hand on the morphology of the coasts. Long-standing touristic centres such as Monaco and Nice have partly rocky coasts and very coarse sand, while more modern resorts, for example St-Tropez and Hyères, can offer spacious beaches with fine sand. The sub-marine land formations have naturally the same geological structure as the coast. Steep shelving, shallows and precipitous rock formations require constant vigilance from those in boats. There are excellent opportunities for experienced sub-aqua sportsmen and sportswomen.

Climate

Coastal Area

Most of the built-up areas near the coast are extraordinarily well favoured from the point of view of climate. Although the annual precipitation is between 550 and 820 mm (22 and 32 in) and is, therefore, not very different from that in northern regions, the annual sunshine total amounts to about 3000 hours. In the east especially, where the mountains rise like an amphitheatre and the slopes are exposed to the sun for the whole of the day, cool north winds are kept at bay. In the west the Mistral occasionally makes its unpleasant presence felt. For the coastal area favourable pressure distribution provides clear sunny days with fresh winds and predominantly dry air in winter. In this season average day temperatures of 6–12 °C (42–57 °F) are reached; maximum temperatures are 2–4 °C (4–11 °F) higher, corresponding approximately to conditions to the south of Rome. Frost and snow are rare on the coast. The windiest month is March which is also rainy; April and May are the most suitable months for a health cure. Summer is not too hot (July average 24 °C (75 °F)). Sultry weather and storms are rare in the vicinity of the coast, but there is a considerable drop in temperature at night and at times heavy dew. Moderate rainfall occurs mainly in autumn and it is almost possible to talk of a rainy season in October (maximum 97 mm (3.8 in)) and November. Precipitation and the frequency of frost increase in relation to altitude and topography.

Climatic conditions in the more northerly upland mountain areas are quite different, as a continental type of climate competes more strongly with the moderating influence of the sea. In this region precipitation occurs throughout the year, without noticeable maxima in spring or autumn. In the higher parts the snow lies for quite a long time; in the high Alpine regions generally excellent conditions for winter sports prevail. Even in the summer months cool "climatic islands" occur here.

Upland Region

The Mistral, a notorious wind, which hurls itself down the Rhône Valley and roars over Provence, occurs when there is low pressure over the Golfe du Lion and simultaneous high pressure over the Massif Central. The constriction of the air currents between the latter and the Alps causes, by means of a kind of jet effect, high wind speeds. At the same time low-pressure areas which are caused by solar heat rising from the North African shotts – saline depressions – and the flat expanses of sandy desert, contribute to causing localised Mistrals. The Mistral generally blows in periods of from three to ten days, normally beginning about 10 a.m. and lasting until sunset. When such a period comes to an end several pleasant days without any wind follow.

Mistral

Flora and Fauna (Plants and Animals)

As a consequence of the favourable Mediterranen climate the flora is exceptionally varied. Silver-grey olive trees, which are found everywhere on the slopes up to 500 m (1640 ft) and more above sea-level, orange and lemon plantations, vines, palms, cypresses, pines, aloes, agaves, cacti and many more are now taken for granted as typical plants of the Côte d'Azur, but were in some cases brought here from various other countries in Roman times.
Of the original vegetation which has suffered from human intrusion as well as catastrophic fires in forest and plain, pines take a leading place (Aleppo, maritime, stone and northern pines), in addition there are holm, kermes and cork-oaks, hornbeam and sweet chestnut. The principal plant of the Garrigue (in Provençal Garoulia), a special form of the maquis (undergrowth of hard-leafed evergreens, bushes, shrubs, etc.), is the kermes oak. The outer surface of its leaves are thickened and covered with a wax layer, and the underside is protected

Flora

with a felty coating and this prevents evaporation occurring too quickly.

The large number of sweetly scented bushes and herbs (lavender, rosemary, thyme, cistus, etc.) is striking. Edible fungi often occur in the forests, particularly truffles in Vaucluse which are tracked down with the help of trained dogs. The flowers of the Riviera have become a legend, the intensive cultivation of cut flowers such as mimosa for export (in winter) or of sweet-smelling blossoms (violets, roses, lavender, oranges, etc.) for perfume production plays an important role in the economy, particularly in the vicinity of Grasse.

Fauna

For climatic reasons, larger wild mammals tend to be restricted to sub-alpine Provence. Nearer the coast, smaller species are seen infrequently. Thrushes and other song-birds, quails, pheasants, partridges, hares, roebuck, chamois, trout, white-fish, river crabs are much sought after outside the few protected zones. In terrain which is difficult to reach there are usually large numbers of reptiles (tortoises, lizards, geckos, adders, vipers – only above 1000 m, etc.) and insects.

Local seafood which is particularly popular includes mussels, prawns, cuttlefish, John Dory, sea-eels, perch, bream, barbel and roach.

Economy

General

The natural potential of Provence has led to land development which is characterised on the one hand by agriculture, forestry and fishery (the last named partly in decline), and on the other hand, by reason of a rapid development of industry, mining, energy production and tourism, a heavy concentration of population and the urbanisation of entire stretches of the coast.

Water Exploitation

A decisive factor in the provision of water is the landform with its deeply incised valleys, especially in the catchment area of the Durance. The numerous dams and canals leading to the south are not only used to generate electricity, but also to control the water-supply by holding back floodwater, thus creating a reserve for periods of drought, irrigation (for example in the Crau) and providing a supply of drinking-water. The waters of the larger rivers, especially the Rhône, are used for cooling the reactors in nuclear fuel plants.

Mining

A not unimportant role is played by bauxite-mining in the vicinity of Brignoles (about 70 per cent of the whole French supply); this supply is important for the industrial area of Marseilles. Of regional importance is the limestone and cement industry between Marseilles and Cassis. Productive salt-pans are located in the area of the Etang de Berre and near Hyères and Giens.

Industry

The favourable geographical situation of the coastal area is of extreme economic importance. Marseilles, at the "gateway to Africa and the East" has become a first-class industrial and commercial centre, and the zone of the Etang de Berre is a major petro-chemical Europort. An annual turnover of about 100 million tonnes (about 90 per cent of the imports consists of oil) makes the port of Marseilles one of the largest in Europe. With an annual refining capacity of 40 million tonnes, this industrial zone holds second place in France (a pipeline from Fos to Karlsruhe in Germany is 782 km (486 miles) long). As well as large complexes of the chemical and petro-chemical industries, there are also aluminium works which produce about 85 per cent of the total output. In addition there are large iron and steel plants, aircraft and engineering works and shipyards. Another important branch of the economy is the food industry (sugar, bread, cakes and pastries, jams, milling and abattoirs).

In addition to Marseilles, Toulon is also notable as a regional economic centre, owing to its natural advantages as a military and commercial port.

Agriculture and forestry have great importance as suppliers of basic materials. In the mountainous regions near the coast supplies of timber (olive, oak, beech and erica arborea=brier roots, especially for pipes) are much in demand. The production of olive oil and cork play a somewhat diminishing agricultural role. Between Toulon and Menton some 8000 specialist firms are engaged in the growing of flowers (principally under glass). The blossoms are used for the production of perfume and ethereal oils. Extensive vegetable- and fruit-growing as well as numerous vineyards are principally to be found in the fertile valleys of the hinterland but also on the artificially irrigated fields of the Crau. The products are not only valuable for the local food and canning industry but are also exported. The less fertile land (the gravelly areas of the Durance karst and the high terrain of the Alpine foothills) serves either as pasture or for growing fodder for cattle and sheep. Increasing demand for veal in the tourist centres has led to a considerable increase in the rearing of cattle. Flocks of sheep are pastured everywhere between the Crau and the Maritime Alps. The main source of income for the farmers on the plateau between the Durance and the coast is the harvesting of lavender, together with a small amount of cereals and hay.

Agriculture

Fishing both on the sea and in inland waters only plays a subordinate commercial role today. On the other hand inshore fishing and fishing on the high seas is of increasing popularity among tourists.

Fishing

The centre of the highly developed and traditional perfume industry is the little town of Grasse and the countryside around it. Here more than 30 large concerns annually produce several million kilograms of flower blossoms (orange, rose, jasmine, thyme, rosemary, mignonette, violet, etc.). There are also undertakings producing synthetic perfume and these are gaining in importance. The distillation of lavender is primarily confined to the catchment area of the Verdon, where almost 80 per cent of the world's lavender oil is produced.

Perfume Industry

Already in the first half of the 18th c. the great beauty and mild climate of this coastal region was talked about in circles where people could indulge in journeys for pleasure and recuperation. At first it was the wealthy English, who overwintered first in Nice and later also in Cannes. Nice, the climate of which was found to be very healthy, became fashionable as a health resort. War and revolution caused a considerable reduction in the already burgeoning tourism, but the Côte d'Azur experienced a considerable rise in prosperity in the 19th c., not least through

Tourism

Colourful publicity for Provençal flower-essences

the building of railway lines and roads. The pattern of settlement was considerably altered when promenades along the shore, splendid gardens, luxury villas and well-appointed inns were built, and there arose here an attractive winter health resort area of international status. Cannes, Nice, Monaco and Menton were the resorts preferred by the European aristocracy. The First World War brought another crisis. However, through skilful advertising wealthy people from all over the world were attracted to Provence for holidays or for their health. After 1930 new settlements on coast and beaches grew up, dependencies of villages situated farther inland, and this relieved pressure on the older seaside resorts, while their beaches attracted more summer visitors. From the original health resorts, which were visited only in winter, there arose a holiday area with visitors all the year round, and with summer as the high season.

The favourable climatic conditions, the beauty of the coasts with their bays and sandy shores, convenient sites for building and the relative proximity of the winter sports area resulted after the Second World War in the development of a tourist region which has few equals and which fulfils the requirements of today's visitors. In the wake of modern mass tourism there succeeded hectic building of hotels, holiday colonies, second homes, marinas, camp sites and leisure complexes. The coast has excellent communications and is accessible by land, sea and air. The mountainous hinterland of Haute Provence is not so easily accessible, and here the main lines of communication follow the river valleys.

With the increase in local holiday traffic, difficulties have arisen, including bottlenecks on roads, pollution and shortage of accommodation. There has also been a considerable increase

in criminal activity (theft, stealing from vehicles, "mugging").
Recently, in addition to local and holiday tourism, business
meetings and congresses have contributed to the growth of the
tourist industry. Cannes, Nice and Monte Carlo in particular
have made great efforts to stage various events – fairs, festivals
and congresses – and the international airport Nice-Côte
d'Azur has been of great service in this respect.

Famous People

The mathematician and physicist André-Marie Ampère, born in
Lyon, did fundamental work in the development of natural
science. He developed a theory of electro-magnetism, built an
electro-telegraph and discovered the direction of circulation of
a magnetic field surrounded by a conductor through which the
current was flowing. Even today the measure of the strength of
a current is named after him. Ampère died at the age of 61 in
Marseilles.

André-Marie Ampère
(22.1.1775–10.6.1836)

Paul Cézanne, born in Aix-en-Provence, came to painting after
studying law for a short time. At first he modelled himself on
classic masters, then through Camille Pissarro turned to the
group of Impressionists. The novelty of this form of art was
working in the open air outside the studio. From his words "La
réflection modifie la vision" ("Contemplation alters what one
sees") he is counted as one of the forerunners of modern art.

Paul Cézanne
(19.1.1839–22.10.1906)

Marc Chagall, born in Vitebsk (White Russia), studied at the
Petersburg Academy of Art and then lived in Paris from 1910 to
1914; in 1923 he went back to the Soviet Union, but finally
turned his back on his homeland. After another period in France
he lived from 1941 to 1964 in the USA but then in St-Paul-de-
Vence. To a great extent his work has roots in the Jewish
tradition of the East. As well as a great number of paintings he
did book illustrations and also stained-glass work.

Marc Chagall
(7.7.1887–28.3.1985)

Alphonse Daudet first saw the light of day in Nîmes, but spent
his youth in Lyon. In 1860 he obtained the post of Private
Secretary to the Duke of Morny, through whose patronage he
gained entrée to interesting literary circles and thus acquired
the basis for a commercially successful career in writing.
Provence plays a great part in his works; the windmill near
Arles, where he was supposed to have written the "Lettres de
mon Moulin", though he never lived there, is today a leading
French tourist attraction. He created the well-known figure of
Tartarin of Tarascon an ironically-drawn Frenchman of the
south on whom the ever-present discrepancy between fantasy
and reality plays many tricks.

Alphonse Daudet
(13.5.1840–16.12.1897)

His early artistic work was typified by melancholy which he had
experienced in the workers' settlements of the Borinage, the
Belgian industrial area. When he joined his brother Theo in
Paris Vincent van Gogh's style of painting changed. He was
completely overcome by the intensity of light and colour when
he went to live in Arles (1888). With vehement energy he
painted picture after picture, even when the first signs of an

Vincent van Gogh
(30.3.1853–29.7.1890)

17

imminent mental illness were making themselves felt. On 29 July 1890 Vincent van Gogh took his own life.

Henri Matisse
(31.12.1869–3.11.1954)

In his early days as an artist Matisse belonged to the school of Impressionism. Then he changed to become one of the most important artists to overcome the direction into which this style was leading; his paintings became more two-dimensional and more intensive in colour. Matisse and the painters of his circle were first disparagingly called "Les Fauves" ("The Wild Ones"). Fauvism preferred to compose pictures with large expanses of colour, abstaining from the delicate shades of Impressionism, and the effect was obtained only by colour and contrast.

Darius Milhaud
(4.9.1892–22.6.1972)

The composer Darius Milhaud who was born in Aix-en-Provence and was a pupil of the famous Conservatoire de Paris, belongs to the Groupe des Six, which included Arthur Honegger; the group had been formed in 1918 and its aim was to give new life to contemporary music. Milhaud was an extraordinarily prolific composer; his works include operas ("Christophe Colomb", "Medée", etc.), ballet music, opera, symphonies and chamber music. From 1947 until 1962 he gave lessons in composition at the Paris Conservatoire.

Frédéric Mistral
(8.9.1830–25.3.1914)

Frédéric Mistral was born in Maillane, not far north of St-Rémy, the son of a farmer. The impetus for his literary work and his enthusiasm for the sonorous Provençal dialect came from his earlier acquaintance with Joseph Roumanille who was 12 years his senior. In 1859 appeared the first of the major works of Mistral, the novel "Mirèio" (in French "Mireille").
Mistral (the name is not a pseudonym!) is the most important innovator of the Provençal language and its poetry. With Théodore Aubanel and Joseph Roumanille he founded in 1854 the group of the Félibres, the members of which devoted themselves totally to this revival. Their work and aims are still highly esteemed in Provence. In 1904 Mistral received the Nobel Prize for Literature.

Nostradamus
(Michel de Nostre-Dame),
14.12.1503–2.7.1566)

Michel de Nostre-Dame was born in St-Rémy-de-Provence. After studying medicine he became the Personal Physician of Charles IX of France. Like many humanists he Latinised his name and henceforth called himself Nostradamus. Considerable success in treating patients in several epidemics led him into disfavour with his colleagues and he was compelled to go into hiding. At this time there began his intensive preoccupation with astrological and cosmological subjects. From his observation of the constellations he drew conclusions which he set down in his sombre esoteric prophecies. This work which is in rhyme and is called "The Centuries" appeared in Lyon in 1555. It aroused enormous interest and continued to exert influence in later centuries.

Gérard Philipe
(4.12.1922–25.11.1959)

The actor Gérard Philipe, born in Cannes, lived only for 37 years. Better known than his stage appearances were the films in which he appeared abroad ("Fanfan la Tulipe", "Le Diable au Corps", etc.). He is buried in the upland village of Ramatuelle near St-Tropez.

Pablo Picasso
25.10.1885–8.4.1973)

Spanish by birth and French by choice Pablo Picasso is considered the greatest modern genuis of pure art. His early

André-Marie Ampère

Frédéric Mistral

Nostradamus

works reveal the influence of Impressionism but about 1907 he turned towards Cubism. However, few of his pictures are abstract. Among his representational work there are not only paintings, but also individual graphics (drawings, etching, lithographs) and book illustrations. His activity with ceramics was extremely fruitful and led in part to Surrealistic works. A centre of his creativity was the pottery village of Vallauris near Cannes which even today lives to a great extent on Picasso's reputation and where, on the market place, one can see his bronze sculpture "Man with a Sheep".

History

First signs of human life (cave finds at Baoussé-Roussé near Menton).	300,000 BC
Stone Age culture, decorated and painted pottery; cave-dwellings, burial-grounds (finds at Roquepertuse near Velaux).	4000–3000
Ligurians take the coastal area and set up strongpoints; development of modest trade along the Riviera.	about 800
Greeks from Phocaea in Asia Minor found the port of Massalia, later Marseilles.	about 600
Further Greek settlements on the coast, increasing clashes with the Celto-Ligurian population.	600–100
Roman incursions into the present-day area of Provence: Provincia Gallia Narbonensis.	150–50 BC
The Teutons suffer a devastating defeat near the Montagne Ste-Victoire by Marius.	104–102 BC

History

50/49 BC	Julius Caesar conquers Massalia (Latin Massilia).
BC/AD	Various magnificent buildings of the Imperial Age appear (victory monument near La Turbie and triumphal arch in Cavaillon).
2nd c. AD	Extension of the Gallo-Roman towns and the first beginnings of Christianity.
3rd c. AD	Arrival of nomadic peoples.
4th–5th c.	Christianity gains in importance; coffins are produced in Marseilles and the Church of St-Victor is built.

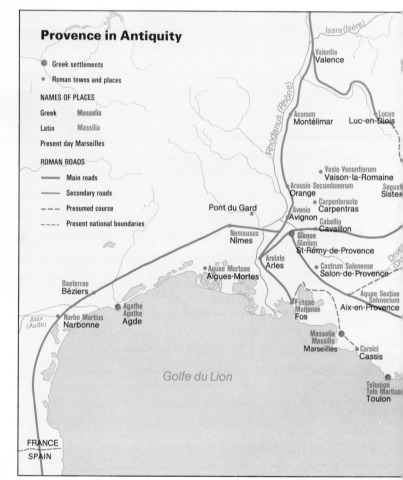

Provence in Antiquity

● Greek settlements

● Roman towns and places

NAMES OF PLACES

Greek   Massalia

Latin   Massilia

Present day Marseilles

ROMAN ROADS

—— Main roads

—— Secondary roads

--- Presumed course

---- Present national boundaries

Isara (Isère)

Rhodanus (Rhone)

Valentia / Valence

Acunum / Montélimar

Lucus / Luc-en-Diois

Vasio Vocontiorum / Vaison-la-Romaine

Arausio Secundanorum / Orange

Segust / Sister

Carpentoracte / Carpentras

Pont du Gard

Avenio / Avignon

Cabellio / Cavaillon

Nemausus / Nîmes

Glanon / Glanum / St-Rémy-de-Provence

Drue / (D)

Aguae Mortuae / Aigues-Mortes

Arelate / Arles

Castrum Salonense / Salon-de-Provence

Baeterrae / Béziers

Fossae Marianae / Fos

Aquae Sextiae Saluvorium / Aix-en-Provence

Atax (Aude)

Narbo Martius / Narbonne

Agathe / Agde

Massalia / Massilia / Marseilles

Carsici / Cassis

Golfe du Lion

Telunion / Telo Martius / Toulon

FRANCE

SPAIN

The Riviera passes into the control of the East Goths.	510
The Franks gain the ascendancy.	536
Normans and Saracens attack the coastal area; the emergence of many refuge settlements (villages perchés). Building of baptisteries (baptismal churches).	7th–8th c.
Charles Martel defeats the Saracens and invades Provence.	714–741
Charlemagne brings peace to the region, ruling through counts and bishops.	768–814

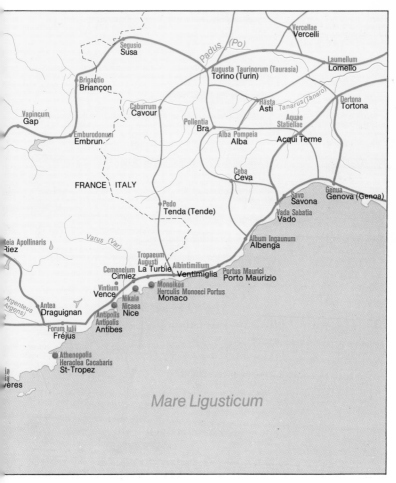

History

879	After the break up of the Frankish Kingdom, the Duke of Boson proclaims himself King of Provence.
9th c.	Spasmodic incursions by the Saracens who settle in the Massif des Maures.
11th c.	First Romanesque church building.
12th c.	Flowering of the ports as a consequence of the Crusades.
1112	The Dukes of Barcelona assume the sovereignty.
1175	Founding of Silvacane Abbey.
1246	Charles of Anjou becomes Duke of Provence by marriage.
12th–14th c.	Flourishing of Courtly poetry (troubadours), especially at the Court of the Dukes of Les Baux.
1308	The Grimaldi family from Genoa purchases the estates of Monaco.
1309–77	Avignon is the Papal residence.
1348	Countess Jeanne (also Queen of Naples) sells Avignon to the Pope.
1388	Nice is incorporated in the Dukedom of Savoy.
1434–80	Flowering of the province under René of Anjou ("Good King René").
1486	After the Council of Aix, Provence is united with the French Kingdom.
1524	Building of the Château d'If on the island of Marseilles.
1536	Charles V penetrates into Provence.
1545	More than 3000 Huguenots and other Protestants are put to death in the Lubéron Mountains.
1580–95	Marseilles develops into an important trading centre.
1629	Great epidemic of plague.
1635	Louis XIV makes Toulon a naval port.
1658–61	After uprisings Marseilles is subjected to the central power of Louis XIV.
1691	The French take over Nice.
1710	Prince Eugen of Savoy advances to the Riviera.
1720–22	Years of severe plague.
1715–50	Flowering of the art of faience in Moustiers-Ste-Marie and Marseilles.
1789	French Revolution; scenes of violence in many Provençal towns.

Siege of Toulon by the young Bonaparte; Nice annexed by French.	1793
Napoleon proceeds via Antibes in the direction of Paris on the route which was later called the "Route Napoléon".	1815
The painter Paul Cézanne is born in Aix-en-Provence.	1839
Piedmont-Sardinia cedes the Maritime Alps to France (alteration of the French eastern border).	1860
German troops occupy the Riviera; in Toulon the French fleet is scuttled.	1942
Within the framework of the invasion strategy which has been proceeding since the beginning of June in Normandy, in mid August enormously strong Allied forces land on the Côte des Maures. With the support of the Resistance they take Toulon, Marseilles and Nice.	1944
Italy cedes the territory of Col de Tende to France.	1947
The town of Fréjus is stricken by a catastrophic flood caused by a breach in the Malpasset Dam.	1959
The airport Nice-Côte d'Azur is opened and quickly becomes of more than regional importance.	1962
The painter Pablo Picasso is buried in Vauvenargues.	1973
A new policy of decentralisation begins under the newly elected President François Mitterrand; the aim is to bring more independence to the political Regions.	1981
Huge forest fires destroy almost the entire stock of trees, especially in the Esterel Mountains.	1982

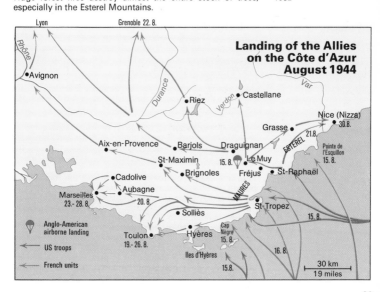

Landing of the Allies on the Côte d'Azur August 1944

23

History of Art

Pre- and Early History

The first monuments of significance date from the time of pre-and early history; these include the finds from the Sanctuary of Roquepertuse near Velaux, from the Oppidum of Entremont near Aix-en-Provence and from Cavaillon near Avignon. 46,000 Bronze Age rock carvings are open to the skies in the Val des Merreilles above Tende.

About 600 BC Greeks from Phocaea bring the first breath of free Classical Mediterranean culture to the Riviera with the founding of Massalia (Marseilles). There are also traces of settlement in Antibes, Nice and the well-preserved wall at St-Blaise.

Roman times

There are many remains of the Roman era including the arena and baths of Cimiez (part of Nice), fine granite pillars in Riez, the remains of the settlements of Glanum and St-Rémy, five remaining monuments in Arles, the arena and port of Fréjus, the great monument near La Turbie, the triumphal arches in Orange, Carpentras and Cavaillon and the temple near Vernègues. There are many more examples of theatres, amphitheatres in Nîmes, Orange, Vaison. There is the incomparable Pont du Gard, the mill at Barbegal, aqueducts and bridges.

Ancient Christendom

From the Early Christian period and the Carolingian era dates remarkable round buildings (baptisteries), which can still be admired today in Fréjus, Aix-en-Provence, Venasque and Riez. The Church of St-Victor in Marseilles is one of the most important monuments of this epoch.

Romanesque

In the 12th c. architecture in this region experiences a considerable uplift, which manifests itself particularly in secular building in the Romanesque-Provençal style. Under the influence of the Cistercians there arise churches in uncomplicated forms with simple façades and plain interiors, generally with a single aisle; the square bell-towers reveal the influence of Lombardy. The best-known buildings of this period are the cathedrals at Aix-en-Provence and Avignon and the abbeys of Sénanque, Thoronet and Silvacane.

Gothic

French Gothic which is influenced by mysticism reaches its zenith in Avignon with the Church of St-Pierre and the famous Papal Palace. Other leading buildings of this time are the Basilica of St-Maximin and the cathedrals of Fréjus and Grasse.

Renaissance

Few architectural monuments remain from the Renaissance but, on the other hand, it left a legacy of very many paintings, most of which were done during the Regency of René of Anjou. The most important example is the "Maria in the Burning Bush" by Nicolas Froment in the Cathedral of Aix-en-Provence.

Inspired by the Italian Renaissance, a remarkable school of painting flourished in Nice, the head of which, Louis Bréa (about 1440 to 1523) is considered the "Fra Angelico of Provence". Works of the school of Bréa, which are charac-terised by a naïve purity and simplicity, are to be found in numerous rural churches of south-eastern Provence.

During the time in which Baroque art was gaining momentum, above all in Italy and Germany, Classicism was developing in France. This movement consciously and intentionally dissociates itself from the Baroque, and in essence also preserves a greater formal strictness and discipline. Yet in south-eastern France the influence of the Italian view of art cannot be ignored and here one can confidently speak of Baroque art.
The most prominent examples of this form of art are to be found in the old town of Aix-en-Provence; as a single work the Pavillon de Vendôme, a little outside the town, is outstanding. Also belonging to this period is the good ceramic work of Moustiers-Ste-Marie. Definitely influenced by Baroque was the Marseilles painter and architect Pierre Puget (1620–94), who was at the same time probably the most important French sculptor of the 17th c.; as well as many other striking sculptures he created the caryatides on the portal of the old Town Hall of Toulon.

18th c. Classicism is reflected in the works of Van Loo and Fragonard. Their favourite themes are landscapes bathed in light and blossoming gardens; works by both painters can be seen in the art museums of Grasse and Nice.

Classicism

In the 19th c. an architectural style based on neo-Romanesque-Byzantine historical models is widespread. A shining example is the Church of Notre-Dame-de-la-Victoire in St-Raphaël and another the Church of Notre-Dame-de-la-Garde in Marseilles which can be seen from a long way off.

Neo-Romanesque

More and more artists of more modern and contemporary painting have been attracted to the Riviera since the end of the 19th c. Impressionists, the master of whom is Cézanne, born in Aix-en-Provence, include Berthe Morisot who painted in Nice, Monet in Antibes and Renoir in Cagnes. In 1892 Signac, an exponent of Pointillism, chose St-Tropez as his domicile and brought others, including Bonnard and Matisse, with him. The reaction in the form of Fauvism was principally represented by Dufy and Matisse who were later resident in Nice. Picasso, one of the initiators of Cubism, spent his time principally in Vallauris, Cannes and Mougins. The Cubist Léger was active in Biot, the Surrealist Chagall found in Vence themes for his colourful dream pictures. Other famous artists lived and worked on the Riviera including Braque in St-Paul-de-Vence, Kandinsky in La Napoule, Cocteau in Menton and Van Dongen in Cannes. Their works can be seen in many local museums.
The Cité Radieuse (Radiant City), built by Le Corbusier between 1947 and 1952 in Marseilles, is an impressive example of contemporary architecture, with modern marinas and leisure and residential layouts, such as Port-Grimaud and Port-Camargue; and here also should be mentioned the important art centre, Fondation Maeght in St-Paul-de-Vence.

19th and 20th c.

Villages Perchés

In addition to the long line of scarcely distinguishable coastal sectors, bays, capes and villages with exceptionally picturesque land- and townscapes and the many interesting little ports along the Côte d'Azur, as well as the old towns of the hinterland, the numerous so-called "villages perchés" deserve a mention. These are hill settlements, also known as "Nids d'Aigle" (literally eagles' nests), situated on the hilltops, slopes, outcrops, ridges or terraces, and which were once used as refuges against foreign incursors or would-be conquerors, especially those threatening attack from the sea. They are situated relatively close to the coast but in places which are difficult of access. Lack of space compelled the inhabitants to build their houses on the smallest possible piece of ground, as close together as possible and frequently intermingled. Although these hill villages are being abandoned by more and more of their inhabitants, largely on account of difficulty of access and quite often a lack of drinking-water, nevertheless they are popular as a place to stay with artists and Bohemians.

Language of Provence

Provençal, which is widely spoken in south-eastern France, has considerable differences from classical French. It is known as "langue d'oc" ("oc" being the word which was originally used for "yes") throughout southern France, whereas in the rest of the country the word was "oil" and French spoken elsewhere was called "la langue d'oil".

Like all living Romance languages, Provençal was derived from vulgar Latin, which had penetrated into the country with Roman colonisation. In Provence about the year 1000 this dialect was the basis of the language of the troubadours and of Courtly poetry, a trend which was to be paralleled in German-speaking countries with the Minnesänger. This old Provençal was basically an artificial language. From the 13th c. the concept of "Proensal" gained currency at the expense of the former idiom known as "Lenga Romana". In subsequent centuries although Provençal was still being used as a spoken language, it was surpassed in written French, and more particularly in the field of literature, by "classical" French which had developed from the northern French tongue, the so-called "langue d'oil".

It is certainly no accident that at the time when nation-states were beginning to come into being, that is in the first half of the 18th c., there arose in Provence a new awareness of its own history and a new assessment of its own language. in 1854 the Association of Félibres was founded, a group of poets of whom Frédéric Mistral was the most important. One of the principal contributions of the Provençal renaissance of that year was the comprehensive stock-taking of the linguistic heritage of the south of France. The conscious nurture of the "Langue d'Oc" and the pride of the people of southern France in belonging to the area where it is spoken, are now increasingly apparent.

Basically Provençal differs from standard French through the richness of its vowels. Whereas in classical French unstressed vowels tend to become reduced to a voiceless "e" or in some cases to disappear altogether, Provençal still makes use of the whole range of vowels. The chief characteristics are the maintaining of "a" in an open syllable (Provençal "pra" = French "pré"), the mutation of this "a" to "ié" (Provençal "marchié" – from the Latin "mercatus"), the distinction of four final vowels (a, e, i, o; Provençal a, e; French e), the "o" ending of the first person of the verb, the regional distinction between Nominative and Accusative and the shaping of certain sounds. There are, of course, unusual features in the vocabulary, both in the stock of words and in meaning.

Recommended Routes

Those who follow the complete route described below and who want to have sufficient time to visit the principal points of interest, must allow about four weeks for the itinerary (including, thanks to convenient and fast motorways, getting to the area). Even when the detours are omitted, the whole tour will still take three weeks.

Timetable

Places which are included in the A–Z section under a main heading appear below in **bold type**. All the places mentioned, whether they are under main headings or are places in the vicinity of the former, are included in the Index (p. 232).
The visitor from Great Britain who travels in his own vehicle, should allow some two to three days for the outward journey, even if using fast – and often expensive – motorways. Visitors travelling by air or rail will find adequate car hire facilities in the major centres (see Practical Information – Car Hire).

Note

The area covered in this guide is entered at **Montélimar** in the Rhône Valley. From here the visitor should not take the motorway to the east of the river but take the RN86 which runs parallel to the Rhône. To the south the imposing dam of **Donzère-Mondragon** is reached.

Main Itinerary

From here a worthwhile day tour runs east to the elevated township of **Grignan**, where there once lived the Marquise de Sévigné, well known for her published letters.

Excursion

Still going south, just before Pont St-Esprit, a turning to the west leads to a very rewarding circular tour through the Gorge of the **Ardèche**.

Soon the main route reaches **Marcoule**, well known for its nuclear power station. Not far to the south the route, now following a country road, crosses the Rhône and comes to **Orange**. The visitor who wishes to concentrate on Provence will avoid the main route to the west, leading to Nîmes and Montpellier, and will continue via Mont Ventoux (probably with detours) to Avignon (see below).

Main Itinerary

Instead of carrying on from Orange, the tourist can chose the round trip via **Vaison-la-Romaine**, **Mont Ventoux** and

Detour

27

Recommended Routes

Carpentras, joining the main itinerary near **Châteauneuf-du-Pape**.

Main Itinerary

From Châteauneuf-du-Pape, continue south-west into the countryside of Languedoc-Roussillon. Passing the **Pont du Gard**, the Roman aqueduct, and **Nîmes**, the chief town of the Département of Gard, drive to **Montpellier**, the most south-westerly point of this itinerary. Turn east again and on the road among the coastal lagoons enter the **Camargue** after passing through Port-Camargue and **Aigues-Mortes**, once a Crusader port. The Camargue, the extensive delta area of the Rhône, interspersed with lagoons, has as its most popular resort the town of **Saintes-Maries-de-la-Mer**.

The main road reaches **Arles** (where those who have elected not to take the alternative via Montpellier rejoin the itinerary) and the ruined town of **Les Baux**. Now cross the **Alpilles** chain and continue to **St-Rémy-de-Provence, Tarascon** and **Avignon**. There is a fast motorway from here to Marseilles, but by far the more rewarding and not much longer alternative is to continue through the Vaucluse. On this stretch lie **Fontaine-de-Vaucluse**, where once lived the humanist Petrarch, the mountain "village perché" of **Gordes** (close by is the old Cistercian Abbey of **Sénanque**), the ochre quarries of Roussillon, and the crest of the Montagne du Lubéron at the southern foot of which stands the Cistercian Monastery of **Silvacane**. The next large town on this stretch is **Aix-en-Provence**.

Detour

From the motorway – there is a parallel main road/Route nationale – leading from Aix to Marseilles, one can branch off westward to the **Etang de Berre** and **Martiques** before entering the city of **Marseilles**.

Main Itinerary

From Marseilles the road runs a little distance inland along the Côte à Calanques.

Detour

Shortly after leaving Cassis one can turn inland and drive through the Massif de la Sainte Baume to **Saint-Maximin-la-Sainte-Baume**.

Main Itinerary

East of Cassis the route continues at varying distances from the coast with most impressive viewpoints at intervals. A succession of places is strung along this road – **Bandol**, the port of **Toulon**, **Hyères** with the Îles d'Hyères lying offshore, then along the foot of the Massif des Maures are **Le Lavandou**, Ramatuelle and **St-Tropez**.

Either take the coast road to Fréjus or drive inland through the **Massif des Maures** and then for a short distance down the Valley of the Argens and again north to the town of **Draguignan**. Finally continue to **Fréjus**.

St-Raphaël lies at the foot of the **Massif de l'Esterel**. After driving a short distance through this mountain region, follow the scenically fine coastal road known as the "Corniche de l'Esterel" to **Cannes**, continuing to Vallauris, a little way inland, and **Cagnes-sur-Mer**. From here the **Route Napoléon** (see below) begins, which will be described on the return journey. Above Cagnes lie the villages perchés of St-Paul and **Vence**.

Detour

From Cagnes it is possible to drive into the mountains along the valleys of the Var and the Tinée. Cross the Col St-Martin to

In the steps of the great Corsican: the Route Napoléon

reach the national park of **Mercantour**, which is continued beyond the French-Italian frontier as the Parco Nazionale di Valdieri. Return to the coast either by the same route or on the mountain road to Menton (see below) via the Col de Turini and Sospel, a charming and rewarding road for those who enjoy driving.

After the detour mentioned above, the coast road comes to **Nice**, the starting-point of the three parallel corniches, the legendary roads through the coastal mountains via **Beaulieu**, **Monaco** and **Roquebrune-Cap-Martin** to **Menton**, near the French-Italian border, the most easterly point of the area covered in this guide.

Main Itinerary

The return journey follows the itinerary already described as far as Cagnes-sur-Mer (see p. 28). Then it is recommended to chose the **Route Napoléon**, running inland to the north-west. This is a most rewarding mountain road leading to **Grasse** and **Castellane**, at the start of the **Grand Canyon du Verdon**, and via **Digne** and **Sisteron** to **Gap** which marks the limit of the area described in this book. By continuing to Grenoble and Lyons the tourist can rejoin the route by which he came to Provence.

Provence from A to Z

Note

In the following description of places the individual headings are so arranged that they follow a circular walk or a circular drive. The description of the places in the surroundings is in general given in alphabetical order.

Aigues-Mortes   D2

Région: Languedoc-Roussillon
Département: Gard
Altitude: sea-level
Population: 4500

Location

The little town of Aigues-Mortes lies on the western edge of the Camargue, the delta of the Rhône, which is here dotted with numerous lagoons. Four navigable canals link the town with the sea, 6 km (4 miles) distant.

History

The town owes its name as the "town of the dead waters" (aquae mortuae), to the bogs and shallow ponds of the surroundings. Until the silting up of the waterways leading to the sea Aigues-Mortes was an important place, founded by St Louis in the 13th c. as a Crusader port, which from time to time had up to 15,000 inhabitants.
In the Hundred Years War, the great controversy about the succession to the French throne, the Burgundians supported by England conquered the town in 1418 and settled here. Afterwards the Gascons laid siege to Aigues-Mortes, penetrated the town one night and defeated the Burgundians. Their corpses were thrown into the west tower of the town walls and covered with salt in order to prevent decay.

**Town Walls

Because of the narrow streets in the Old Town a visit on foot is recommended. There are car parks on the northern edge of the Old Town (near the Tour de Constance) and outside the south-west town wall.
The massive walls were erected between 1267 and 1275; they form a square which is still complete and which surrounds the town. The ring of walls has 15 towers and is penetrated by 10 gates protected by towers; it comprises an area which has sides of 567 m (620 yd), 497 m (544 yd), 301 m (329 yd) and 269 m (292 yd).

Tour de Constance

The mightiest tower in the town walls, the so-called "Tour de Constance", forms the northern corner of the ring of walls, from which it is separated by a moat filled with water and spanned by a bridge. With its 54 m (177 ft) height it is the epitome of a medieval defensive construction. From the earliest times it

◄ *Glory of antiquity: Triumphal Arch in Orange*

Aigues-Mortes: Town walls and the Tour de Constance

served as a State prison for it was considered impregnable. Among those imprisoned here were, at the beginning of the 14th c., members of the Order of Templars, who had been taken prisoner by Philipp IV on the pretext of heresy and immorality, from the 17th c. many Huguenots and finally a group of Protestant women who were released in 1768 by clemency of the Governor; among these prisoners was the well-known Marie Durand, who spent 38 years in this dungeon and who is renowned in France for her steadfastness.

It is interesting to climb up to the little turret which is crowned by an iron cage in which there was a navigational light at the time when Aigues-Mortes was still a port. From here there is a charming panoramic view of the surrounding countryside.

A circuit of the surrounding walls starts from the Porte de la Gardette, a few steps east from the Tour de Constance. A broad path on the inside of the walls enabled the defenders quickly to reach any point of the defences in order to repulse the attackers. It is also worth while following the ring of walls on the outside. There is a good view of the Tour de Constance and the town walls on the west from the bridge spanning the canal (Chenal Maritime).

Aix-en-Provence D3

Région: Provence-Alpes-Côte d'Azur
Département: Bouches-du-Rhône
Altitude: 177 m (581 ft)
Population: 125,000

Aix (Provençal Ais) the former capital of Provence, lies barely 30 km (19 miles) north of Marseilles in a fertile plain surrounded by mountains.

Shortly after the destruction of the Celtic settlement (121 BC) to the north near Entremont, Aix-en-Provence was founded by Caius Sextius as the first Roman settlement in Gaul and called "Aquae Sextiae Saluviorum". Its medicinal springs, which had been known for a long time, and its favourable position from the point of view of communications on the Via Aurelia, led to a rapid development of the new foundation. After serious setbacks, caused by migrations and attacks by the Saracens, Aix became the capital of the county of Provence and also, especially in the time of the art-lover René of Anjou, a cultural centre of Provençal poetry. In 1481 the town passed to France. It was badly affected in the Wars of Religion. From 1630 there were violent clashes with Richelieu and Mazarin which could only be settled by the good offices of Michel, the brother of Mazarin and Archbishop of Aix. The painter Cézanne (1839–1906) was born and died in Aix.

History

The lightly radio-active hot springs, rich in minerals (36 °C (97 °F)), were already known in Roman times. There chief constituents are bicarbonates, calcium, sulphates, silicates, chlorine and magnesium. They are therapeutically applied both orally and externally especially for veneral diseases, diseases of the stomach, female disorders and mobility diseases.

Medicinal Springs

* Cours Mirabeau

The broad Cours Mirabeau, laid out in 1651, borders the Old Town in the south, separating it from the newer parts. This idyllic shady promenade is planted with old plane trees (which, however, are regularly and heavily pruned); in the middle of the roadway stand three beautiful fountains, the centre one of which, the so-called "Fontaine Chaude", is fed with warm spring water, and on the Place du Général de Gaulle, which is the western boundary of the line of streets, stands the great Fontaine de la Rotonde. There are several impressive buildings in the street, among them the Hôtel des Villiers (No. 2; 1710), the Hôtel d'Isouard de Vauvenargues (No. 10; 1710), the Hôtel d'Arbod Jouques (No. 19; early 18th c.), the Hôtel de Forbin (No. 20; 1656) and the Hôtel de Maurel de Pontèves (No. 38; 1647–50; now the office of the Principal of the University). At the east end of the Cours Mirabeau stands the Chapelle des Oblats, part of the Carmelite Monastery designed by a pupil of Puget and restored about 1700. North of the Cours Mirabeau the Old Town extends as far as the Hôtel de Ville (Town Hall) and is largely a pedestrian precinct.

Museum of Natural History

Near the central one of the three fountains on the Cours Mirabeau, Rue Clemenceau leads into the heart of the Old Town. At the end of the little Place St-Honoré Rue Espariat branches off to the left, and near it stands the Museum of Natural History. Its collections, particularly the dinosaur eggs, are well known in specialist circles in Provence. The museum

Location
Rue Espariat 6

Opening times
Mon.–Fri. 10 a.m.–midday and 2–6 p.m.

is housed in the Hôtel Boyer d'Eguilles, a town mansion built in the late 17th c.

Place d'Albertas

The Place d'Albertas lies a short way west of the Museum of Natural History. On its south side stands a town house of three wings grouped round a fountain. Here the visitor should turn right and follow the Rue Aude in a northerly direction (noting on the left the 16th c. Hôtel Peyroneti), then continuing along Rue du Maréchal Foch, with the Hôtel d'Arbaud (17th c.) on the left, until the Place de l'Hôtel de Ville is reached.

Place de l'Hôtel de Ville

The Place de l'Hôtel de Ville, the central point of the Old Town, is adorned with a fountain (1755) around which the busy flower market takes place every day. On the west side of the square stands the Hôtel de Ville (Town Hall), built between 1652 and 1668 and modelled on Italian Baroque; it encloses the courtyard which has a notable iron lattice-work gate. It was badly damaged during the French Revolution. The first floor houses the 18th c. Bibliothèque Méjanes (350,000 volumes) as well as the Fondation Saint John Perse (mementoes of the diplomat and winner of the Nobel Prize for Literature in 1960).

Tour de l'Horloge

On the right side of the façade of the Hôtel de Ville rises the Tour de l'Horloge (Clock-tower of 1510), which was erected on the Roman foundations of a former town gate. In 1661 the astronomical clock below the balustrade was installed.
On the south side of the square stands the former Halle aux Grains (grain market), built between 1759 and 1761 and embellished with sculptures by Jean Pancrace Chastel. It now houses the post office.

Musée du Vieil Aix

Location
Rue Gaston de Saporta 17

Opening times
Tues.–Sun. 10 a.m.–midday and 2–6 p.m.
(winter 2–5 p.m.)

Passing through the clock-tower and following the Rue Gaston de Saporta (fine town houses), one reaches the Musée du Vieil Aix (museum of civic history), which is located in the 17th c. Hôtel Estienne de St-Jean.
Also in Rue Gaston de Saporta are the Hotel de Château Renard (finely decorated staircase) and the Hôtel de Maynier d'Oppede, once the seat of the Faculty of Letters.

St-Sauveur

Location
Rue J. De la Roque

In the north of the Old Town stands the Cathédrale St-Sauveur (St Saviour's Cathedral). It was built in various stages from the 12th to 17th c.; dedicated in 1534.

In the Gothic doorway (15th–16th c.) where the stone figures were severely damaged during the French Revolution, there are beautiful carved walnut doors (principally created between 1508 and 1510 by Jean Guiramand; normally they are concealed behind protective shutters, which the Sacristan will open on request). The lower part of the doors, already reveals elements of the Early Renaissance.

Aix: Cours Mirabeau . . .   *and the Tour de l'Horloge*

The cathedral is entered through a Romanesque doorway, to the right of the Gothic part of the façade. On the right is an Early Christian Baptistery, dating from the 6th c. and renewed in 1577. On the right of the nave is the triptych "Virgin of the Burning Bush" by Nicolas Froment (1435–84). In the central aisle and in the right side aisle are Flemish wall tapestries (1511; representations of the suffering and history of the Virgin, with likenesses of English courtesans; now partly being restored).

Interior

Behind the High Altar lies the Chapelle de St-Mitre, dedicated to the patron of the town, whose tomb can be found in the first chapel on the right. There is a small Romanesque cloister adjoining the church.

*Musée des Tapisseries

The Musée des Tapisseries (Gobelin Museum) is housed in the Ancien Eveché (former episcopal palace; 1648) adjoining the cathedral on the east. On show are tapestries from Beauvais (Picardy) which date from the 17th and 18th c. and include scenes from "Don Quixote de la Mancha" by Cervantes.

Location
Place des Martyrs de la
Résistance

Opening times
Tues.–Sun. 10 a.m.–midday
and 2–5.30 p.m.

Établissement Thermal (Thermes Sextius)

The Établissement Thermal (thermal baths), which is reached from the cathedral by following Rue du Bon Pasteur in a south-westerly direction was built in the 18th c. on the foundations of

Location
Cours Sextius

the Roman Baths of Sextius (2nd c. AD). The water which issues at a temperature of 36 °C (96 °F) is distinguished by being absolutely bacteriologically pure. It is used both for drinking and bathing, especially for metabolic disturbances, circulatory disorders, nervous diseases and post-operative complaints.

Pavillon de Vendôme

Location
Rue Celony 32

Not far west of the Établissement Thermal, outside the town walls as they were at that time, stands the pavilion built in 1664–67 for the Duc de Vendôme and reconstructed in the 18th c. It is surrounded by a little park. The sculptural decoration is noteworthy.

* Atelier Paul Cézanne

Location
Avenue Paul Cézanne 9

Opening times
Tues.–Sun. 10 a.m.–midday and 4–5.30 p.m. (summer 2.30–6 p.m.)

The studio of the famous painter Paul Cézanne, born in Aix, is situated to the north outside the Old Town and is reached along Avenue Pasteur. In addition to mementoes of the master painter there is an audio-visual information exhibition, etc.

Quartier Mazarin

Fontaine des Quatre Dauphins

The area to the south of the Cours Miabeau is called the "Quartier Mazarin" and is rectangular in shape; it is bounded on the south by the Boulevard du Roi René and bordered by the Boulevard Carnot which in places follows the Old Town Walls. Part of this area is the Place des Quatre Dauphins with the fountain (1667) of the same name which is adorned with sculptures of four dolphins.

Musée Paul Arbaud

Location
Rue du 4 Septembre 2a

Opening times
Mon.–Sat. 2–5 p.m.

Standing to the north of the Fontaine des Quatre Dauphins the Hôtel d'Arbaud is one of the finest town mansions of the quarter. It was built in the 18th c. and now houses the Academy of Aix and the Musée Paul Arbaud. This collection has important examples of faience and pictures and also possesses a large library.

Musée Granet (Museum of Fine Arts and Archaeology)

Location
Place St-Jean-de-Malte

Opening times
Wed.–Mon. 10 a.m.–midday and 4–6 p.m.

The Musée Granet to the east of the Fontaine des Quatre Dauphins is one of the most comprehensive museums of Provence. It is housed in the former palace of the Commandant of the Order of Malta (Palais de Malte), dating from 1671. Most of the exhibits were formerly the property of the collector and painter François Marius Granet (1775–1849); they include Celto-Ligurian sculptures from the Oppidum d'Entremont (see p. 38), Greek reliefs, Roman fragments, an Early Christian sarcophagus, medieval sculpture and works of European painters (including Jost van Cleve, Hans Holbein the Younger, Rubens, Rembrandt, Cézanne and Pissarro).

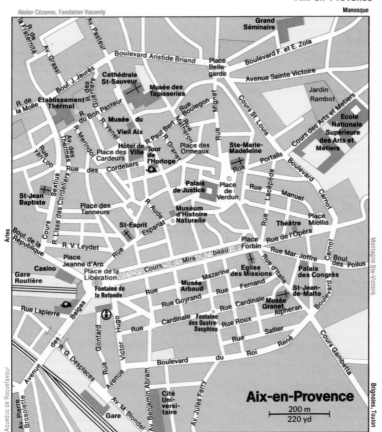

The Church of St-Jean-de-Malte, which adjoins the palace on the east, was once part of the property of the Commandant of the Order of Malta. Erected late in the 13th c. it is the earliest Gothic building in the town. In 1682–93 it was extended by having chapels added to it. The bell-tower of the 14th c. is 67 m (220 ft) high.

St-Jean-de-Malte

Cité Universitaire

The Cité Universitaire is located in the Quartier des Fernouillères. The foundation of the University with its Faculty of Philosophy (1409) dates from the reign of Louis II. University institutions are still housed in the old buildings in the Place de l'Université, but in 1950 it became necessary to remove a considerable part of the University out of the Old Town. There are now about 10,000 students in Aix.

Location
South of the Boulevard du Roi René

*Fondation Vasarely

Location
Avenue Marcel Pagnol

Opening times
Wed.–Mon. 9.30 a.m.–
12.30 p.m. and 2–5.20 p.m.

The Fondation Vasarely lies in the district of Jas de Bouffan in the west of the town. In an unconventional modern building, 87 m (286 ft) long, are 42 monumental works and 800 studies of the Hungarian-French painter Victor Vasarely (b. 1908). Among the notable exhibits are spatial objects which include the observer as an element of movement and which allow differing impressions according to the position of the observer.

**Oppidum d'Entremont

Location
3 km (2 miles) north

The excavation site of the Celto-Ligurian settlement of Oppidum d'Entremont lies to the north of Aix (reached on road D14). Of this strategically well-sited settlement (Upper and Lower Towns) about 4 ha (10 acres) have been excavated where fragments of pillars indicate the layout of individual buildings and parts of the settlements. A mosaic floor and remains, which lead to the conclusion that there were so-called "charnel-houses" here, provide evidence of a sanctuary situated on the highest point, which was destroyed in 123 BC.

Vauvenargues   D3

Location
12 km (7 miles) east

Road D10 leaves Aix in a north-easterly direction and eventually traverses a charming landscape above the northern bank of the Bimont Reservoir. Above the river which supplies this reservoir lies the village of Vauvenargues, the surroundings of which are well known for their profusion of game. The pretty village church dates from the 12th and 16th c. The Renaissance castle in which Luc de Clapiers, Marquis de Vauvenargues, wrote his famous maxims, was inherited in 1958 by Picasso, whose grave is in the park.

**Croix de la Provence

South of Vauvenargues rises the crest of the Montagne Ste-Victoire.
From the hamlet of Cabassols to the west a very attractive footpath (part of the GR9 footpath) leads up to the Croix de la Provence (945 m (3100 feet); 30 minutes). From here there is a magnificent panorama extending from the Camargue in the west over the Massif des Maures as far as the Alps in the east.

Ventabren   D3

Location
15 km (9 miles) west from
Aix-en-Provence

Ventabren is a picturesque village perché (hillside villages) dominated by a ruined castle high above the Valley of the Arc. The 11th–12th c. Parish Church of St-Denis is worth visiting; there is a magnificent view from the castle ruins over the Etang de Berre and Martigues on the southern bank of the river.

*Roquefavour Aqueduct

4 km (2½ miles) to the south of Ventabren along a charming lateral valley of the Arc, one comes to Roquefavour Aqueduct, an imposing construction conveying the Durance Canal over the valley towards Marseilles. The aqueduct (three storeys; internal height 83 m (272 ft); length 375 m (410 yd)) was constructed between 1842 and 1847.

4 km (2½ miles) west of Ventabren in the Valley of the Arc lies the Celtic rock-sanctuary Roquepertuse (footpath from the junction of the D65 and D10). Most of the important finds made here can be seen in the Borély Museum in Marseilles (see entry).

· Roquepertuse

Alpilles

D2

Région: Provence-Alpes-Côte d'Azur
Département: Bouches-du-Rhône
Highest point: La Caume 387 m (1270 ft)

The chain of the Alpilles (Little Alps) extends east of the Rhône between St-Rémy-de-Provence (see entry) to the north and Les Baux (see entry) to the south. In spite of its relatively modest height the steep limestone massif has a thoroughly Alpine appearance. Geologically the Alpilles are a continuation of the Lubéron (see entry), the mountain range adjoining on the east which runs parallel to the northern bank of the Durance. The first discoveries of bauxite were made in the Alpilles.
The highest point of the Alpilles is the Caume (387 m (1270 ft)). The summit, from which there are excellent views, can be reached on a road (sometimes closed), which branches off to the east on road G5, the stretch joining St-Remy and Les Baux. The panorama extends as far as the mouth of the Rhône and the Camargue in the west and to Mont Ventoux and the Valley of the Durance in the east.

Antibes

D5

Région: Provence-Alpes-Côte d'Azur
Département: Alpes-Maritimes
Altitude: sea-level
Population: 63,000

The town of Antibes lies to the east of Cannes at the west end of the Baie des Anges (Bay of Angels) which reaches as far as Nice. Cap d'Antibes, which extends to the south into the Mediterranean, closes off the huge sweep of the bay. The actual area of the town occupies the Peninsula of Garoupe. Flower-growing is of great importance to the economy (about 3 sq. km (1.2 sq. miles) under glass; roses, carnations, etc.).

Location

Antibes was founded in the 5th c. BC by the Greeks from Phocaea Antipolis, that is the town lying opposite the settlement of Nikaia Polis (Nice). The settlement became a Roman municipium, later a bastion against the barbarians. From the 14th c. onwards it was a frontier town between Savoy and France. Later the old fortifications were remodelled by Vauban and Fort Carré, of which only a few remains still exist, was built. The castle in the old town was for many years the seat of a bishop and a holiday residence of the Grimaldi family.
Today Antibes, Cap d'Antibes (see p. 41) and Juan-les-Pins form a three-part community.

History

Antibes has a fine situation on the north-east side of the cape

· Townscape

View of the Old Town of Antibes

between the little bays of Anse St-Roche in the north and Anse de la Salis in the south.

Above Anse St-Roche rises the picturesque Fort Carré (16th c.), a relic of the town defences. Near by is a sports and youth centre.

South of the old fort lies the harbour (Port Vauban) which was laid out by Vauban himself.

Cathedral

Location
Avenue Amiral-de-Grasse

South of the harbour (there is a good general view from the Avenue de Verdun on its south side) there stands on the coastal road (Avenue Amiral-de-Grasse) the Church of the Immaculate Conception, which in the Middle Ages was an episcopal church. The nave dates from the 17th c., so that there is not much to see of the former Romanesque building (12th c.). The church houses a notable altar-painting by Louis Bréa ("The Madonna with Rosary", 1515) as well as a figure of Christ dating from 1447.

Château

Location
Place du Château
Musée Picasso

The former castle of the Grimaldis stands to the south of the cathedral. Today it contains the interesting Musée Picasso, a collection of modern art (about 150 works of Pablo Picasso, paintings, pottery, and the wall tapestry "Judith and Holofernes" by Jean Cocteau).

Musée Archéologique

The coastal promenade continues south to the Bastion St-André, also a relic of the Vauban fortifications. Here is situated the Musée Archéologique Terrestre et Sous-Marine (Museum of Antiquities and Subterranean Archaeology). Among the exhibits are ancient amphorae, some of them from shipwrecks, and coins.

Address
Avenue Amiral-de-Grasse

Opening times
Tues.–Sun. 9 a.m.–midday and 2–6 p.m.; closed November

Cap d'Antibes   D5

The spit of land about 4 km (2.5 miles) long, which leads to Cap d'Antibes, is dotted with villas and gardens. Its highest point is the Plateau de la Garoupe (78m (256 ft); lighthouse) on which there is an observation platform and an orientation table. The panorama includes the town and the coast with the offshore Îles de Lérins (see surroundings of Cannes) as well as the Esterel Mountains and the Maritime Alps rising behind them.

Location
south of Antibes

Also on the plateau stands the old Pilgrimage Chapel of Notre-Dame-du-Bon-Port; among its internal features are an icon from Sebastopol (14th c.) and two gilded wooden statues.

ˈNotre-Dame-du-Bon-Port

The Jardin Thuret is situated not far west of the Plateau de la Garoupe on the Boulevard du Cap. The garden commemorates the botanist Gustave Thuret who laid it out about 1856. In the botanical garden, which has many exotic plants, the eucalyptus tree, originating in Australia, was first planted.

Jardin Thuret

To the south-west not far from the end of the cape (where is a rock pool and a luxury restaurant) one comes to the Batterie du Grillon. This former defensive work now houses the Musée Naval et Napoléonien (Naval and Napoleonic Museum).

Musée Naval et Napoléonien

Juan-les-Pins   D5

Picturesque Juan-les-Pins lies on the Golfe Juan which extends between Antibes and Cannes (see entry). The name is derived from an old pine grove. Juan-les-Pins is an international and very popular resort with many hotels and a casino.

Location
west of Antibes

Biot   D5

If you leave Antibes on the Biot road you reach in 3 km (2 miles) the aquarium "Marine Land" with its trained dolphins, etc. Biot, once a chief place of the Ligurians, is a village with steep little streets and bumpy paths climbing up a hill slope. It is notable for its arts and crafts (gold and silver work, ceramics, glass-blowing, carving in olive-wood, weaving, silk-screen printing). In the Church of Ste-Madeleine-St-Julien are two beautiful altar-pictures from the school of Nice.

Location
8 km (5 miles) north

Twenty minutes' walk away is the Musée Fernand Léger with an enormous mosaic visible from afar on its outside wall.

Musée Fernand Léger

Ardèche (Gorges de l'Ardèche)   C2

Régions: Languedoc-Roussillon and Rhône-Alpes
Départements: Gard, Ardèche

Location

The Ardèche is a tributary on the right bank of the Rhône which it joins near Pont St-Esprit, about 100 km (66 miles) north of the Mediterranean coast.

Course of the river

The Ardèche, which has a total length of 120 km (75 miles), rises at a height of 1467 m (4815 ft) in the area of Vivarais on the eastern edge of the Massif Central. It drops steeply in its upper course.
The most impressive reach of the river from the point of view of scenery is between Vallon-Pont d'Arc and Pont St-Esprit, a stretch which is also designated as the "Gorge de l'Ardèche". The following description is confined to this part of the river which is about 30 km (17 miles) long as the crow flies.

Note

Boats can be hired at many places on the road which follows the gorge. Canoeing down the Ardèche is a popular sport. Occasionally there are rapids in the river; also when there is heavy precipitation the water-level can rise rapidly by several metres – due to the porosity of the surrounding limestone country. For these two reasons boating is advised only for experienced canoeists. During the high season (May and June) very many boats are on the river. At least 6 hours should be allowed for this excursion.

Warning

The scrub and bushes which cover a large part of the higher slopes are extremely dry in summer and, therefore, fire is always a danger. Because of the extensive nature of the area and its lack of paths these fires are practically impossible to fight. One should, therefore, be especially careful with inflammable objects, including cigarettes, etc.

** Circular tour through the Gorges de l'Ardèche

The circular tour described below is approximately 150 km (93 miles) long. In addition to the wildly romantic scenery of the gorge this trip is also impressive for the karst caves, especially those of the Aven d'Orgnac which are among the most important caves in France open to visitors. The vistas which are disclosed on this drive are extremely impressive, especially the many ever-changing views downwards to the rushing turquoise river.

Timetable

The visitor who wants ample time to appreciate the scenery is recommended to devote a whole day to this tour.
Leaving Pont St-Esprit the road crosses the Rhône (not far north of the confluence with the Ardèche) on an old stone bridge nearly 1000 m (1994 yd) long. There is an exceptionally charming view of the river frontage of the Old Town.
From Pont-St-Esprit you follow for a short distance the N86 and then bear left on to the D901 (signposted "Gorge de l'Ardèche"); this road, which is not within sight of the river, gradually climbs to the undulating higher slopes which are covered with scrub and bushes. Near Laval-St-Roman one

turns right off the D901 on to the D174 and, following the signs "Aven d'Orgnac", in 9 km (6 miles) reaches the village of Orgnac l'Aven, near which is the cave.

Aven d'Orgnac is one of the greatest caves in the country which are open to the public. In this dripstone cave, which was discovered on 19 August 1935, there is an almost constant temperature of 13 °C (55 °F), so that in addition to stout footwear warm clothing is recommended. A visit (with a guide) lasts about an hour.

°°Aven d'Orgnac

In the hall of the building at the entrance a plan of the cave can be seen on the wall and over it are displayed a number of objects which have been found there (bones, pottery, etc.). The cave is entered by an artificially constructed tunnel which leads to the "Great Hall" with its almost 25 m (82 ft) high stalagmites. Visitors are photographed inside the cave and can take the photographs away with them when they leave.

Only the parts of the extensive system of caves which were opened up by 1939 are accessible to the public. Continuations were discovered from 1965 and to a great extent have been explored. Near the entrance stands a memorial to Robert de Joly (1887–1968), the discoverer and first investigator of the cave.

Not far north-west of the Aven d'Orgnac one finds the Aven de la Forestière, a dripstone cave, with an interesting cave zoo; it was discovered in 1966 and since 1968 has been accessible to the public. It must be said that it is not nearly so impressive as the Aven d'Orgnac.

Aven de la Forestière

Leaving Orgnac l'Aven one follows the D317 which later

Aven d'Orgnac: dripstone cave

becomes the D176, west. In a few kilometres there is a
rewarding view on the right. On the far side of the bridge one
turns right and follows the sign "Route Touristique des Gorges
de l'Ardèche". The road (D290) now follows the course of the
river for the most part. At first it runs through rock galleries; here
there are some little grottoes including the Grotto of the Tunnel.

°Pont d'Arc

About 4 km (2½ miles) from Vallon-Pont d'Arc a large bridge-
like rock arch can be seen on the right and through it flows the
River Ardèche. The arch has headroom of 34 m (112 ft) above
the normal water-level and a breadth of 60 m (197 ft) at the
water-level. The sandy stretches on the banks are popular as
stopping-places for people in boats. The best view of the Pont
d'Arc is from a point a short distance away after driving round
a little bluff.
The road continues at varying distances from the river, which in
this reach has dug its bed many hundred metres deep into the
chalk. At the viewpoints (belvédères) there are parking places;
falling rocks are often a danger on this stretch.
On this part of the route are the viewpoints of Belvédère du
Serre de Tourre, Belvédère de Gaud, Belvédère d'Autridge and
Belvédère de Gournier. Beyond the last named the D590
branches off and on this road one comes in just over 5 km (3
miles) to the Aven de Marzal.

°Aven de Marzal

The dripstone cave Aven de Marzal was systematically
investigated in 1892 by the famous French speleologist
Edouard Martel (1859–1938), then it was forgotten again. Not
until 1949 was the cave rediscovered and it is now open to
visitors. The guided visit of the cave lasts about an hour; warm
clothing is recommended.
The cave is notable for its wealth of stalactites and stalagmites,
sinter formations and crystals, the colours of which range from
pure white through shades of ochre to brown. In the cave
museum can be seen equipment (ladders, boats, diving
apparatus, etc.) which was used in the various phases of the
investigation of the Aven de Marzal.

Grotte de la Madeleine

On the right away from the tourist road and near the above-
mentioned fork lies the Grotte de la Madeleine (reached on a
narrow road). It has beautiful dripstones (among them the
completely irregular so-called "excentriques") and sinter
formations. A guided tour lasts about an hour. Near by is the
viewpoint Belvédère de la Madeleine.

°°Belvédères de la Corniche

The stretch of the D290 beyond the turning of the D590 follows
the river; this section is known as the "Haute Corniche" and is
especially charming. Here are the best viewpoints – Belvédère
de la Cathédrale (a view of the Cirque de la Madeleine), Balcon
des Templiers and Belvédère de la Maladrerie (a magnificent
view of the huge bend of the Ardèche), Belvédère de la
Rouvière, Belvédère de la Coutelle, Grand Belvédère (at the
end of the gorge), Belvédère du Colombier and Belvédère du
Ranc-Pointu (above the last bend of the river with a fine view
into the Rhône Valley). The return route to St-Esprit, where the
tour started, is via St-Martin d'Ardèche.

A shorter alternative

The visitor with little time at his disposal can curtail the tour by
taking the last part, the Haute Corniche, in the opposite
direction from Pont St-Esprit. In this case the views become

Pont d'Arc . . .   *and bends of the River Ardèche*

more impressive as far as the Balcon des Templiers. Finally one can visit the Aven de Marzal.

Arles   D2

Région: Provence-Alpes-Côte d'Azur
Département: Bouches-du-Rhône
Altitude: 9 m (30 ft)
Population: 51,000

The ancient town of Arles lies on the Rhône south of the point where the river divides into two arms and traverses the Camargue before flowing into the Mediterranean.

Location

Arles was originally a Greek settlement (from 46 BC), a Roman colony (Arelate) and competed with Massilia (Marseilles) as a port. Quite early in its history it had a Christian community and was the venue in 314 for the first Council of the Roman Empire in the West. In 406 the city was the seat of the Roman Civil Government for the whole of Gaul. From the 10th c. it belonged to the Kingdom of Burgundy and in 1481 it fell with Provence to France. In 1888 the painter Vincent van Gogh resided here. Today Arles extends over 750 sq km (290 sq. miles) and in area is the largest commune in France (Paris is only 105 sq. km (41 sq. miles)).

History

The beauty of the maidens of Arles was immortalised by Georges Bizet in his two-part concert suite "L'Arlésienne".

Note

If you are following the route described in this guide then you will enter the town from the south-west. You are recommended to leave your vehicle outside the Old Town, which is partly surrounded by walls, and to visit the town on foot.

Collective tickets at a reduced rate are available and give admittance to all the sights in the town. They can be obtained at all ticket offices.

*Arènes (amphitheatre)

Location
Rond-Point des Arènes

Opening times
1 June–14 Sept. 8.30 a.m.–
12.20 p.m. and 2–7 p.m.
15 Sept.–31 Oct. 8.30 a.m.–
12.20 p.m. and 2–6.30 p.m.
1–30 Nov. 8.30 a.m.–12.20
p.m. and 2–5 p.m.
1–31 Dec. 8.30 a.m.–2.20
p.m. and 2–4.30 p.m.
1 Jan.–28 Feb. 9–11.50 a.m.
and 2–4.30 p.m.
1–31 March. 9–11.50 a.m.
and 2–5.30 p.m.
1–30 April. 8.30–11.50 a.m.
and 2–6.30 p.m.
1–31 May. 8.30–12.20
and 2–7 p.m.

The Roman amphitheatre is the most complete ancient monument in the town. The great oval was built shortly after the foundation of the Roman colony and once had accommodation for 21,000 spectators. With a length of 136 m (149 yd) and a width of 107 m (117 yd) the arena was one of the largest in Gaul. In the Middle Ages it was converted into a fortress by the addition of towers and the walling up of the arcades. When the arena was thoroughly restored in the 19th c., three of the towers were left. The one over the entrance can be climbed and from it there is a charming view over the roofs of the Old Town and of the nearby ancient theatre. Nowadays in summer bullfights take place in the arena.

Seating for the spectators was once on 34 rows of tiered steps; the arena itself is built into the bedrock of the site. In ancient times a wooden floor was provided over the rock; the holes in which the supporting joists were fixed can still be seen in the wall surrounding the arena.

Théâtre Antique (Roman theatre)

Location
Rue de la Calade/Rue du
Cloître

The Roman theatre, which was built in the time of Augustus with seating for 8000 on 33 tiers of steps, was as large as the theatre in Orange (see entry). In the early Middle Ages the

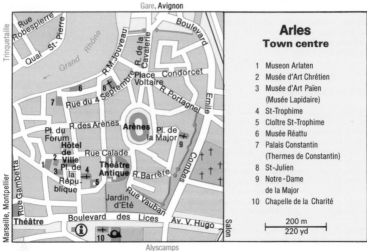

Arles
Town centre

1 Museon Arlaten
2 Musée d'Art Chrétien
3 Musée d'Art Païen
   (Musée Lapidaire)
4 St-Trophime
5 Cloître St-Trophime
6 Musée Réattu
7 Palais Constantin
   (Thermes de Constantin)
8 St-Julien
9 Notre-Dame
   de la Major
10 Chapelle de la Charité

200 m
220 yd

Arles: bird's-eye view of the Roman buildings

theatre was used as a quarry and with the material which it provided the town wall was erected. Of the rear wall of the stage only a few stumps of pillars and two more or less complete columns remain. Since the theatre is now again used during the summer, it is protected on the outside by screens and the interior is somewhat spoiled by the necessary technical apparatus.

Most of the relics brought to light during excavation are to be found in the Musée d'Art Païen (Museum of Pagan Art, see p. 48) – the most important of these is the "Venus of Arles" (a representation of the goddess Diana), which was discovered near a fountain and is now in the Louvre in Paris.

Opening times
see Arènes (amphitheatre)

St-Trophime

The Church of St-Trophime, once the cathedral, the patron of which was a Greek disciple who brought Christianity to Provence, was founded it is believed in the year 606. In its present form it is a Romanesque basilica (built 1152–80), the interior of which reveals Early Gothic forms.

Location
Place de la République

The façade facing the square has a magnificent doorway – a masterpiece of Provençal sculpture. It was placed in front of the existing Carolingian building in the 12th c. and shows a certain similarity to the doorway of the Church of St-Gilles (see entry). On the pillars are figures of saints and Apostles (on the extreme inside of the front on the left is St Trophime being crowned with a mitre by two angels and on the right the Stoning of St Stephen). Above the door in the tympanum can be seen the

**Doorway

47

Last Judgment with Christ in glory, surrounded by the symbols of the Evangelists and with the Twelve Apostles at his feet. This frieze is continued on the left and the right in the portrayal of the Last Judgment (the "chosen" on the left and the "damned" on the right); below, on the capitals on the left the Annunciation and on the right the Birth of Jesus.

Both side doorways are considerably smaller than the main doorway and were added in the 17th c. Through them one enters the rather dim interior. All three aisles are very narrow and high and show the transition from Romanesque to Gothic. In the first bays on the right and the left are large Gobelin tapestries. The choir and the choir ambulatory are High Gothic (15th c.).

** Cloisters

The Cloisters of St-Trophime adjoin the church on the south-east. They are accessible through the building in the Place de la République to the right of the façade of the church and the courtyard lying behind it. The opening times are the same as for the Amphitheatre (see p. 46)

In the cloisters pillars alternate with columns in pairs, the capitals of which are decorated with fine sculptures of Biblical scenes; on the pillars are figures of Apostles and saints, and between them reliefs of stories of Christ and the saints. The north and east wings (12th c.) are the oldest parts, the south and west wings date from the 14th c.; thus the cloisters reveal both Romanesque and Gothic elements. The Chapter House adjoins the cloisters; in it are two Gobelin tapestries and in the gallery a small lapidarium. The other rooms adjacent to the cloisters are used for temporary exhibitions. The stairs leading to the galleries and to the rooms above also provide access to the terrace-like roof gallery which encircles the cloisters and provides a charming view of the latter.

Musée d'Art Païen (Musée Lapidaire)

Address
Place de la République

Opening times
see Arènes (amphitheatre)

The Musée d'Art Païen (Museum of Pagan Art) or Musée Lapidaire (lapidarium) is located opposite St-Trophime in the former Church of Ste-Anne (1630). it exhibits works of the Roman Age and especially of Hellenism. Most of the exhibits come from the Roman theatre, the former Forum and other ancient buildings in Arles.

Hôtel de Ville

Diagonally across on the right the Hôtel de Ville (Town Hall) adjoins the museum; it was re-erected in the late 17th c. The Belfry (1553) dates from the period of the earlier building.

Obelisk

In the Place de la République stands an Egyptian obelisk which was found in the amphitheatre (Arènes) and which was set up here in 1676.

Musée d'Art Chrétien

Address
Rue Baize

Opening times
see Arènes (amphitheatre)

The Musée d'Art Chrétien (Museum of Christian Art) lies a short distance north-west of the Musée Lapidaire. Housed in the chapel of the former Jesuit college which was built in 1652, it possesses one of the most important collections of Early Christian sarcophagi (4th c.); many of them come from the

St-Trophime: Doorway . . .   *and Cloisters*

Necropolis of the Alyscamps (see p. 50) and from the Early Christian burial-place of St-Genest in the present-day suburb of Trinquetaille. The sarcophagi are decorated with reliefs showing scenes from the Old and New Testaments.

The so-called "Cryptoporticus", a partly subterranean arcade of the ancient Forum (see below), can be reached from the museum.

Museon Arlaten

The Museon Arlaten (Museum of Arles) is a foundation (1891) of the famous Provençal poet Frédéric Mistral. The Palais de Laval-Castellane in which it is situated immediately adjoins the Museum of Christian Art. Mistral, a Nobel Prize-winner of 1904, donated the amount of his prize, in order to create in his native region the museum which is now the most important collection of Provençal folk art; it contains furniture, costumes, ceramics, tools and farming implements.

Address
Rue de la République

Opening times
Tues.–Sun. (daily in summer) 9 a.m.–midday and 2–6 p.m.

Forum

The Forum, the market and meeting-place of the Roman town, was situated on the south side of the present-day Place du Forum, north of the above-mentioned museums. The best-preserved part is the so-called "Cryptoporticus" (crypto doorway about 40 BC), a horseshoe-shaped loggia 89 m (97 yd) by 59 m (65 yd) in extent, built to compensate for the slope of the site.

Address
Place du Forum
Entrance to the Cryptoporticus from the Musée d'Art Chrétien

Thermes de Constantin

Address
Rue D. Maisto

The Thermes de Constantin (Baths of Constantine), the Roman bathing complex, dates from the 4th c. AD and is situated in the north of the town near the arm of the river called the "Grand Rhône". Of the once-extensive series of buildings, which resembled a palace, only the Caldarium (warm bath) and parts of the Hypocaust (underfloor heating) and the Tepidarium (warm air room) remain.

Musée Réattu

Address
Rue du Grand Prieuré

Opening times
see Arènes (amphitheatre)

The Musée Réattu, housed in a former building which had been the Grand Priory of the Knights of Malta of the 15/16th c., originated in the collection of the painter Réattu (1760–1833) and exhibits drawings and paintings of Provençal artists of the 18th and 19th c., as well as a collection of contemporary art and a photographic gallery (largely due to the generosity of Pablo Picasso).

*Alyscamps

Location
Avenue des Alyscamps

Opening times
see Arènes (amphitheatre)

Not far from the south-east corner of the Old Town extend the Alyscamps (the so-called Elysian Fields), an extensive Roman burial-place which, according to the legend of St Trophime, was dedicated as a Christian cemetery and, in the Middle Ages, was so famous that the dead were brought here for burial from considerable distances. The marble sarcophagi, which were later neglected, sold or destroyed, were not assembled again until the 18th c. Along the idyllic Allée des Tombeaux (Street of Graves) the only coffins now standing are the plain stone ones of the early Middle Ages. At the end of the Allée is the Church of St-Honorat (12th c.), the only remains of which are the choir and the adjoining chapels of the 15th to the 18th c. Inside near the entrance is a sarcophagus dating from the 4th c. AD.

Pont de Langlois

Location
Rue Gaspard Monge

The now reconstructed Pont de Langlois, a canal bridge made famous by the well-known painting of Vincent van Gogh, is situated outside the town to the south. The lift bridge is no longer used.

Musée Camarguais

Location
11 miles south-west on road D570

Opening times
daily 9 a.m.–midday and 2–6 p.m.

In the marshy Plaine de Meyran, just on the far side of the Canal du Rousty, the Musée Camarguais (Museum of Camargue) was established in an old farmstead. It contains agricultural exhibits and objects of rural life from the area of the delta of the Rhône; adjoining is a 3.5 km (2 mile) long ecological educational footpath.

Moulin de Daudet

See Montmajour

The evocative Alyscamps

Avignon   D2

Région: Provence-Alpes-Côte d'Azur
Département: Vaucluse
Altitude: 23 m (75 ft). Population: 92,500

The former Papal Residence of Avignon is situated on a tongue of land which is bordered in the north-west by the Rhône and in the south by its tributary the Durance.

Location

Avennio (or Avenio), the capital of the Gallic Cavares, later became a thriving Roman colony. In turn the town fell into the hands of the Burgundians and the Franks. In the 13th c. it was acquired, together with Provence, by Charles of Anjou. Between 1309 and 1377 there resided here Popes Clement V (1305–14), John XXII (1314–34), Benedict XII (1334–42), Clement VI (1342–52), Innocent VI (1352–62), Urban V (1362–70) and Gregory XI (1370–78), a nephew of Clement VI. Only the return of Gregory XI to Rome ended the almost 70 years of "Babylonian Exile" of the Church. After his death when schism set in, the Popes Clement VII (1378–94) and Benedict XIII (1394–1424) resided in Avignon until 1403. The town with the surrounding county of Venaissin remained a possession of the Curia until the Revolution united the "Papal city" with France in 1791.

History

After the Popes had employed Italian masters, especially the Sienese Simone Martini who died here in 1344, there flourished in Avignon right until the 18th c., an important school of painting.

*Town Walls

The whole of the Old Town is surrounded by a complete ring of walls which date from the years 1350–68, although they were considerably restored in the 19th c. Into the walls, which have a total length of some 5 km (about 3 miles), 39 towers were inserted at irregular distances.

*Palais des Papes (Papal Palace)

Location
Place du Palais

Opening times
Easter to 30 June
daily 9–11.30 a.m. and
2–5.30 p.m. (guided tours)
1 July–31 Sept.
daily 9 a.m.–6 p.m.
1 Oct. to Easter
daily 9–11 a.m. and 2–4 p.m.
(guided tours)

The immediate reason for the erection of the Papal Residence was the removal of the Curia from Rome to Avignon under Clement V. His successor, John XXII (Pope 1314–34), chose the palace of the Bishop of Avignon, his nephew Arnaud de Via, as his official seat and initiated the first extensions. The present aspect of the fortress-like block of buildings is due mainly to the erection of the east and north-east wings (Palais Vieux=Old Palace) by Benedict XII (Pope 1334–42) and the west wing (Palais Nouveau=New Palace) by Clement VI (Pope 1342–52). Later Popes who resided in Avignon were only responsible for small extensions and completions.

Exterior

The east of the Place du Palais is dominated by the mighty façade of the Palais Nouveau, more of a fortress than a centre of spiritual power. The irregular buildings of the façade are articulated in the lower part by great pointed arches over wall columns. Over the entrance gateway are two octagonal towers with pointed spires. On the right the façade is flanked by the Tour de la Gache and on the left by the Tour d'Angle, two somewhat insubstantial stump towers protruding from the surface of the wall. On the left set back a little towards the façade, is the Palace Vieux, articulated completely by wall pillars and pointed arches. At the corner of the building rises the Tour de la Campane with its battlemented pinnacle; it is thus a defensive tower. Near the Palais Vieux, above a mighty open stairway, stands the Cathedral of Notre-Dame des Doms (see p. 54).

Interior

Although the entire furnishings of the inside of the Papal Palace, except for some remains of sculptures and frescoes, have disappeared, the interior of the complex of buildings offers a compulsive impression of space. Passing through the Porte des Champeaux, the entrance from the open-air stairway, one crosses the Grande Cour, the great inner courtyard, around which the old and new parts of the palace are grouped and in which, from time to time, open-air dramatic performances take place.

In the left-hand rear corner of the courtyard is the entrance to the Consistoire (Consistory), and, opposite, the Cloister of Benedict XII (see below). In the Hall of the Consistory measuring 11 m (36 ft) by 48 m (158 ft) can be seen the remains of some frescoes of Simone Martini; adjoining the longer wall lies the Chapelle St-Jean Chapel of St John), the lower part of the chapel tower. Here there are some well-preserved frescoes whch were created between 1346 and 1348 and have been ascribed to the Italian Matteo Giovanetti. They represent the life histories of St John the Baptist and St John the Evangelist.

"Babylonic exile of the Church": The Papal Palace in Avignon

Opposite the entrance to the Consistory Hall lies the Cloister of Benedict XII, dating from 1339 and completely restored in 1940; this was the site of the previous palace of John XXII. A staircase leads to the covered gallery above the cloister (notice the alternation of double and considerably smaller simple windows up above). Adjoining this gallery is the former Banqueting Hall (Grand Tinel or Magnum Tinellum). It is situated immediately above the Consistory Hall and has the same measurements; the wooden vaulted ceiling is modern. Hanging here can be seen four huge Gobelin tapestries (18th c.); from the short linking corridor in the left-hand corner of the hall which gives access to the Kitchen Tower (Tour des Cuisines), there is a charming view to the south-west over the Old Town. The Chapelle St-Martial, which occupies the upper storey of the chapel tower, is, like its counterpart on the ground floor, decorated with frescoes by Matteo Giovanetti which date from 1344–45. They portray the miracles of St Martial (patron saint of Limousin, 3rd c.).

From the end of the Banqueting Hall one enters the Robing Chamber, the ante-room to the Papal bedroom, in which two Gobelins (18th c.) and a model of the Papal Palace are to be seen. The Papal bedroom, immediately adjoining, is in the Tour des Anges. Of interest here are the (restored) polychromatic tiled floor, the painted beamed ceiling and the walls painted in tempera (predominantly arabesques on a blue ground; in the window niches are painted birdcages). In the Tour de la Garde-Robe, the tower adjacent to the Tour des Anges, is the former study of Clement VI, the Chambre du Cerf (Room of the Stag), so-called from the secular scenes, especially of hunting and

53

fishing, painted on the walls. Also of interest is the painted coffered ceiling. The floor tiles are, like those in the bedroom, of more recent date but copied from old designs.

A staircase now leads into the North Sacristy where there are plaster replicas of numerous tombs of cardinals and other spiritual dignitaries. Then comes the Grand Chapelle (Great Chapel) also called the "Chapelle Clementine", a huge single-naved church with a coffered roof. On the walls hang a considerable number of Baroque paintings; to the right of the altar is the entrance to the South Sacristy in which are replicas of the tombs of Innocent VI, Clement V, Clement VI and Urban V. From the Great Chapel you enter the loggia where through the large traceried Fenêtre de l'Indulgence (Window of Indulgence) there is a view of the Great Courtyard. From this window the Pope used to give his blessing to the assembled faithful. Now you follow the broad vaulted staircase down to the ground floor. Here on the left of the door of the Large Audience Chamber is the two-naved audience hall beneath the Chapelle Clementine. This, too, was embellished by Matteo Giovanetti with wall-paintings (1352; Prophets and Sybils). In the Small Audience Chamber (also called the "Audience des Contredites") ornamental grisaille paintings were introduced in the 17th c.

The way back to the entrance doorway is through the Corps du Garde (Guardroom).

Notre-Dame des Doms

Location
Place du Palais

Near the Papal Palace on the north rises the Cathedral of Notre-Dame des Doms; its present architecture is mainly of the 12th c. but it was altered several times between the 14th and 16th c. On the arch and gable of the main doorway are remains of two frescoes by Simone Martini. The gilded statue of the Virgin on the tower and the Crucifixion group in front of the cathedral are of 19th c. date.

In the interior can be seen a bishop's chair (12th c.) of white marble; in the first side chapel on the north stands the former Romanesque main altar; in the fourth chapel on the south side the partly restored Late Gothic monument to John XXII. At the entrance to the Baptistery Chapel can be seen early 15th c. frescoes (the Baptism of Christ; representations of the donor's family, the Spiefami from Lucca). In the Sacristy is a beautiful silver sculpture ("The Scourging of Christ"). The Chapel of the Resurrection on the south side, which was the gift of Archbishop Cibelli, also contains his tomb.

Rocher des Doms

Location
north of the Cathedral

The Rocher des Doms is a rocky spur which rises to the north of the Papal Palace and then falls steeply down to the Rhône. There is a very good view from the beautiful park on its summit of the Pont St-Bénézet (see below) and the islands of Barthelasse and Piot in the river, as well as Villeneuve-lès-Avignon on the far bank.

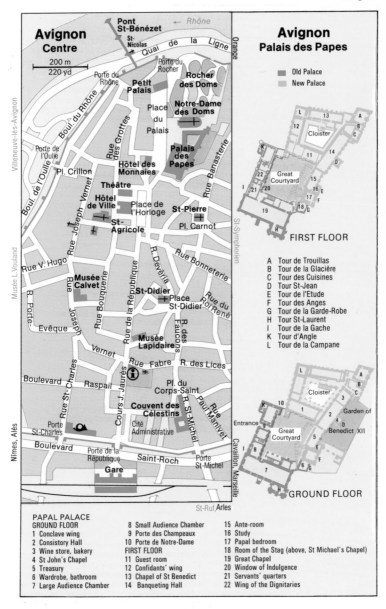

Avignon
Centre

200 m
220 yd

Pont St-Bénézet
St-Nicolas
← Rhône
Quai de la Ligne
Orange

Porte du Rochor
Rocher des Doms

Porte du Rhône
Petit Palais

Boul. du Rhône
Place du Palais
Notre-Dame des Doms

Villeneuve-lès-Avignon

Porte de l'Oulle
Rue des Grottes
Palais des Papes

Rue Banasterie

Pl. Crillon
Hôtel des Monnaies

Boul. de l'Oulle

Rue Joseph Vernet

Théâtre
Hôtel de Ville
Place de l'Horloge
St-Pierre
Pl. Carnot

St-Agricole

St-Symphorien

Musée L. Vouland

Rue V. Hugo

Rue Bourguerie
R. Devéria
Rue Bonneterie

R. Porte-
Musée Calvet

St-Didier
Place St-Didier
Rue du Port René

Rue de la République

R. des Faucons
R. du Pont René

Évêque-
R. Joseph Vernet

Musée Lapidaire

Vernet
Rue Fabre
R. des Lices

Boulevard
Raspail
Rue St-Charles
Cours J. Jaurès

Pl. du Corps-Saint

R. St-Michel
Rue Paul Manivet

Nimes, Alès

Porte St-Charles
Cité Administrative

Couvent des Célestins

Boulevard
Porte de la République
Saint-Roch
Porte St-Michel

Cavaillon, Marseille

Gare

St-Ruf, Arles

Avignon
Palais des Papes

■ Old Palace
■ New Palace

FIRST FLOOR

L 13 A
12 B
Cloister C
11 14 D
K
22 Great Courtyard 15 E
21 20 16
17
19 18 G
H

A Tour de Trouillas
B Tour de la Glacière
C Tour des Cuisines
D Tour St-Jean
E Tour de l'Etude
F Tour des Anges
G Tour de la Garde-Robe
H Tour St-Laurent
I Tour de la Gache
K Tour d'Angle
L Tour de la Campane

GROUND FLOOR

L A
10 1 B
Cloister 3 C
K 4 Garden of
2 D Benedict XII
Entrance Great Courtyard E
8
6 F
7 G
H

PAPAL PALACE

GROUND FLOOR
1 Conclave wing
2 Consistory Hall
3 Wine store, bakery
4 St John's Chapel
5 Treasury
6 Wardrobe, bathroom
7 Large Audience Chamber
8 Small Audience Chamber
9 Porte des Champeaux
10 Porte de Notre-Dame

FIRST FLOOR
11 Guest room
12 Confidants' wing
13 Chapel of St Benedict
14 Banqueting Hall
15 Ante-room
16 Study
17 Papal bedroom
18 Room of the Stag (above, St Michael's Chapel)
19 Great Chapel
20 Window of Indulgence
21 Servants' quarters
22 Wing of the Dignitaries

Avignon

Pont St-Bénézet (Pont d'Avignon)

Location
Quai de la Ligne

The Pont St-Bénézet at the foot of the Rocher des Doms juts out into the river and is probably the most famous bridge in France. Every child in the country knows the old song "Sur le Pont d'Avignon". The fortified bridge was built between 1177 and 1185 and led to Villeneuve-lès-Avignon across the river, but half of it was destroyed in 1668. Approximately in the middle of the remaining part stands the two-storeyed Chapelle St-Nicolas, the lower part of which is Romanesque and the upper Gothic, with a belfry on the gable.

Petit Palais

Location
Place du Palais

Opening times
Wed.–Mon. 9.15 a.m.–
midday and 2–6 p.m.

On the north side of the Place du Palais stands the 14th c. Petit Palais, a Gothic defensive building which once served as an episcopal headquarters and residence. It has a beautifully arcaded courtyard and an old 13th c. central building. Today it houses the Campana di Cavelli collection of paintings (Italian masters of the 13th–15th c.) and a collection including works of the Avignon school of painting.
Not far north the town wall is breached by the Porte du Rocher through which one can get to the Pont St-Bénézet.

Hôtel des Monnaies

Not far south of the Petit Palais, opposite the entrance to the Papal Palace, can be seen the Hôtel des Monnaies, the former Mint. This early 17th c. Baroque building reveals considerable Italian influence; the façade is decorated with large figures of animals, and bears the coat of arms of Pope Paul V, who was descended from the Borghese family and whose Vice-Legate resided here. Today the palace houses the School of Music.

St-Symphorien

Location
Place des Carmes

Some distance to the east of the Papal Palace stands the mainly 15th c. Church of St-Symphorien which belonged to the former nearby Monastery of the Barefoot Carmelites and, therefore, is also called the Église des Carmes. The interior houses a few 16th c. statues and paintings by Pierre Parrocel, a less-well-known member of this family of painters, as well as other works.

Place de l'Horloge

Location
South of the Papal Palace

For some time now the lively Place de l'Horloge has been a pedestrian precinct, where plane trees giving character to the square also provide shade for the street cafés; on the west side is the theatre and the Hôtel de Ville (Town Hall, 1845) with a clock-tower dating from the 14th c.

St-Pierre

Near the square on the west stands the Church of St-Pierre (1356); extended in the late 15th c. and restored in the 19th; it has a fine façade and carved wooden doors of 1500.

St-Agricol

A short distance south-west of the Town Hall one comes to the Church of St-Agricol, a three-naved basilica without transepts, built in the time of Pope John XXII and later extended several times.

The Pont d'Avignon . . .   *and Place de l'Horloge*

St-Didier

To the east of the Rue de la République, the main street of the Old Town leading south from the Place d l'Horloge, stands the single-aisled Church of St-Didier which dates from the 14th c. Inside can be found one of the earliest works of art of the Renaissance, a Way of the Cross created by Francesco da Laurana between 1478 and 1481. He was Italian but had been working in France since 1476. More recently wall-paintings dating from the 14th c. (Crucifixion, etc.) have been uncovered in the church.

Location
Place St-Didier

*Musée Calvet

The Musée Calvet has its origin in the private collection of the doctor, a native of Avignon, François Esprit Calvet (1729–1810) together with municipal collections. Since 1833 it has been housed in the Hôtel de Villeneuve-Martignan which dates from 1750. The contents embrace antique sculptures, medieval paintings of Provençal masters, as well as an instructive cross-section of French painters from the 16th to the 19th c., together with collections of coins and ceramics.

Address
Rue Joseph Vernet 65

Opening times
Wed.–Mon. 9 a.m.–midday
and 2–6 p.m.

Musée Requien

The Musée Requien is located close to the Musée Calvet. As well as a large scientific library, it possesses geological and

Address
Rue Joseph Vernet 67

botanical collections (including a large herbarium). Opening times are Tuesday to Saturday, 9 a.m.–midday and 2–6 p.m.

*Musée Lapidaire

Address
Rue de la République 27

Opening times
Wed.–Mon. 9 a.m.–midday and 2–6 p.m.

The Musée Lapidaire (lapidarium) can be found in the former Baroque Jesuit church, which is joined by a bridge to the Jesuit college (now a secondary school) and which was founded in 1564. The exhibits include Roman mosaics, fragments of the former triumphal arch, reliefs, ancient sculptures, etc.

Couvent des Célestins

Location
Rue St-Michel

Right in the south of the Old Town near the Port St-Michel is the former Célestine monastery, founded in the 14th c., which was once the largest monastery in the town. The interesting church has a large apse by Perrin Morel; in the cloister (about 1400), which unfortunately is only partially preserved, is a 17th c. gateway.

Musée Louis Vouland

Address
Rue Victor Hugo

Opening times
Tues.–Thurs. 10 a.m.–1 p.m. and 3–6 p.m.

In the west of the Old Town near the Porte St-Dominique can be found the Musée Louis Vouland, with French furniture, especially of the 18th c., pictures, Gobelin tapestries and ceramics. Of interest here is also the collection of Chinese porcelain and a number of ivory sculptures.

St-Ruf

Location
Boulevard Gambetta

Some distance to the south, outside the Old Town on the other side of the station, stands the artistic Church of St-Ruf, the remains of a monastic foundation (Abbatiola Sancti Rufi) which goes back to Carolingian times; it was formerly the place of honour for the relics of St Justus.

Cavaillon   D3

Location
25 km (16 miles) south

The town of Cavaillon (a centre of melon-growing and of the canning industry) lies on the right bank of the Durance and on the western edge of the Montagne du Lubéron (see entry).
In the centre of the town stands the notable former Cathedral of St-Véran which was presumably founded in the 12th c. as its Romanesque Provençal architecture reveals. There are beautiful capitals in the apse and a fine cloister.
The synagogue, not far north-east of St-Véran is a very fine building which was originally in Rococo style but was later altered on many occasions and today houses the little Musée Judeo-Comtadin (Jewish museum).
In an old chapel of the hospital (Rococo façade) can be found the Archaeological Museum where among the interesting exhibits is a Merovingian altar-table.
South-west of St-Véran, on the edge of the town, can be found

the only remaining building of the Roman era, the little triumphal arch of the former Roman Oppidum Cabellio.

Villeneuve-lès-Avignon   D2

A bridge over the southern part of the island of Barthelasse leads from Avignon to the little town of Villeneuve-les-Avignon, which was laid out by Philippe the Fair as a bastion against the Papal residents.

Location
3 km (2 miles) west

On the bank of the Rhône opposite the Pont St-Bénézet (see p. 56) stands the Tour Phillipe le-Bel, built in 1307. In the Church of Notre-Dame, dedicated in 1333, are some good panels and a noteworthy treasury.
South of the church can be found the Musée de l'Hospice; in the chapel is the grave of Pope Innocent VI (1362) and a "Coronation of the Virgin" of 1452.
From Fort St-André with two mighty round towers, which dates from the 13th c., there is a magnificent view. In the northern part of the main street (Rue de la République) can be found on the right the ruins of the former Chartreuse du Val de Bénédiction (Carthusian monastery); it was founded in 1356 by Pope Innocent VI whose tomb can be found in the church. To the north of the monastic church is the Petit Cloître (Little Cloister) and the elongated Cloître du Cimetière (20 m (66 ft) by 80 m (263 ft)), adjoining which were the monks' cells.

Bandol   D3

Région: Provence-Alpes-Côte d'Azur
Département: Var
Altitude: sea-level
Population: 7000

The port of Bandol lies on the pretty bay between Marseilles and Toulon.

Location

Townscape

Bandol, known as a health resort, possesses a casino and three beaches: Plage du Casino (500 m (550 yd) long, fine sand), Plage de Rènecros (500 m (550 yd) long, fine sand) and Plage Dorée (500 m (550 yd), coarse sand and pebbles). The promenades, Allées Alfred-Vivien and Allées Jean-Moulin, are charmingly planted with palms, pines and flowers.
In the church the Baroque woodwork is worth seeing. The surroundings of Bandol are among the best wine-producing areas of the French Mediterranean coast.

Île de Bendor   D3

The Île de Bendor is a rocky island only 7 minutes away from Bandol by boat. Its attractions include a reconstructed Provençal harbour, the Musée de la Mer (Marine Museum), the Fondation Paul Ricard (art exhibitions, courses; with a huge

Location
1 km (½ mile) south

Ferry
Every 30 mins

painting by Salvador Dalí), the Exposition Universelle des Vins et des Spiritueux (wine and spirits exhibition), the Centre International de Plongée (diving centre), a little zoo and a sea-water swimming-pool.

Sanary-sur-Mer   D3

Location
4 km (2 miles) south

Sanary-sur-Mer is a pretty former fishing village surrounded by wooded hills and with an extensive colony of villas. To the west of the village on a hill stands the Chapel of Notre-Dame-de-Pitié (1560) which is worth seeing and from which there is an excellent view.

Six-Fours-La-Plage   D3

Location
10 km (6 miles) south

Six-Fours-la-Plage is a large community of several parts situated at the foot of a hill (210 m (689 ft)), magnificent view of the Roads of Toulon (see Toulon) with the Fort de Six-Fours. At the foot of the hill stands the Church of Vieux-Six-Fours, part of which is a well-preserved Romanesque building; it contains a fine 16th c. winged altar.

There is an extensive complex of holiday homes along the shore.

Cap Sicié

Cap Sicié, south of Six-Fours-la-Plage, is the imposing steep slope of a wooded promontory. To the east in the sea can be seen the two rocks Les Deux Frères (The Two Brothers). Not far west on the 358 m (1175 ft) high summit of the cape is the Pilgrimage Church of Notre-Dame-du-Mai from which there is an excellent panorama.

Îles des Embiez

About 5 km (3 miles) south of Six-Fours-la-Plage, on the southern edge of the Bay of Sanary, lie the Îles des Embiez. The Île de la Tour-Fondue (95 ha (235 acres)) is the chief island of this diverse group and has been developed into a centre for water sports. The south of the island (64 m (210 ft) high and steeply sloping) is characterised by a salt-works, vineyards and bathing beaches. The Observatoire de la Mer (marine observation station and marine museum) is worth a visit.

St-Cyr-sur-Mer   D3

Location
9 km (6 miles) north-west

St-Cyr-sur-Mer a community of several parts, has highly developed agriculture (flowers, capers, olives, grapes) and a ceramic industry.

The principal tourist area is the stretch of coast between the yacht harbours of Les Lecques in the north-west and La Madrague in the south.

The Musée de Tauroentum (once the site of a Roman villa) has well-preserved mosaics (1st c. AD), the remains of pillars and amphorae.

Les Baux de Provence   D2

Région: Provence-Alpes-Côtes d'Azur
Département: Bouches-du-Rhône
Altitude: 280 m (919 ft)
Population: 500

The ruined town of Les Baux is situated in the extreme west of
Provence on the crest of the Alpilles (see entry) north-east of
Arles.

Location

In the Early Stone Age this elevated site was settled. In the 12th
and 13th c. Les Baux (Provençal Li Baus=The Rocks) was the
chief town of a county which embraced a great part of
Provence and numbered more than 3000 inhabitants. The Cour
d'Amour, the rendezvous of the troubadours, was famous as
the centre of Courtly poetry which was later to find a parallel in
German-speaking countries in the Minnesang. Under Louis
XIII Les Baux, at that time a stronghold of Huguenots, was
destroyed in 1632. Not until the time when the Grimaldi were
Dukes of Les Baux was an attempt made to revive the town but
without noticeable success.
At the beginning of the Industrial Age another aspect quickly
became important. In the surroundings in 1821 rich deposits of
a mineral were discovered which provides the most important
basic material for aluminium production and which was named
"Bauxite" after the town.

History

*Lower Town

The entire place can only be visited on foot; parking is available
outside the entrance to the Lower Town. The ruins occupy the
plateau of a rock mass which rises above the Lower Town.
Passing the former Town Hall (17th c.) and the Porte
Eyguières, the ancient town gate, follow the Rue de l'Église to
the attractive little Place St-Vincent, the south side of which is
formed of hewn rock walls. There is a fine view from this square
towards the west.
The sturdiness of the Church of St-Vincent, dedicated to St
Vincentius, a martyr of the 4th c., makes a surprising impression
of space. Its present-day form dates from the Romanesque and
Gothic periods. The chapels leading off the right-hand aisle
have been hewn into the soft stone; in the centre one is a font
which has been contrived from the actual rock. The right aisle
is of 10th c. date, that is of the Carolingian era. The nave dates
from the 12th c. and is Romanesque. The left-hand aisle
(15th c.) is from High to Late Gothic; immediately below here
the princes of Les Baux were buried. Their tombs in the
subterranean galleries beneath the church are not open to
visitors.
All the windows of the church are modern work and were the
gift of Prince Rainier of Monaco, the successor to the last
Dukes of Les Baux.
Opposite the church the square is shut off by the Chapelle des
Pénitents-Blancs (17th c.); there are modern pictures inside.
On the left near the church stands the Hôtel des Porcelets, a
building of the 16th c., which now houses the Musée d'Art
Moderne (open daily 9.30 a.m.–midday and 2–6.30 p.m.). On

exhibition are works of contemporary artists, especially from the Provençal region.

A lane going gently uphill on the left of the museum passes on the right the former Protestant Church (Temple Protestant) and leads to the late 16th c. Hôtel de Manville with its beautiful inner courtyard. This is now the office of the Mayor; on the ground floor is a picture gallery and on the second a permanent art salon of modern masters, as well as documents and photographs dealing with the past and present of Les Baux.

From the Hôtel de Manville one can go farther along Rue des Fours and Rue du Trencat, a chemin creux (sunken road) cut into the rock, and come to the entrance to the Upper Town.

* *Upper Town

Entrance Fee

At the entrance to the Upper Town (ticket office) in a 14th c. house is the Musée Lapidaire (lapidarium), with finds from the graves of a Celtic necropolis which has been excavated in the vicinity and other archaeological exhibits, as well as an instructive series of large slides concerning the mining of bauxite.

On the far side of the ruined little Chapel of St-Claude-et-St-Blaise (14th c.) you come to a large bare rock plateau, the edge of which falls almost vertically to the foothills below. This steep slope should be approached with the necessary precaution for it is completely unsecured and the often violent and gusty winds here can be dangerous.

Quite near the end of the plateau stands a monument to the Provençal poet Charloun Rieu (1846–1924) who belonged to the Association of Félibres around Frédéric Mistral. This association was responsible for the renaissance of the Provençal language and culture. From here there is a grandiose panorama into the Valley of the Rhône, the Plain of the Crau and to the Alpilles.

The way to the ruined town runs parallel to the eastern edge of the plateau. The phenomenon of wind erosion which can be observed everywhere on exposed surfaces is impressive.

Only scanty remains of the former castle have survived. A comprehensive and highly impressive panorama can be enjoyed from the rocky crests which border the Upper Town and which can be climbed by steep paths and ladders.

The Lower Town can be reached by a direct path which passes the old Columbarium (an Early Christian burial-place with niches for the urns containing ashes).

Beaulieu-sur-Mer   D5

Région: Provence-Alpes-Côte d'Azur
Département: Alpes-Maritimes
Altitude: sea-level
Population: 5000

Location

Beaulieu-sur-Mer, highly regarded as a marina, lies in the eastern part of the Côte d'Azur about half-way between Nice and Monaco.

Les Baux: View of the Lower Town from the castle ruins ▶

Beaulieu-sur-Mer

Townscape

Protected from the north winds by ranges of hills, Beaulieu-sur-Mer is a popular summer and winter holiday resort. Abundant vegetation thrives in the especially mild climate.

The Baie des Fourmis, fringed by a palm-lined promenade, is picturesque. On a spit of land, which closes off the bay towards the north-east, stands the Villa Kerylos, an imitation of an ancient Greek mansion. This building, which since 1928 has been owned by the Institut de France, has a remarkably fine interior with marble and bronze work, mosaics and furniture of the finest materials. However, only a very small number of these objects are in fact antique.

From the Baie des Fourmis the Avenue des Hellènes, the Boulevard Maréchal Leclerc and the fine Boulevard Alsace-Lorraine lead north-east to the well-equipped yacht harbour which is one of the best of its kind on the French Mediterranean coast.

Petite Afrique

Not far east of Beaulieu the modern holiday seaside settlement of Petite Afrique (Little Africa) has been laid out. It is protected by steep cliffs up to 300 m (985 ft) high and has a good pebble beach.

Eze   D5

Location
4 km (2½ miles) north

The two-part settlement of Eze has an extremely charming situation not far from the Moyenne Corniche (see Corniches de la Riviera). In the narrow streets can be found many handicraft enterprises (ceramics, pewter-work, carving in olive-wood) and perfumeries.

Eze Village . . .

and its Exotic Garden

Eze-Village, the old refuge settlement, has a picturesque situation on a conical rock crowned by the ruins of a castle from which there are marvellous views; it is still surrounded by its 17th c. walls. Of interest are the Musée d'Histoire Locale et d'Art Religieux (local and religious art) and the Chapelle des Pénitents Blancs (often closed) with modern frescoes by J. M. Poulin. The Jardin Exotique (exotic garden; flowering shrubs, cacti; good view) is very pretty.

Eze-Village

The fishing village of Eze-Bord-de-Mer, dominated by high cliffs, lies on the coast. This place was already well known in ancient days and in more recent times has been developed into an important tourist centre.

Eze-Bord-de-Mer

St-Jean–Cap-Ferrat
D5

This friendly villa colony is situated on the promontory of the same name which extends out into the sea. It has excellent holiday residences and attractively laid-out gardens.
To the east of the picturesque centre of the village the Chapel of Ste-Hospice, with a bronze Madonna and a 16th c. tower, stands on the Pointe Ste-Hospice.
High above the sea in a magnificent park on the road towards Beaulieu can be found the Musée Île-de-France founded by Ephrussi de Rothschild. It houses a ceiling fresco by Tiepolo, paintings, furniture and other works of art from the 14th to the 19th c. from Europe and the Far East; its formal gardens can also be visited.
The most southerly tip of the peninsula is Cap Ferrat with its lighthouse (well worth the climb) and a statue of the Virgin Mary.

Location
4 km (2 miles) south-west from Beaulieu-sur-Mer

Cagnes-sur-Mer
D5

Région: Provence-Alpes-Côte d'Azur
Département: Alpes-Maritimes
Altitude: 77 m (253 ft)
Population: 36,000

Cagnes-sur-Mer which consists of several sections, is situated about 12 km (7 miles) west of Nice on the far side of the River Var which flows into the Mediterranean at this point.

Location

*Haut-de-Cagnes

Inland on a conical hill lies the picturesque old village of Haut-de-Cagnes, with narrow little streets and houses built close together within the enclosing walls. It is overlooked by the former Château Grimaldi (14th c.). The castle was taken over in 1536 and rebuilt at the beginning of the 17th c. Since 1939 it has been owned by the town and furnished as a museum (ethnographical collection, information about olive-growing, works by Chagall, Matisse, Renoir, etc.); from the tower there is an extensive view.
On the way towards the centre of the old village stands the Chapel of Notre-Dame-de-la-Protection with fine 16th c.

frescoes not discovered until 1936 and the Renoir house, Maison
Les Colettes, a good example of Provençal architecture.

Cros-de-Cagnes

The old fishing port of Cros-de-Cagnes, about 2 km (1 mile)
south of the old village at the mouth of the Cagne, is now a large
seaside resort and yacht harbour.

La Colle-sur-Loup   D5

Location
6 km (4 miles) north-west

This place, which is popular with artists, lies amid the fertile
foothills of Vence (vineyards, flower-growing). Of interest are
the restored 12th c. church and the chapel dating from the same
period which is owned by the monks of Lérins.
Near by is the Château de Montfort of King François I.

Villeneuve-Loubet   D5

Location
3 km (2 miles) south-west

Villeneuve-Loubet, originally an elevated farming village
situated some 2 km (1 mile) from the coast on the left bank of
the Loup, has a castle, built originally in the 12th c., with a
30 m (98 ft) high defensive tower; the castle is not open to
the public. In the house where the famous chef Escoffier
(1846–1935) was born there is a Museum of Cuisine
(Tues.–Sun. 2–6 p.m.) with culinary objects of the 14th to
20th c. A chain of hills, some 50 m (165 ft) high separates the
old part of the village from the coastal settlement which was
begun in 1930. Here gigantic houses built in pyramids and
the newly created Marina-Baie-des-Anges characterise the
landscape.

Camargue   D2

Région: Provence-Alpes-Côte d'Azur
Département: Bouches-du-Rhône
Area: 60,000 ha (148,260 acres)

Location

In the strictest sense the Camargue is only the marshy area
between the Grand Rhône and the Petit Rhône, the two arms
of the river which divide just short of Arles. The western arm
(Petit Rhône) here also forms the boundary between the
regions of Provence-Alpes-Côte d'Azur and Languedoc-
Roussillon.

Landscape

In spite of the enormous amount of tourism, parts of the
Camargue are still completely isolated and flat. The Camargue
(Provençal Camargo) is an area with a thoroughly individual
and often quite melancholy character. The part nearest the sea,
around the lagoon of the Etang de Vaccarès, consists almost
entirely of lagoons and reed-infested marshes or dry salt
expanses and dunes on which, in places, umbrella pines,
juniper bushes and tamarisks thrive. Waterfowl (recently a

considerably increased colony of flamingoes, heron, etc.) and even birds of prey are numerous. Turtles and beavers can also be found here. In winter especially, men on horseback herd half-wild small black cattle and light grey horses. These well-known Camargue horses are hired out in the holiday season everywhere – in many places there are centres with Promenades à Cheval (horse-riding).

**Drive through the Camargue

The most favourable starting-points for a drive through the Camargue are Arles and St-Gilles (see entries). Road D570 coming from Arles is joined after 15 km (9 miles) by the D37 from St-Gilles and continues in a south-westerly direction among rice fields and vineyards. As one approaches the sea the countryside takes on an increasingly steppe-like character and halophytes (plants which are tolerant of the high salt content of the ground) take the place of cultivated plants.

In the southern part of the Camargue an area of about 15,000 ha (over 37,000 acres) has been protected since 1928 as a plant and animal reserve. In 1976 near the Etang de Ginès, a small lake by the shore, the Centre d'Information de Ginès (Information Centre open daily 9 a.m.–midday and 2–6 p.m.; dedicated to the first President of the Camargue Nature Park Foundation, François Huet, 1905–72) was set up. It provides information on large instructive slides about the flora and fauna of the area, its geological history and ecology. The bird sanctuary situated between the Information Centre and the

Parc Régional de Camargue

In the Camargue: flamingoes . . .   *and white horses*

lake can be viewed through large panoramic windows; telescopes are available.

The D570 comes to an end in Saintes-Maries-de-la-Mer (see entry).

Etang de Vaccarès

From Stes-Maries the visitor can return by the same road for about 21 km (13 miles) until the junction with the D37 is reached (on the right; signpost "Etang de Vaccarès"). On the far side of Méjanes this road runs close to the Etang de Vaccarès surrounded by a girdle of reeds. This lake which has an area of about 6000 ha (14,826 acres) – varying according to the water-level – is by far the largest of the Camargue but its average depth is only about 50 cm (20 in). The lake is also a protected area. Near Grand Romieu the D36 B bears off to the right; this is a charming scenic stretch. It follows (often with fine views) the eastern shore of the lake which towards the south gives way to a number of level lagoons dotted with sandbanks.

Salins du Midi

Near Salins-de-Giraud lie the "salt pans", where salt is obtained by the gradual evaporation of sea-water. Not far south of the village huge white heaps of salt are deposited. From an artificial hill there is an extensive panorama of the mountains of sea-salt and the huge evaporation basins, the water of which is coloured by microbes with shades of brown, red and violet.

The road, in places now rather narrow, runs south between the embanked Rhône and the salt-pans. It ends near the Plage de Piemançon, a broad beach of fine sand where the Camargue ends at the Golfe du Lion. The return journey can be made considerably more quickly on the D36, the course of which is parallel to the Rhône and which shortly before reaching Arles joins the D570 (see p. 67).

Cannes
D5

Région: Provence-Alpes-Côte d'Azur
Département: Alpes-Maritimes
Altitude: sea-level
Population: 73,000

Location

The exclusive resort of Cannes marks the western end of the Côte d'Azur in its real sense. It has a sheltered situation on the wide Gofe de la Napoule, with the island group of the Îles de Lérins offshore.

History

Evidence of an early settlement on Mont Chevalier is given by finds of the Celto-Ligurian Age. In the 2nd c. BC the Romans are said to have erected the Castrum Marsellinum here. In the 11th c. there was a watch-tower around which later a small walled town was grouped. The town did not spread into the plain until it was discovered to be a healthy place by the Englishman Lord Brougham (1778–1868) who had fled from Nice to Cannes to avoid a raging cholera epidemic. In 1838 the harbour was laid out and 30 years later a beginning was made with a promenade along the shore. Because of its exceptional mild climate (average in winter 9.8 °C (50 °F)), its rich subtropical vegetation and its beach, Cannes is a tourist centre at all times of the year. The International Film Festival (April–May) is of particular importance.

Mountains of salt: the Salins du Midi

Old Town

The Le Suquet quarter, the Old Town, slopes up to Mont Chevalier (67 m (220 ft)), the summit of which is crowned by the 11th c. watch-tower. A few yards south of this we come to the Musée de la Castre which contains Egyptian, Phoenician, Etruscan, Greek and Roman antiques as well as art from the Far East and Central America.

Not far to the north stands the Late Gothic Church of Notre-Dame de l'Espérance (1521–1648) with a notable 17th c. Madonna on the High Altar and a wooden statue of St Anne (about 1500).

The Boulevard Jean-Hibert runs westward along the shore, passing the Square Leclerc, to the magnificent Square Mistral. Then the 3 km (2 mile) long Boulevard du Midi connects with the Corniche de l'Esterel (Corniche d'Or).

Quartier Anglais

Opposite the Boulevard du Midi extends the Quartier Anglais (English Quarter) with its sumptuous villas. The Boulevard Leader leads up to the Croix des Gardes (164 m (538 ft) above sea-level), situated in a mimosa copse (blossom time Feb.–March); this is a fine viewpoint with the best light towards evening. 1 km (¾ mile) to the north-west is the Rocher de Roquebillière (130 m (427 ft)) above the little river of the same name.

*Vieux Port

To the east below the Old Town lies the Vieux Port (Old Port); at its north-eastern corner is the Gare Maritime (Marine Railway Station; 1957).

To the north the port is bordered by the pretty Allées de la Liberté which are lined with plane trees. Here in the morning the fine Marché aux Fleurs (Flower Market) takes place. At the western end of the Allées stands the Hôtel de Ville (Town Hall; 1874–76). The Rue Félix-Faure, which runs parallel on the north, and its eastern extension, the Rue d'Antibes, are the main shopping streets of the town.

Le Cannet

From the northern edge of the Inner Town the broad Boulevard Carnot leads northwards to the beautifullly situated villa settlement of Le Cannet from which there are fine views.

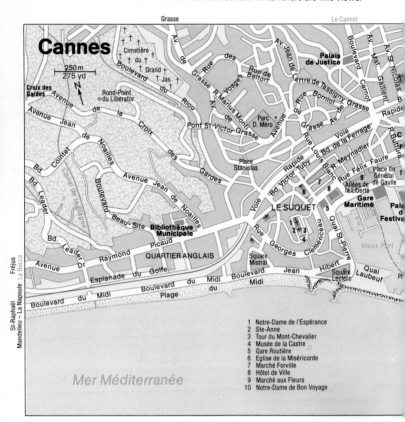

1 Notre-Dame de l'Espérance
2 Ste-Anne
3 Tour du Mont-Chevalier
4 Musée de la Castre
5 Gare Routière
6 Eglise de la Miséricorde
7 Marché Forville
8 Hôtel de Ville
9 Marché aux Fleurs
10 Notre-Dame de Bon Voyage

*Palais des Festivals

On the east side of the fort stands the Palais des Festivals, opened in 1982. It is an impresssive complex of buildings with three large auditoriums (the most modern technical apparatus includes sound studios, simultaneous interpretation arrangements, audio-visual equipment and large projectors). There are 11 conference rooms, 2 exhibition halls (one of which has 14,000 sq. m (16,745 sq. ft) of undivided useful space), a casino, a night-club and a restaurant. In this building the annual film festival is held.

Address
Boulevard de la Croisette 1

*Boulevard de la Croisette

The centre of tourist activity is the Boulevard de la Croisette which extends eastward from the new Palais des Festivals

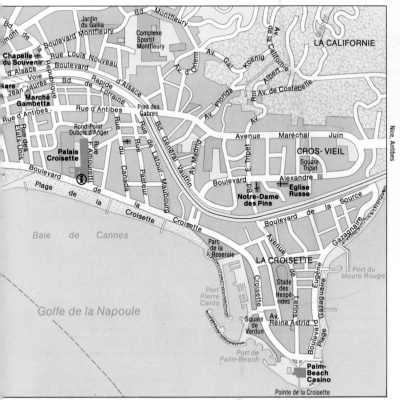

ILES DE LERINS

LEVEL 4

LEVEL 3

LEVEL 1/2

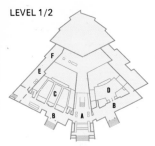

GROUND-LEVEL

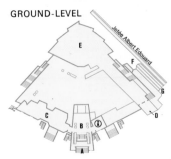

Cannes
Palais des Festivals

LEVELS 5 and 6 (no plan)
Roof Terrace 1700 sq. m (2033 sq. yd)

LEVEL 4
A Rooms I and J (each 80 seats)
B Room K (150 seats)
C Large Reception Hall ''Les Ambassadeurs''

LEVEL 3
A Room a (300 seats)
B Rooms b, c, d and e (each 40 seats)
C Rooms f, g and h (each 50 seats)
D Ante-room
E Foyers
F Internal Corridor (Rue Interieure)
G Grand Auditorium
H Claude Debussy Theatre
I Press Club
K Television Studio
L Press Conference Room (300 seats)
M Radio Studio
N Press Offices

LEVEL 2
F Organisers' Offices
   Audio-Visual Production
   Projection Rooms and
   Interpreters' Booths

LEVEL 1
A Palais Corridor (Rue de Palais)
B Foyers
C Grand Auditorium (hall with 2400 seats)
D Claude Debussy Theatre (1000 seats)
E Administration of the Palais des Festivals

GROUND-LEVEL
A Main Entrance   E Casino
B Entrance Hall   F Le Bistingo
C Reception and   Restaurant
   Exhibition Hall   G Entrance to Car
D Casino Entrance   Park

ⓘ Information

BASEMENT LEVEL 1 (no plan)
Exhibition Area 14,000 sq. m (16,744 sq. yd)

BASEMENT LEVEL 2 (no plan)
Parking for 900 cars; lorry ramp, store, workshops

along the Rade de Cannes (fine sandy beach); from it there is a magnificent view of the gulf and the offshore Lerin Islands (Îles de Lérins; see below). On its left side stands the Palais Croisette (the former Palais des Festivals) with the Service de Tourisme (Municipal Tourist Bureau; information). In these streets there are luxury hotels and high-class shops.

The eastern section of the boulevard bends south at the fine Parc de la Roseraie, skirts the new port layout of the Port Pierre Canto and ends at the southern tip of the Pointe de la Croisette by the Port de Palm-Beach and the Palm Beach Casino. On the east side of the peninsula the pleasant Boulevard Eugène-Gazagnaire (fine bathing beach) leads north to the Port du Moure Rouge.

La Californie

From the eastern part of the Boulevard de la Croisette one can go northwards through the district of Cros-Veil on the far side of the railway line (the Église Russe (Russian Church), on the Boulevard Alexandre-III is well worth seeing) to the especially charming part of the town known as "La Californie". This area is overlooked by the Observatoire de Super-Cannes (325 m (1067 ft); observation tower, orientation table and the terminus of the old funicular). Below on the Boulevard des Pins is the notable Mémorial St-Georges (to the memory of the Duke of Albany).

Farther north lies the pretty Villa Fiesole on the avenue of the same name.

Îles de Lérins   D5

The island group of the Îles de Lérins lies between the Golfe de la Napoule and the Golfe Juan. The two principal islands are Ste-Marguerite and St-Honorat.

Location
4 km (2 miles) south

Ferry
several times a day

As early as the 5th and 6th c. the islands were an important centre of ecclesiastical erudition and monastic life. In the year 660 the monastery assumed the Rule of St Benedict. Attacks by the Saracens and later by pirates from Genoa affected the monks very severely and in the 16th c. the convent began to decline into obscurity.

Ste-Marguerite 3 km (2 miles) long and up to 1 km ($\frac{1}{2}$ mile) wide, is the largest island of the group and is covered with eucalyptus and pine woods. On its northern side stands a fort (17th c.; fortified by Vauban), which served for a long time as a prison. Towards the end of the 17th c. the man known as the "Masque de Fer" (Man in the Iron Mask), who was surrounded in secrecy and whose identity has never been established, was held prisoner here.

Ste-Marguerite

About 700 m (765 yd) from Ste-Marguerite (ferry) lies the Île St-Honorat, 1.5 km (1 mile) long and up to 400 m (438 yd) wide and also covered with pine woods. On a tongue of land in the south lie the monastery buildings which were once fortified and, it is believed, were a foundation of St Honoratus, Bishop of Arles, who died in 429.

St-Honorat

In the south by the sea stands the impressive Château St-Honorat the tower built in the 11th c. as a refuge against pirates

The famous seashore promenade of Cannes: the Boulevard de la Croisette

and later altered; there are beautiful cloisters on the ground floor and on the first floor (extensive view).

There were formerly seven chapels scattered about the island, but today the only two remaining are the Chapelle St-Sauveur, an Early Christian smooth-wall building, with a diameter of almost 10 m (33 ft), and the Chapelle de la Trinité, an early medieval cemetery chapel.

Mandelieu–La Napoule   D4

Location
5 km (3 miles) west

The twin villages of Mandelieu–La Napoule, which are bisected by the motorway, are situated between the mouth of the rivers Siagne and Argentier at the foot of the Massif du Tanneron.

Picturesquely situated by the sea and popular as a holiday place, the village sector of La Napoule-Plage is overlooked by a restored castle (14th c.; art exhibition) standing on a porphyry rock. From the nearby hill of San Peire (131 m (430 ft) ruined chapel; 45 minutes' walk) there is a fine view.

Théoule-sur-Mer   D4

Location
7 km (4 miles) south-west
of Cannes

In the western part of the Golfe de la Napoule lies the resort of Théoule-sur-Mer which has an 18th c. soap-works by the sea, remodelled into a manor house, and a harbour which dates from the 17th c. The slopes are lined with tiers of apartments in old Sardinian style; in the vicinity of the yacht harbours Port de la Rague and Port de la Galère to the south lies the Pointe de l'Aiguille, above which the settlement of Théoule-Superieur is highly regarded as a place in which to spend holidays.

Vallauris – Golfe-Juan   D5

The locality above the Golfe-Juan with the seaside estate of the same name was originally called "Vallis Aurea" (Golden Valley). This little town with its potteries, its vineyards and orange groves once belonged to the monks of Lérins.

Location
5 km (3 miles) north-east

The only relic of the Middle Ages is the Romanesque chapel, in the beautiful crypt of which Picasso painted between 1952 and 1959 his picture "War and Peace". The monastery which was fortified in the 12th c. was destroyed in 1569 and rebuilt during the Renaissance. Today it houses the Musée National Picasso (modern art) and the Musée de Vallauris. In front of the church (market in the morning) stands Picasso's sculpture "Man with a Sheep".

Pottery has been important in Vallauris since the time of the Romans. After the Second World War the activity of Pablo Picasso gave the place a fresh impetus. Today there are about a hundred potters working in Vallauris and their products are sold in the streets. The biennial pottery fair assures the future of this craft.

Pottery

Vallauris: a potter's shop . . .   *and a sculpture by Picasso*

Carpentras   C3

Région: Provence-Alpes-Côte d'Azur
Département: Vaucluse
Altitude: 102 m (335 ft)
Population: 26,000

Location

The little industrial town of Carpentras lies between Mont
Ventoux to the north-east and the Plateau de Vaucluse to the
south-east, in a plain which is open to the Rhône. The River
Alzon flows past the north of town centre.
The town is descended from the ancient Carpentoracte which,
from 1320 until the French Revolution (1789), was the capital
of the Papal county of Venaissin.

St-Siffrein

In the town centre rises the former Gothic Cathedral of St-
Siffrein, built between 1405 and 1519. It is a single-aisled
building, the nave of which is flanked on both sides by chapels.
The stump of a tower is to be seen on both sides of the west
façade which was altered in the 17th c. but nevertheless
remains incomplete; in more recent times another tower was
added on the south.
The church is entered through a door in the south wall (the
Porte Juive = Jews' Door) which is decorated with remarkable
figures and which reveals the typical Flamboyant Style of Late
Gothic. The nave, without transepts, is richly decorated and
includes a number of remarkable panels as well as a radiant halo
of gilded wood (1694) by Jacques Bernus. In a chapel to the
left of the choir is a collection of religious art.
On the north side of the church are the remains of the
Romanesque building and a Roman triumphal arch, dating
from the 1st c. AD, which had been incorporated in the
Romanesque church and on the narrow sides of which
prisoners and trophies of war are represented.

Palais de Justice

Opening times
Mon.–Fri. mornings

Adjoining the north side of the church is the Palais de Justice
which was built in 1640 in imitation of Italian Baroque style. It
was formerly the episcopal palace. The interior has some
magnificently furnished rooms including the Bishop's Room
(18th c. prayer-desk), the Council Room and the Criminal
Court (cartouches with views of the towns of the Venaissin).

Museums

Address
Boulevard Albin-Durand

Opening times
Wed.–Mon. 10 a.m.–midday
and 4–6 p.m.

The most important museums of Carpentras are housed in a
large common complex in the west of the Inner Town.
The Musée Comtadin has collections of the ethnology of the
surroundings. The Musée Duplessis possesses several notable
panels created by local painters (Duplessis, Lebrun, etc.) as
well as some of Italian and Dutch origin; the Musée Sobirats
houses artistic handicraft, the Musée Lapidaire has finds from
the Iron Age to the early Middle Ages as well as a collection of
Natural History.

Bibliothèque Inguimbertine

The Library, opposite the museum block on the north, commemorates Bishop d'Inguimbert (Bishop 1735–57); he was a bibliophile who bought up numerous libraries. Later the collection was increased by donations, so that today there are about 220,000 volumes available as well as manuscripts, prints, etc.

Address
Boulevard Albin-Durand

Opening times
Mon. 2–6.30 p.m.
Tues.–Fri. 9.30 a.m.–
6.30 p.m.
Sat. 9.30 a.m.–midday

Synagogue

The Synagogue of Carpentras is the oldest remaining in France. It was built in the 15th c. and restored in the 18th c. and again in 1958. On the ground floor and in the basement are the ritual baths, some partly dating from the 14th c., as well as the kosher bakery; on the first floor is the place of worship which received its present furnishings in the 18th c.

Location
Place de la Mairie

Opening times
Mon.–Fri. 10 a.m.–midday
and 3–5 p.m.

Hôtel-Dieu in Carpentras

The Hôtel-Dieu (hospital; 1750) also goes back to the time of Bishop d'Inguimbert. This two-storeyed Classical building at the southern end of the town centre comprises an inner courtyard with two fountains; a monumental staircase leads up to the upper floor. On the ground floor the pharmacy with its original furnishings is of interest.

Address
Place Aristide Briand

Opening times
Mon., Wed., Thurs. 9–
11.30 a.m.

Venasque

South-east of Carpentras the village of Venasque has a picturesque situation in the Vaucluse. Here the 13th c. church and the baptistery (6th and 12th c.) are worthy of note.

Location
11 km (7 miles) south

Castellane

Région: Provence-Alpes-Côte d'Azur
Département: Alpes-de-Haute-Provence
Altitude: 724 m (2376 ft)
Population: 1500

The township of Castellane lies in the south-east of Provence on the Route Napoléon and on the River Verdon (see entry), which to the west of here flows through the well-known gorges. Castellane is, therefore, of touristic importance as the starting-point for a visit to the Grand Canyon du Verdon.

Location

Townscape

On the northern edge of Castellane there are some remains of the old walls, the most important relic of which is the Tour Pentagonale (Five-angled Tower).
At the western end of the Old Town with its narrow streets rises

Castellane: Notre-Dame du Roc . . .

and Clock-tower

the picturesque Tour de l'Horloge (14th c. clock-tower). Of interest here are the Fontaine aux Lions (Lion Fountain; partly Romanesque) and the Church of St-Victor, originally 12th c. but altered later on several occasions.

Notre-Dame du Roc

Over the little town towers a mighty almost cubic block of rock, 104 m (604 ft) high on which stands the little Chapel of Notre-Dame du Roc. To the rear of the parish church on the eastern end of the Old Town (not particularly important) a rewarding path leads to the rear of the limestone block and past the Stations of the Cross up to the top, from which there is a good view of Castellane and of the river as it flows into the gorge.

Châteauneuf-du-Pape   C2

Région: Provence-Alpes-Côte d'Azur
Département: Vaucluse
Altitude: 117 m (384 ft)
Population: 2000

Location

The famous wine town of Châteauneuf-du-Pape lies between Orange and Avignon in a gently undulating landscape near the left bank of the Rhône away from the main roads.

Viticulture

Châteauneuf-du-Pape is situated amid the greatest concentration of the Rhône vineyards. The red wine produced here is one of the best in the country and has normally the greatest specific gravity (sugar content of unfermented grape juice). The impetus for the standardisation of the quality of wine and the corresponding grading originated in Châteauneuf (see Practical Information – Wine). There are many opportunities to visit the wine cellars and to sample the products ("visites de cave" and "dégustation de vins").

Townscape

Châteauneuf-du-Pape is clustered about the ruins of the castle, which the Popes erected during the time of their exile in Avignon and from which the place gets its name. Only the high tower and remains of the walls are still to be seen but the panorama is impressive.

The Musée du Père Anselme (daily 9 a.m.–midday and 2–6 p.m.) exhibits an interesting collection concerning the history of viticulture which was introduced here by the Popes.

Corniches de la Riviera   D5

Région: Provence-Alpes-Côte d'Azur
Département: Alpes-Maritime

Nice (see entry) is the starting-point of three different Corniches (the name implies a road jutting out on the edge of a mountain), well-known roads of which the Moyenne Corniche and the Grande Corniche are the most beautiful in Europe; they are built on the slopes or at the foot of the Maritime Alps in the direction of Menton (see entry).

General View

The distance between Nice and Menton on all three routes is about 30 km (19 miles).

*Corniche du Littoral

The Corniche du Littoral running along the seashore – it is also called Corniche Inférieure or Petite Corniche – has beautiful views but it cannot compare with the two more elevated Corniches and in addition it carries heavy traffic which, especially in the many built-up areas through which is passes, leads to congestion.

**Moyenne Corniche

The Moyenne Corniche is constructed half-way up the slopes which face the sea. It crosses many bridges where there are fine views and passes through rock galleries. The road, which was completed in 1939, terminates in Monaco (see entry). It is certainly the most beautiful of the three stretches because it is nearer the sea than the Grande Corniche and offers opportunities to view the beauties of the coast one by one.

Digne

**Grande Corniche

The highest stretch is the Grande Corniche which attains an elevation of 530 m (1740 ft). It was built in the time of Napoleon I and thanks to its height offers a magnificent extensive panorama over the highly structured coastline.

Note

The visitor who uses the Grande Corniche as part of a round tour from Nice is advised to choose the Moyenne Corniche for the outward run, because it reveals the magnificence of the landscape in individual views, while the return journey on the Grande Corniche gives once more a superb general view.

Digne   C4

Région: Provence-Alpes-Côte d'Azur
Département: Alpes-de-Haute-Provence
Altitude: 608 m (1995 ft)
Population: 16,000

Location

The town of Digne lies in the heart of Provence, approximately on a line joining Grenoble to Cannes, in the foothills of the Alps.

Townscape

The 15th c. Cathedral of St-Jérôme has an elevated situation in the Old Town. In the Romanesque former Cathedral of Notre-Dame-du-Bourg (12th–13th c.) can be seen remains of wall-paintings of the 14th–16th c. as well as a Merovingian altar.

*Serre-Ponçon (Barrage et Lac de Serre-Ponçon)

There is a rewarding drive from Digne to the north (at first not on the direct road D900 but west of this on the D900 A) through the Clue de Barles and Clue de Verdaches, two romantic gorges; then over the Col de Maure (1747 m (4421 ft)) to the Barrage de Serre-Ponçon (see Gap – Surroundings). After leaving Le Vernet on the return journey one can take the D900 instead of the D900 A and cross the Col du Labouret (1240 m (4070 ft)).

Donzère-Mondragon   C2

Région: Rhône-Alpes
Département: Drôme
Altitude: 64 m (210 ft)

Location

The Rhône Dam was constructed near the two little villages of Donzère and Mondragon (between Montélimar and Orange), and this gives it its name.

Rhône Dam Donzère-Mondragon

Between Donzère (in the north) and Mondragon (in the south)

Rhône Barrage near Donzère and Mondragon

the 28 km (13 mile) long Canal de Donzère avoids a very narrow stretch of the Rhône, into which flow the rivers Conche and Ardèche (see entry).

The Usine de Bollène, one of the river power stations, lies not far north of the village of the same name. As well as the buildings housing the turbines, it includes a lock for canal traffic. The construction, which was completed in 1952, is 240 m (788 ft) long and 15 m (49 ft) high. On the downstream side a road crosses the canal and on the west side of this there is a car park. The interior of the power station is not open to the public.

A short way downstream from Bollène there is a very good view of the canal from the suspension bridge, across which runs road D994 to St-Esprit.

Not far north of the river power station the Complexe Eurodif, a diffusion plant for the enrichment of uranium as nuclear fuel, is in course of construction. With its associated plants it will be of great importance for the economic development of the area of Tricastin. Eurodif is a joint project of Belgium, Spain, France and Italy.

Eurodif

Draguignan   D4

Région: Provence-Alpes-Côte d'Azur
Département: Var
Altitude: 181 m (594 ft)
Population: 28,000

Esterel

Location

Draguignan is situated about 27 km (17 miles) inland from Fréjus, north of the Massif des Maures and the Valley of the River Artuby which border these mountains.

History

In Roman times the place was called Antea. In the 5th c. the district was Christianised by Hermentarius, the first Bishop of Antibes. According to legend the Bishop had won the confidence of the inhabitants by killing a dragon which had threatened the whole countryside and laid it to waste. The name of the town also recalls this episode; it appears to be derived from "dragon" and the legendary monster figures in the arms of the town.

In the 17th c. when Anne of Austria was acting as a Regent for her under-aged son Louis XIV, the town was surrounded by a stout defensive wall. During the French Revolution Draguignan was the district capital and then the capital of the Département of Var.

Townscape

The old town centre of Draguignan is clustered about the clock-tower (Tour de l'Horloge) which stands on a rock from which there is a fine view. Normally the tower is closed but the key can be obtained at the Office de Tourisme (Tourist Office, south of the Old Town in the Boulevard Clemenceau). Not far north-west in Rue de la Juiverie there is a museum housed in a former Ursuline convent; as well as ceramics, furniture, French and Flemish paintings of the 17th c., the museum has one of the 14th c. manuscripts of the "Roman de la Rose" the most important work of Courtly poetry in France (12th c.).

Esterel (Massif de l'Esterel)   D4

Région: Provence-Alpes-Côtes d'Azur
Départements: Var and Alpes-Maritimes
Altitude: up to 618 m (2028 ft)

Location

The Esterel Mountains rise immediately behind the coast between St-Raphaël in the west and Cannes in the east. They are bordered in the north by the Valley of the Argentière and in the west by the Valley of the Reyran.

Landscape

The Esterel Mountains are formed of old volcanic rock, predominantly of porphyry, the characteristic red colour of which is a feature of the landscape. The proliferation of conifers, cork-oaks and coriaceous trees, which formerly covered the entire massif, has in recent years fallen victim to devastating forest fires and the new thin vegetation is scarcely as high as a man.

* Mont Vinaigre

The highest peak of the Esterel Mountains is Mont Vinaigre (618 m (2028 ft)) near to its northern escarpment. It can be reached from Fréjus (see entry) on road N7, from which in

11 km (7 miles) a narrow forest road branches off. There is
an extensive panorama from the summit.

From the coastal village of Agay (see St-Raphaël – Surroundings), situated on the Corniche de l'Esterel (see below), a road
leads inland and encircles (mostly as a single-track road) the
Pic de l'Ours (496 m (1628 ft)). This summit in the eastern part
of the mountain range, from which there is an extensive view,
is best reached from the nearby Col Notre-Dame, to which the
mountain road climbs up with numerous bends. From this
stretch of road there are magnificent views of the deeply
fissured rocky coast. It takes about half an hour's climbing to
reach the summit of the Pic de l'Ours on which there is a radio
and television transmitter. The panorama from here is highly
impressive.

* Pic de l'Ours

The Corniche de l'Esterel (N98) is a charming road which
winds its way along the rocky coast between St-Raphaël and
Cannes. It runs through the resort of Boulouris, passes the
impressive Cap du Drammont (lighthouse; offshore the little Île
d'Or) and the village of Agay which has a fine situation on a
bay; on the Pointe de la Baumette is a memorial to the aviator
and writer Antoine de St-Exupéry. The road then continues
through Anthéor with the Pic du Cap Roux (452 m (1482 ft);
rewarding view) rising on the left, Le Trayas, Miramar (with a
marina), La Galère (in the holiday complex of Port-la-Galère
are remarkable grotto-like houses) and Théoule-sur-Mer.
Cannes is then reached via La Napoule.

* Corniche de l'Esterel

Red porphyry rocks of the Esterel Massif

Etang de Berre   D3

Région: Provence-Alpes-Côte d'Azur
Département: Bouches-du-Rhône
Area: 15,000 ha (37,056 acres)

Location

The Etang de Berre is a huge lagoon to the north-west of
Marseilles. It is connected to the Mediterranean by the Caronte
Canal to the west; in the south is the Chaîne de l'Estaque, a
ridge up to 279 m (916 ft) high; to the west extends the Plain
of the Crau.

Landscape

The Etang de Berre is a popular recreation area for the people
of Marseilles and district; nevertheless on the southern shore an
extremely active industrial zone has developed. Satellite towns
have also arisen.
Near the eastern shore of the lake lies the international airport
Marseille-Marignane.

Martigues

See entry

Fontaine-de-Vaucluse   D3

Région: Provence-Alpes-Côte d'Azur
Département: Vaucluse
Altitude: 80 m (263 ft)
Population: 500

Location

The little village of Fontaine-de-Vaucluse, well known for its
spring, lies in the west of Provence about 30 km (19 miles) east
of Avignon.

History

Fontaine-de-Vaucluse was made famous by the Italian poet
and humanist Francesco Petrarca (Petrarch; 1304–74); he was
born in Arezzo in Italy but took up residence in the former Papal
town of Avignon and later withdrew to his country seat in the
Vaucluse where he devoted himself entirely to his literary
pursuits.

Description

The village, which has an uncommonly picturesque situation at
the end of the valley and which is dominated by the ruins of the
castle of the Bishops of Cavaillon, owes its name to the hollow
which surrounds it ("vallis clausa"). It is reached by a branch
road; near the centre there are a number of car parks for visitors.

In the house in which Petrarch is believed to have lived there is
a little museum devoted to the poet and his works. Near the
Place de la Colonne (see below) stands the 11th c.
Romanesque Church of St-Véran, in the crypt of which is the
grave of St Véran, who was Bishop of Cavaillon in the 6th c.

**Fontaine de Vaucluse

In the centre of the village lies the pretty Place de la Colonne, shaded by plane trees. Here stands a column erected in 1804 commemorating the 500th anniversary of Petrarch's birth. All round the square there are restaurants, some of which have terraces by or above the river.

The Fontaine de Vaucluse, which is a resurgent spring of the River Sorgue, is reached from here by a roadway 800 m (875 yd) long which is generally only passable on foot because of the numerous stalls set up here (herbs of Provence, olive-wood carvings, leather goods, souvenirs, etc.). There is no longer any facility for parking here. On the right at the edge of the village and by the river stands a cave museum (daily 10 a.m.–midday and 2–6.30 p.m.), which in particular provides information about the nearby spring. Also close at hand is the Musée des Restrictions, with souvenirs from times of war and need (1870, 1914–18 and 1939–45).

Farther along the road is a paper-mill with a great water-wheel; here paper is made according to a 15th c. process (a visit is possible). On a bluff on the far side of the deep turquoise river rises the ruined castle.

The roadway continues upwards into the narrowing valley beside the river, which is fringed with ancient plane trees and which rushes down here in foaming cascades during winter and spring floods. Set into the rock on the left above the spring is a tablet, placed here in 1963 by the Dante Society in memory of Petrarch and his beloved Laura.

The actual Fontaine de Vaucluse is a funnel-shaped spring at

The River Sorgue rises in the Fontaine de Vaucluse

85

the foot of a vertical 200 m (656 ft) high rock wall. Here water seeps out of the limestone of the Plateau de Vaucluse and, depending on rainfall, the levels of water and the force of the spring vary considerably.

Fréjus   D4

Région: Provence-Alpes-Côte d'Azur
Département: Var
Altitude: 8 m (26 ft)
Population: 33,000

Location

The town of Fréjus is situated in the eastern section of the French Riviera between the Massif des Maures and the Massif de l'Esterel. Not far to the south-east the River Argens flows into the Mediterranean.

History

Whether the site of the Forum Julii, founded by Caesar, was already settled in pre-Roman times has not been conclusively proved. Its quickly increasing importance, however, is shown by the building of a harbour before the birth of Christ. In the 4th c. Fréjus became the see of a bishop, and in the 10th c. it suffered severely from attacks by the Saracens. From the 12th c. onwards the development was frequently influenced by epidemics of plague. The harbour had to be finally abandoned in the 18th c. because of silting up. In August 1944 Allied forces landed here.
The breaching of the Malpasset Dam in 1959 was a catastrophe. The mighty rush of water down the valley caused 421 deaths and enormous damage.

Cathedral

Location
Place Formigé

Opening times
Tues.–Sun. 9.30 a.m.–
midday and 2–6 p.m.

Guided tours

The cathedral, built in the 11th and 12th c., is almost completely surrounded by other buildings; only the doorway leading into the narthex (lobby) is visible from the outside. Above rises the tower with its spire, rectangular in the lower part but octagonal above.
The narthex of the cathedral is entered through the south doorway with its impressive Renaissance doors (1530), which, however, are usually protected by wooden shutters and are shown only on guided tours. The carving represents scenes from the life of the Virgin, St Peter and St Paul.

* Baptistery

To the left of the narthex is the Baptistery, an eight-sided building of the 4th–5th c. with eight ancient pillars. The font in the middle is sunk into the floor.

Interior

In the two-aisled cathedral can be seen, left of the entrance, two marble tombs (17th c.), a wooden Crucifix (16th c.) and a beautiful 16-part altar-picture (15th c.) by Jacques Durandi (school of Nice); in the chapel to the left of the High Altar are two other bishops' tombs (14th and 15th c.).

* Cloister

Steps from the narthex give access to the Cloister which is composed of delicate pillars. The coffered ceiling has a cycle of

In the Cloisters of Fréjus

pictures of scenes from the Apocalypse, not all of which have been preserved, dating from the 14th to the 15th c. In the centre of the cloister is a well.

On the north side of the cloister is a double staircase, the steps of which were once used as seats for the nearby Roman amphitheatre (see below). The upper storey of the cloister was originally also enclosed on all four sides but a great deal was destroyed in the French Revolution, so that only one side of the gallery now remains. In the adjoining room can be found the Musée Archéologique with a Roman mosaic floor and other finds of the Greek and Roman eras.

Musée Archéologique

Amphitheatre

The Roman Amphitheatre (Arènes; 1st–2nd c. AD) measures 114 m (125 yd) by 82 m (90 yd) and once had accommodation for 10,000 spectators. To a great extent it is unrestored and also largely free of modern buildings. On the north side the oval leans against the slope, while on the south side an elaborate vaulted construction supports the steps from below.

Location
Rue Henri Vadon

Opening times
Wed.–Mon. 9.30 a.m.–
midday and 2–6.30 p.m.

Aqueduct

In the north-east of the town on road N7 there are still some remains of the Roman aqueduct which tapped the River Siagnole near Mons, a distance of 50 km (31 miles).

Roman Theatre

Not far west of the aqueduct are the remains of a Roman theatre laid out in a semicircle.

Pagoda

Outside the town to the north on road N7, stands a Buddhist pagoda, a somewhat unconventional sight with its vivid coloration, built by Indo-Chinese during the 1914–18 war.

Barrage de Malpasset   D4

Location
10 km (6 miles) north

First of all one follows road D37 which leads to the A8 motorway, but just before the junction with the motorway one turns to the right and follows the Valley of the Reyran upstream. The road which in its final part is not made up, goes under the motorway and ends not far below the Barrage de Malpasset, the dam which burst in 1959. Ninety minutes should be allowed to wander around the remains of the dam; there is an explanatory diagram and a general sketch by the path.

Looking at the gigantic blocks of reinforced concrete which were torn away by the flood wave and which today lie strewn about everywhere, gives one a vague idea of the enormous force of the water as it rushed towards the sea from the reservoir.

Le Muy   D4

Location
11 km (7 miles) west

The lively community of Le Muy at the confluence of the rivers Nartuby and Argens, is situated in an area of intensive agriculture. The 15th c. church and the round Tour Charles-Quint (Tower of Charles V) are notable. Anglo-American parachute troops landed here on 15 August 1944.

About 2.5 km (1½ miles) south-west on the slope of the Montagne de Roquebrune (up to 372 m (1022 ft)); fine views and peculiar rock formations stands the Chapelle Notre-Dame-de-la-Roquette to which there are pilgrimages on 25 March, on the second Monday after Easter and on 8 September.

Gap   C4

Région: Provence-Alpes-Côte d'Azur
Département: Hautes-Alpes
Altitude: 733 m (2406 ft)
Population: 31,000

The busy Départemental town of Gap is an important traffic junction on the Route Napoléon; it lies on the River Luye in the north of Provence and in about the same latitude as Montélimar.

History

The place was already populated when the Romans penetrated into this region. Almost every trace of the Roman settlement of Vapincum disappeared during the succeeding centuries,

Fréjus: Ancient theatre . . .   *and Malpasset Barrage*

especially as the place lay on the crossing of important
north–south and east–west routes and was always much
sought after and consequently fought for. In the year 558 the
Lombards laid the town waste; in 1650 plague removed two-
thirds of the population and in 1692 Savoy troops burned
down almost all the houses. In March 1815 Napoleon arrived
on his way back from Elba and passed through Gap on his
march to Paris.

*Townscape

Gap has an unusually charming situation with the backdrop of
the Alps on the north of the town. Because of its pleasant
climate Gap is popular as a health resort, but has also a good
reputation as a starting-point for the winter sports areas.
In the Avenue du Maréchal Foch, a little to the east of the town
centre, can be found the Musée Départemental (museum)
which houses Gallo-Roman antiquities, ceramics and material
on local and regional history.
The 19th c. cathedral in the town centre is in the Romanesque
style.

*Serre-Ponçon (Barrage et Lac de Serre-Ponçon)   C4

Road N94 leads east from Gap to the Barrage de Serre-Ponçon,
a 120 m (394 ft) high dam built between 1955 and 1961,

Location
20 km (12 miles) east

Gap and the backdrop of the Alps

which confines the water of the Durance and forms the great Lac de Serre-Ponçon, about 3000 ha (2415 acres) in extent.

The best excursion is a circular drive; from Gap take the above road as far as Chorges then turn right on to the D3 which winds its way south, with beautiful viewpoints, to the dam; the best general view of the dam is from the Belvédère (viewpoint) a little way north on the road. The D3 continues to the junction of the D900 B. Take this road, cross the Durance and then, at varying distances from the water, follow the southern bank of the reservoir. In about 20 km (12 miles) turn west on to the D954. A little way from the road can be seen the Demoiselles Coiffées (Ladies with Hats), or "Demoiselles du Sauzé", a group of earth pyramids. Still following the bank of the lake you reach the N94 near Savines-le-Lac where once again cross the lake and return to Gap via Chorges (see above).

Gordes   D3

Région: Provence-Alpes-Côte d'Azur
Département: Vaucluse
Altitude: 373 m (1224 ft)
Population: 1600

Location

The hillside township of Gordes lies on the southern flank of the Plateau de Vaucluse about 40 km (25 miles) east of Avignon.

* * Townscape

Gordes has become very well known by reason of its extremely picturesque situation on the slope down from the Plateau de Vaucluse to the Valley of the Coulon. This "village perché" is dominated by its 16th c. castle.

* Musée Vasarely

The Fondation Vasarely has found a home in the fortified castle which is flanked by towers at its corners. Here are exhibited works by the Hungarian-born painter Victor Vasarely (born 1908) who is one of the most important artists of Constructivism. As well as abstract paintings which consist primarily of flat geometric forms, there are also kinetic objects on view.

Opening times
Wed.–Mon. 10 a.m.–midday and 2–6 p.m.

* * Village des Bories

The Village des Bories lies 2 km (1 mile) south of Gordes. From the main road a narrow carriageway branches off to the west; it is enclosed in places by walls made of boulders and in spite of stretches of one-way operation cannot be used for large motor or towed caravans.
Bories are built of flat stones without mortar, that is in drystonework, and are generally without windows. The slope of the roof consists of a kind of false vaulting whereby each layer of stone overhangs the one immediately below, until the

Opening times
daily 9 a.m.–sunset

Gordes: a typical "village perché"

An archaic village: village of "bories" near Gordes

slopes coincide in the middle of the roof. These constructions which are quite common in Provence used to serve generally as herdsmen's huts but, as in the case here, rural farms and whole settlements could consist of bories. Examples of this curiously archaic construction had their precursors in the New Stone Age and were built in Provence until the beginning of the 20th c.; they could be put up by an experienced craftsman with no other tool than a hammer.

The settlement of bories near Gordes was thoroughly restored in the 1960s. It is probably the largest and most complete of its kind still remaining. The village is surrounded by a wall, scarcely as high as a man, enclosing the five groups of huts. Besides houses and stables there are a winepress, bakery, etc.; in a few of the bories farming implements of several periods are exhibited. In a two-storey 17th c. house there is instructive literature about this method of construction and its corresponding forms in other countries.

The view to the south over the hills covered with maquis (evergreen shrubs) is charming.

Other bories, generally standing on their own, are to be found in other places around Gordes.

Roussillon   D3

Location
10 km (6 miles) east of
Gordes

The little hill village of Roussillon has a picturesque situation in the well-known ochre area on the south of the Plateau de Vaucluse. The whole little town reveals the intensive colour of ochre which was mined here and which brought prosperity to to the citizens as a raw material much in demand for the manufacture of paint, until the competition from synthetic pigments became too great. At the entrance to the Upper Town stands an attractive belfry. Farther uphill past the church there is a Belvédère (viewing platform) with an orientation panel. All around in the forests can be seen the ochre rocks, the colours of which vary from violet to light yellowish brown.

The most impressive ochre formations and the most convenient to reach are to be found in a pine wood to the right of road D199 which leads to Apt (see Lubéron).

°Ochre Rocks

La Grande-Motte   D2

Région: Languedoc-Roussillon
Département: Hérault
Altitude: sea-level
Population: 4000

The modern holiday centre of La Grande-Motte lies on the Golfe du Lion, 10 km (6 miles) west of Aigues-Mortes and 20 km (12 miles) south-east of Montpellier. It is actually not part of Provence but of the adjoining Région of Languedoc-Roussillon.

Location

Townscape

La Grande-Motte is one of those holiday centres which are

Among the ochre rocks of Roussillon

93

essentially "drawing-board foundations" in the lagoon and
dune country west of the Camargue. It has developed into a
huge holiday town with a sophisticated infrastructure and an
architectural style which has been successful, particularly as
the temptation to put up uniform concrete skyscrapers has been
resisted.

The place is grouped around the well-equipped marina, on
both sides of which stretches a beach of fine sand. The typical
silhouette is formed by pyramid-shaped blocks of apartments.
On the east side of the harbour is a fine aquarium with more
than 30 tanks. There is a casino in La Grande-Motte.

To the north and east of the main road through the town are
holiday houses, various sports centres and a holiday village.
Sometimes in the nearby lagoons, Etang du Ponant and Etang
de Mauguio, fairly large groups of flamingoes can be observed.
Here there are also opportunities for water sports and for
fishing.

Le Grau-du-Roi   D2

Location
3 km (2 miles) south-east

Le Grau-du-Roi near by is in the Département Gard. It is
somewhat more conventional than La Grande-Motte and in
addition has "developed" into a fishing village. On the beach
near by is a large water-chute. The lagoons lying to the south-
east which extend into the countryside of the Camargue are
used mainly for obtaining sea salt.

Port-Camargue   D2

Location
5 km (3 miles) south-east of
La Grande-Motte

South of Le Grau-du-Roi lies Port-Camargue, the newest and
most easterly of the holiday towns on the coast of Languedoc-
Roussillon. Port-Camargue has excellent boating facilities and
broad sandy beaches. The complex of holiday homes and
apartment blocks, generally only one or two storeys high, are
built out into the lagoon so that many boats can be tied up right

Holiday Centre
La Grande-Motte

1 Shopping centre
2 Pyramid houses and hotels
3 Aquarium
4 Harbour Master's office
5 Camp site
6 Riding ground
7 Holiday houses
8 Golf-course
9 Holiday village
10 Games area

Skyline of the holiday centre of La Grande-Motte

outside the front door. Two broad roads run round the edge of this attractive place and finish on either side of the harbour, keeping traffic away from the residential area.

Grasse   D4

Région: Provence-Alpes-Côte d'Azur
Département: Alpes-Maritimes
Altitude: 333 m (1093 ft)
Population: 38,000

Grasse, at heart still an ancient little town, has a sheltered situation on the slope of the Roquevignon, some distance from the Mediterranean coast on the Route Napoléon, about 18 km (11 miles) north of Cannes

Location

The town is believed to have been settled in the 5th–6th c. in the time of the Merovingians; in the 12th c. Grasse obtained its independence but in the 13th came under the control of the Dukes of Provence. From 1244 until 1790 it was the see of a bishop. The perfume industry which has made Grasse world famous was introduced in the 16th c. by Catherine de Médicis.

History

Grasse is the most important centre of the perfume industry, not only in France but also in the whole of Europe. The material from which the perfume is extracted is provided by the large flower plantations and lavender fields of the surrounding area. In and around Grasse about 30 large firms process throughout

Perfume Industry

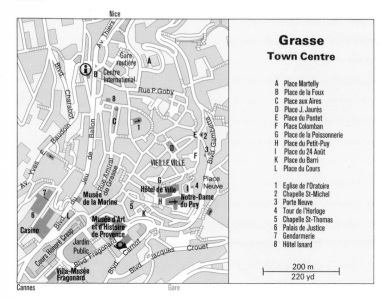

Grasse
Town Centre

A Place Martelly
B Place de la Foux
C Place aux Aires
D Place J. Jaurès
E Place du Pontet
F Place Colomban
G Place de la Poissonnerie
H Place du Petit-Puy
I Place du 24 Août
K Place du Barri
L Place du Cours

1 Eglise de l'Oratoire
2 Chapelle St-Michel
3 Porte Neuve
4 Tour de l'Horloge
5 Chapelle St-Thomas
6 Palais de Justice
7 Gendarmerie
8 Hôtel Isnard

200 m
220 yd

the year several million kilograms of blossoms (orange, rose, jasmine, thyme, rosemary, mignonette, violet, etc.). For the manufacture of perfume from natural raw materials three main methods are used; the first is the old-fashioned distillation process by means of steam; the second is an extraction process in which the perfumes together with fatty deposits are extracted by using alcohol; the third is a method of solution whereby the scents are extracted by chemical means. In order to obtain 1 kg of ethereal oil 1000 kg of orange-blossom for example, are necessary.

To obtain oil of lavender the lavender plants, which are principally gathered by hand, are allowed to dry for a week and then treated with steam in vats. After the mixture is cooled the particles of lavender oils which have a lighter specific gravity float to the top of the brew and can be removed. About 40 kg of lavender plants are necessary to obtain 1 litre of oil of lavender.

Most of the perfume factories in Grasse are open to visitors.

Walk round the town

Because of the narrow thoroughfares in the Old Town, Grasse can only be visited on foot.

The tour begins at the Office du Tourisme (Tourist Office) in the Place de la Foux; not far east of here lies the Centre International de Grasse, a modern congress and conference centre. From the southern end of the square a circular double set of steps enclosing a fountain leads down into the Old Town.

One now reaches the Place aux Aires where the lively market is held every morning and which also has a fountain; on the north side of the square is the pretty Hôtel Isnard built towards the end of the 18th c.

Place aux Aires

Following Rue de l'Amiral de Grasse southwards from the Place aux Aires one comes to the Place du Cours, from where there is a pleasant view over the parts of the town lower down and into the valley. Near by is the Parfumerie Fragonard (visits are permitted).

South of the Place du Cours is the panoramic main promenade of the town, the Cours Honoré Cresp. Here can be found the municipal casino and a number of perfumeries. A little to the south stands the Villa-Musée Fragonard (an 18th c. palace) with pictures by Jean-Honoré Fragonard (1732–1802) who was born in Grasse, and by other artists who were natives of the town.

On the east opposite the observation terrace in Rue Mirabeau stands the former Hôtel de Clapiers-Cabris, a stately palace of 1771. It now houses the Musée d'Art et d'Histoire de Provence (Museum of Provençal Art and History; closed Mondays) with historic furniture, ceramics and a collection devoted to the history of the town.

Musée d'Art et d'Histoire

To the north-east behind the museum and right in the middle of the Old Town stands the former Cathedral of Notre-Dame,

Cathédrale Notre-Dame

Grasse: Place aux Aires . . .

and perfumery laboratory

originally 12th–13th c. and extended in the 17th–18th c. Inside is a remarkable representation of the "Washing of Feet" by J. H. Fragonard, probably the only religious painting by this master of Rococo; there is also the Altar of St-Honorat which has been attributed to Bréa.

To the north, opposite the church, stands the Ancien Evêché, the former bishop's palace, built in the 13th c. and later considerably altered; it is now the Town Hall.

One returns to the Place aux Aires and the Place de la Foux through the narrow picturesque streets of the Old Town.

Cabris   D4

Location
8 km (5 miles) west

Cabris, a picturesque village above the Grasse Basin, is popular with artists. Of interest are the ruins of the 12th c. castle, a church (1606–50) and the Chapel of Ste-Marguerite with a winged altar of about 1500. At the western edge of the village stands the 16th c. Chapel of St-Jean-Baptiste.

*Gourdon   D4

Location
15 km (9 miles) north-east
of Grasse

Near the end of the Gorges du Loup (see below) the little village of Gourdon is situated on a ridge. The fortress, built in the 13th and 17th c. on Saracen foundations, houses a museum (Oriental and French weapons, pictures of the Cologne school of about 1550, primitive painting). The park-like terraces laid out by Le Nôtre partly belong to a botanical research station. From here there is a fine view of Cap d'Antibes and Cap Roux.

*Gorges du Loup   D4

Location
15–20 km (9–12 miles)
north-east

The gorge which the River Loup has cut into the rock is reached from Grasse via Gourdon (see above). The road through the gorge (in a westerly direction D3, in an easterly the far more rewarding D6) runs below rock walls up to 400 m (1313 ft) high, past the Cascade de Courmes (altogether 70 m (230 ft) high) and near to the 25 m (82 ft) high Saut du Loup.

Grignan   C2

Région: Rhône-Alpes
Département: Drôme
Altitude: 197 m (647 ft)
Population: 1200

Location

The township of Grignan lies in hilly terrain east of the Rhône Valley about 30 km (17 miles) south-west of Montélimar.

History

Grignan, which was a barony from the Middle Ages, was made famous by the Marquise de Sévigné (1626–96). The letters, which she wrote to her daughter, the wife of the last Count of Grignan, and to other contemporaries, were published in 1726

The houses of Grignan gathered round the Castle

and became celebrated for their vividness and for the details they give of contemporary life. The Marquise died in the castle at Grignan.

Townscape

The little town nestles below the castle and the church. If the visitor is following the route recommended in this guide, when he comes to Grignan he will be charmed by the whole aspect of the place.

It is advisable to visit the town on foot. There are parking facilities in the Lower Town.

On the northern edge of the Old Town lies the Place Sévigné with a fountain commemorating the Marquise. The little square is dominated by the 12th c. belfry (a defensive civic tower). Continuing past this tower, the road leads to the Upper Town and the castle; below on the right can be seen a Classical pump-room.

Below the castle stands the Church of St-Sauveur, built in the 16th c. for the canonical foundation. The left-hand wall of the nave abuts the hillside. From the gallery of this single-aisled church there is a direct entrance to the castle. With its ribbed vaulting and traceried windows the building reveals elements of Late Gothic. Near the High Altar can be seen the Tomb of the Marquise de Sévigné beneath a marble slab. Continue along the road around the castle.

St-Sauveur

Château

Opening times
Wed.–Mon. 9.30–11.30 a.m.
and 2.30–5.30 p.m.

The castle, which dominates the whole town, dates from the late Middle Ages, but was completely rebuilt in the 16th c. At the time of the French Revolution a great part had to be pulled down by order of the authorities. The present aspect is largely the result of a thorough and successful restoration at the beginning of the present century.

Through the gateway, which is flanked by towers, one enters the castle. Among the rooms which can be visited are the boudoir of Madame de Sévigné and several reception-rooms containing antique furniture and tapestries.

A large terrace-like courtyard, which is enclosed by the Renaissance façade, opens out on the south; from here a splendid view of Mont Ventoux to the south-west may be enjoyed.

Hyères   D4

Région: Provence-Alpes-Côte d'Azur
Département: Var
Altitude: 40 m (131 ft)
Population: 42,000

Location

Hyères, an important agricultural centre (wine, flowers, early vegetables) and the oldest winter health resort of the French Riviera, is situated at the foot of the 294 m (670 ft) high Castéou, 4 km (2½ miles) from the sea and 20 km (12 miles) east of Toulon.

History

Near the present-day town was the Greek foundation of Olbia. The Romans fortified the settlement, and the fortifications were subsequently extended by the Lords of Fos and by Charles d'Anjou. During the Wars of Religion (16th c.) the town suffered considerably. Hyères was "discovered" in the 19th c. as a health resort.

Old Town

The heart of the Old Town is the Place Massillon, where the lively daily market is held and where can be seen the 12th c. Tour St-Blaise, the remains of a residence of the Knights Templar.

To the west in Rue Rabaton is the birthplace of the great preacher Massillon (1663–1742). Passing along Rue Ste-Catherine one reaches the Place St-Paul (orientation table; extensive view) with the church of the same name, originally built in the 12th c. and restored in the 16th, when side chapels were added. Opposite is a charming Renaissance house with little corner turrets. A few yards to the west stands the Porte des Princes, part of a former monastery. To the north of the square in Rue du Paradis is a pretty restored 13th c. house.

South-east of the Place Massillon and the edge of the old town centre stands the 13th c. Porte de la Rade, the former main gate of the town which opens on to the Place Clemenceau. Near by in the Place de la République can be seen a statue of Massillon and the 13th c. Church of St-Louis. East of the apse of the

church, on the Cours Strasbourg, is the theatre and behind it
the attractive Jardin A. Denis.
The busy Avenue du Général-de-Gaulle leads west from the
Place Clemenceau and forms the boundary of the New Town
to the south.

New Town

The impressive Avenue Gambetta leads south from the Place
du Portalet into the New Town. To the east lies the Place
Lefèbvre and here one finds the interesting Musée Municipal
(Municipal Museum) with archaeological, local and natural
history collections.

*Jardins Olbius-Riquier

To the south of the inner town can be found the Jardins Olbius-
Riquier, a fine garden layout of 6.5 ha (16 acres) with a great
many exotic plants.

Notre-Dame-de-Consolation

The suburb of Costebelle lies 3 km (2 miles) south of the town
centre on a 98 m (322 ft) high hill. On the top of the hill there
was a place of pilgrimage as early as the 11th c. There is a fine
view from the Chapel of Notre-Dame-de-Consolation, the
tower of which is surmounted by a statue of the Madonna. A
pilgrimage to this spot takes place on 15 and 16 August. From
the chapel the 306 m (1004 ft) high Mont des Oiseaux (view)
can be climbed in about 1½ hours.

Still farther south are the ruins of the Monastery of St-Pierre
d'Almanarre (Arabic al-manar=lighthouse).

St-Pierre d'Almanarre

Hyères-Plage

By the sea south of Toulon-Hyères Airport lies the resort of
Hyères-Plage with a racecourse and the harbour of Port St-
Pierre-de-la-Mer (marina).

North-east of the airport and on the far side of the mouth of the
River Gapeau are the seaside settlements of L'Ayguade-Plage
and Le Ceinturon-Plage which have beaches of fine sand but
which are often very crowded at holiday times. This area was
once the place from which the Crusaders set sail.

L'Ayguade-Plage,
Le Ceinturon-Plage

Giens (Presqu'Île de Giens)   D4

Near Toulon-Hyères Airport the Presqu'Île de Giens juts out
into the Mediterranean. To the east of this narrow tongue of
land stretches the wide bay of Rade d'Hyères and to the west
extends the Etang des Pesqueirs, closed off on the west by a
dike along which runs the Route du Sel (Salt Road). Here are
the Salins Neufs (New Salt-pans; 500 ha (1236 acres)). These
two spits of land link the coast to the Giens Peninsula, 6.5 km

Location
5–10 km (3–6 miles) south

101

On the ferry from Giens to Porquerolles

(4 miles) long and up to 1.5 km (1 mile) wide, which only became joined to the mainland in Roman times.

On the eastern spit, which is covered with pines, are long sandy beaches, with opportunities for surfing, and the settlement of La Capte. The central point of the peninsula is Giens with its castle ruins (52 m (171 ft) above sea-level; good view). In the west near the village of La Madrague rises the highest point of the peninsula (118 m (387 ft); signal station).

Some 2 km (1 mile) east of Giens the road from Hyères ends at the ruins of the former Fort de la Tour-Fondue, built in the time of Richelieu. Immediately adjoining is the mooring-place of the motor-boats for Porquerolles (see below). To the south of the Giens Peninsula lies the Île du Grand-Ribaud, a rocky island with a lighthouse.

* Îles d'Hyères (Îles d'Or)   D/E4

Location
south to south-east of Hyères

Ferry
from Hyères-Plage to Porquerolles also from La Tour Fondue

Île de Porquerolles

The Îles d'Hyères, also known as the Îles d'Or (Golden Isles) presumably because of their mica-bearing rocks, are an island group belonging geologically to the Massif des Maures (see entry). The islands are for the most part wooded, with steep fissured slopes; they have fine natural harbours and are popular not least because of their beaches which are ideal for bathing.

The Island of Porquerolles, almost 8 km (5 miles) long and about 2 km (1 mile) wide is the largest of the archipelago. On the north coast it has flat beaches; the entire southern and eastern part falls steeply to the sea.

The principal place is Porquerolles on the main bay of the north coast. From here there is a rewarding excursion (about 45 minutes) through beautiful Mediterranean vegetation south to the Phare de l'Ousteau, the southernmost tip of the island (96 m (315 ft) above sea-level; lighthouse).

Going north-east from Porquerolles through the woods along the Plage Notre-Dame, one reaches in just over an hour the Cap des Mèdes. About half-way a path branches off on the right which leads past the Fort de la Repentance to the Sémaphore (signal station; 142 m (466 ft); view).

East of the Île de Porquerolles lies the Île de Port-Cros (6640 ha (16,408 acres). Since 1963 it and the surrounding off-shore area has been a Parc National (nature reserve); only a few people live on this island.

Île de Port-Cros

The luxuriant Mediterranean fauna and flora (primeval forests, nesting sites of rare birds, fishing grounds) and the former Fort du Moulin (17th c.) at the entrance to the harbour of Port-Cros are of considerable interest. West of the harbour lies the little Île de Bagaud (up to 59 m (194 ft) high). From Port-Cros a particularly rewarding walk (1½ hours) leads from the harbour south-east into the Vallon de la Solitude (Valley of Loneliness) and to the imposing Falaises du Sud (almost 200 m (654 ft) high steep cliffs). Also worth while is a 3 hour walk eastwards to the charming Pointe de Port-Man.

Still farther east lies the geologically interesting lonely rocky island, the Île du Levant (8 km (5 miles) long and up to 1.5 km (1 mile) wide). It was formerly the possession of the Abbots of Lérins. It has become well known through the naturist colony of Héliopolis, set up in 1932. Large parts of the island are military territory.

Île du Levant

La . . . , Le . . . , Les . . .

See main name

Le Lavandou

D4

Région: Provence-Alpes-Côte d'Azur
Département: Var
Altitude: sea-level
Population: 4500

Le Lavandou lies at the foot of the Massif des Maures, about half-way between Toulon and St-Tropez, on a broad bay facing south-east.

Location

Townscape

This pretty fishing village, now popular as a holiday resort, may owe its name to the large amount of lavender which grows in the surrounding area. Extensive areas of holiday homes and numerous high-rise buildings are prominent features of the town. From the harbour, in the eastern part of which spacious mooring facilities for yachts have recently been established, ferries leave for the Îles de Hyères (see Hyères).

West of the harbour extends the Plage du Lavandou, a beach of fine sand which is fringed by the Boulevard de Lattre de Tassigny; from the boulevard the visitor may enjoy a comprehensive view of the sea and the islands of Port-Cros and Levant (part of the group of the Hyères Islands). In the south the bay is enclosed by the wooded slopes of Cap Bénat, while far to the east can be seen Cap Lardier.

Road D559 running east from Le Lavandou gives access to sandy beaches, interspersed with rocky stretches.

Cap Bénat

South of Le Lavandou the wooded Cap Bénat extends out into the sea. The road leading to it comes first to the resort of La Favière (yacht harbour, beach) before reaching the settlement of holiday homes at Cap Bénat. On the highest point, Les Fourches (205 m (673 ft)), stands a castle and, on the extremity of the cape, a lighthouse.

Bormes-les-Mimosas   D4

Location
2 km (1 mile) north-west

The old township of Bormes-les-Mimosas extends picturesquely along the flank of a hill. In the Place de la Liberté stands the handsome Chapelle St-François-de-Paule (16th c.), with cypress trees on either side. A statue commemorates the beneficent deeds of St Francis of Paola during the plague of 1481. In the immediate vicinity can be seen a memorial to the landscape-painter Jean-Charles Cazin (1841–1901); some of his work is to be seen in the Hôtel de Ville. Also of interest is the Tour de l'Horloge, an 18th c. clock-tower, and the Church of St-Trophime (also 18th c.; fine winged altar). Bormes-les-Mimosas has a good yacht harbour beyond the Plage de la Favière.

Lubéron (Montagne du Lubéron)   D3

Région: Provence-Alpes-Côtes d'Azur
Département: Vaucluse
Altitude: up to 1125 m (3692 ft)

Location

The Montagne du Lubéron rises in the interior of the region, far to the north of Marseilles. In the south it is bordered by the Durance; in the north the Valley of the Coulon divides it from the Plateau of Vaucluse.

Landscape

The Montagne du Lubéron is a mountainous area of chalk which reaches a height of 1125 m (3692 ft) in the Mourre Nègre. Usually a distinction is made between the Petit Lubéron in the west and the Grand Lubéron in the east, which are separated by the gorge of the Combe de Lourmarin.

A large part of this mountainous area is taken up by the Parc Régional du Lubéron (nature park), established in 1977, which has an area of about 120,000 ha (296,520 acres) and which extends into the neighbouring Département of Alpes-de-Haute-Provence.

In several places in Lubéron can be seen the characteristic so-
called "bories", huts built of boulders without mortar (for
further details see Gordes).

Drive through the Lubéron Mountains

By following the route recommended in this guidebook one
reaches the Lubéron range near the little town of Apt. This is
the most convenient starting-point for a drive through the
mountains.

The town is situated in the basin of the same name, the Bassin
d'Apt, on the little River Calavon. Of interest is the former
Cathedral of Ste-Anne, originally Romanesque but considerably altered in the 14th and 17th c. In the Baroque Chapelle
Ste-Anne is the reliquary of the patroness of the church. The
treasury contains reliquaries from Limoges and illuminated
manuscripts.
The archaeological museum has, in addition to Gallo-Roman
antiquities, a considerable collection of ceramics.

A good 10 km (6 miles) east of Apt is the village of Rustrel. Like
Roussillon (see under Gordes) it is known for its deposits of
ochre. Here the little River Dôa has cut a gorge, called the
"Colorado de Rustrel". This picturesque gorge can be reached
by two roads going south from Rustrel. Footpaths lead to the
ochre rocks.
From Apt road D943 leads south to the Combe de Lourmarin.
It offers fine views of the mountains with their forests of low
trees and bushes (especially gorse, holm-oaks and sweet
chestnuts). Just short of Lourmarin a narrow forest track
branches off to the left, climbs up to the crest of the Grand
Lubéron and in about another 15 km (9 miles) reaches the
Mourre Nègre, the highest point of the range. The last short
stretch must be made on foot; from the top there is a
magnificent panorama.

At the southern end of the Combe lies Lourmarin, overlooked
by its hilltop château; from the 15th–16th c. tower there are
extensive views.

There is a worthwhile excursion from Lourmarin to Cucuron,
about 10 km (6 miles) distant. Of interest here are the church
(Romanesque and Gothic) and the little regional museum,
housed in the Hôtel des Bouliers (pre- and early history; Gallo-
Roman finds).
Mourre Nègre (see above) can also be climbed from Cucuron.
The Plain of the Durance and the Abbey of Silvacane (see
entry) are reached via Cadenet.

Apt

Rustrel

Lourmarin

Cucuron

Marcoule

C2

Région: Languedoc-Roussillon
Département: Gard
Altitude: 50 m (164 ft)

The nuclear research centre of Marcoule lies in the west
opposite Orange on the right bank of the Rhône.

Location

The nuclear research centre of Marcoule

Usine Nucléaire (nuclear power centre)

The extensive complex is situated right by the river, the waters of which are used for cooling the reactors. The principal task of the centre is, however, not the production of electrical energy, but nuclear research and the obtaining of radio-active substances for medicine, science and industry as well as the processing of nuclear fuels. For this purpose the adjoining nuclear reactor Phénix (first fast breeder in the world) was started up in 1973.

Belvédère de Marcoule

The best general view of the plant is to be had from the elevated Belvédère (viewpoint), to which a private road leads (June to September closed at 7 p.m.; otherwise at 5.30 p.m.). Orientation is facilitated by a large panoramic photograph with explanatory text and by a small exhibition.

Marseilles   D3

Région: Provence-Alpes-Côtes d'Azur
Département: Bouches-du-Rhône
Altitude: sea-level
Population: 880,000 (entire district over 1 million)

Location

Marseilles, the second largest city and the most important port of France, is situated to the east of the delta of the Rhône on a broad curving bay, which is enclosed on the north by the Chaîne de l'Estaque towards the Etang de Berre (see entry).

The town was founded in the 7th c. BC under the name of "Massalia" by Greeks from the town of Phocaea in Asia Minor. Until well into the time of the Roman Empire it was a centre of Greek culture. The town experienced its first flowering in the middle of the 6th c. BC, after Phocaea had been destroyed by the Persians, and the population was soon increased by streams of refugees. Massalia expanded to the north-east towards the present-day Butte des Moulins. Trade flourished, especially with the Ligurians who, it is generally believed, had their principal settlement in the nearby Oppidum of Entremont (see under Aix-en-Provence).

History

The intervention of the Romans after the Second Punic War in favour of the Greeks culminated in the destruction of the Saluvian tribe in 154 BC, whereupon the first town on Gallic soil to be founded by the Romans followed at what is now Aix. The quarrel between Caesar and Pompey led to a fateful clash with the Romans, when the people of Massalia sided with Pompey. Caesar conquered the town, added to it the extensive territory of the Province of Arles and promoted the development of the Forum Julii (Fréjus).

Already in the 1st c. AD an extension of the now-Roman town of Massilia was carried out by draining the extensive marshes to the east. The wall which had been built in the Imperial Age enclosed the settlement until well into the 11th c.; at that time the town was composed of an Upper Town (temple, forum and other public buildings) and a Lower Town (port, dock installations, etc.).

After the fall of the Roman Empire the town came under the domination of the Western Goths, then of the Franks and finally passed to the Kingdom of Arles. After its destruction by the Saracens it was rebuilt in the 10th c. and became subject to the Vicomtes de Marseille; in 1218 it became free until 1250 when Charles of Anjou conquered Marseilles which was united to France in 1481. The importance of the harbour increased enormously at the time of the Crusades. In the Middle Ages defences were constructed as opportunity offered, for example the Tour St-Jean on the north side of the harbour entrance, erected by the Knights of the Order of St John, a bastion near the present-day Pilgrimage Church of Notre-Dame-de-la-Garde by François I and extensions to the Château d'If. Under Mazarin the Forts of St-Jean and St-Nicolas were reinforced at the harbour entrance.

During the French Revolution which led to violent clashes between the Jacobins and the merchants, the most unruly elements withdrew to Paris where they made popular the "Marseillaise" which had been written and set to music by the army officer, Rouget de Lisle, in Strasbourg.

In the 19th c. there were large-scale extensions to the town, with numerous examples of splendid architecture, including the Triumphal Arch on the Place d'Aix and the Palais Longchamps. The increase of French influence in North Africa from 1830 and the opening of the Suez Canal resulted in a great demand for accommodation, etc. (many new dwellings; "bidonvilles"=tin-can towns; extension of the harbour, etc.), a trend which has continued until the present day and which has led to a similar townscape to that of other European centres of population.

The economic situation of the town is primarily determined by the importance of the port. A third of French maritime trade is

Economy

handled by the independent Port Autonome de Marseille. The annual turnover of goods amounts to about 100 million tonnes (almost 90 per cent imports), of which the greatest part (over 90 per cent) is handled by the new installations of Fos-sur-Mer and Lavéra which extend a long way to the west (transport of mineral oil, mineral oil products and ores).

With some 700,000 passengers annually Marseilles is the third passenger port of France; a great proportion of this traffic is attributable to the busy ferries across the harbour basins.

La Canebière

The principal traffic artery of the extremely busy Inner City, in which people of a great variety of races can be seen, especially in the port area, is the Canebière (Provençal Canebiero), a broad highway which begins at the harbour. This street, about 1 km ($\frac{1}{2}$ mile) long carries a great deal of traffic and is lined with shops and offices. The name is derived from cannabis (hemp) and means "ropewalk".

Stock Exchange

Not far from the port on the left of the Canebière stands the Bourse (Stock Exchange), an impressive building of 1852–60, with the Musée de la Marine de Marseille (marine museum; collection of pictures and other artistic exhibits of the Marseilles Chamber of Trade; many drawings and plans of 17th c. ships).

Greek Ramparts

The redesigned Centre de la Bourse (Stock Exchange Centre; department store, etc.) gives access to the excavation site,

▼ *View of Marseilles from the Château d'If*

where remains of the Greek fortifications of the port of Massalia (3rd–2nd c. BC) were uncovered and which has been laid out as a park. On the ground floor of the Stock Exchange Centre can be seen a collection of the finds.

South of the Canebière, at Rue de Grignan 19, which is reached by way of Rue Paradis, is the Musée Cantini (old porcelain; temporary exhibitions).

Musée Cantini

Not far from the Stock Exchange there is a wide crossing of the Canebière, with the broad Cours St-Louis on the right leading into the long Rue de Rome, and on the left the busy Cours de Belsunce with its continuation, the Rue d'Aix. This is the intersection of the main routes running north–south and east–west.

About 250 m (275 yd) farther on one reaches the intersection with the Boulevard Dugommier (left) and the Boulevard Garibaldi (right). At the end of the Canebière stands the neo-Gothic Church of St-Vincent-de-Paul.

*Palais Longchamp

At the eastern end of the Boulevard Longchamp, which runs approximately in the same direction as the Canebière, stands the Palais Longchamp. It was built by Espérandieu in 1862–69 at the end of the canal from the Durance to Marseilles. The impressive museum buildings have a pillared hall, with fountains on either side; on the left is the Musée des Beaux-Arts containing paintings and modern sculpture, together with works of the caricaturist Honoré Daumier (1808–79); on the

Location
Boulevard Longchamp

right is the Musée d'Histoire Naturelle (Natural History Museum). Behind the Palais lies the large Zoological Garden.

Musée Grobet-Labadié

Location
Boulevard Longchamp

The Boulevard Longchamp terminates in a circular open space, where stands the Palais Longchamp (see above); on the southwest side is the Musée Grobet-Labadié, a mansion containing furniture, sculptures, tapestries and paintings. The house was presented to Marseilles by Madame Grobet.

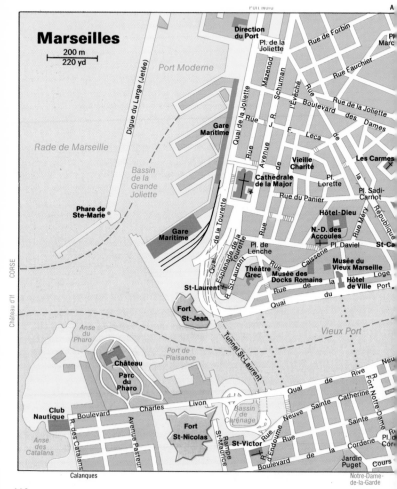

*Vieux Port (Old Harbour)

At the end of the Canebière in the west of the town lies the picturesque Vieux Port (25 ha (62 acres); 4–7 m (13–23 ft) deep). It can now only be used by small vessels. Boats leave the Old Harbour for the Château d'If (see p. 115) and also for the Calanques (see p. 117) near Cassis. The lively waterfront, especially the Quai des Belges on the east side (fish market every morning), is a focal point for tourists. At the harbour entrance two forts stand sentinel, the Fort St-Jean on the left the Fort St-Nicolas (viewpoint) on the right.

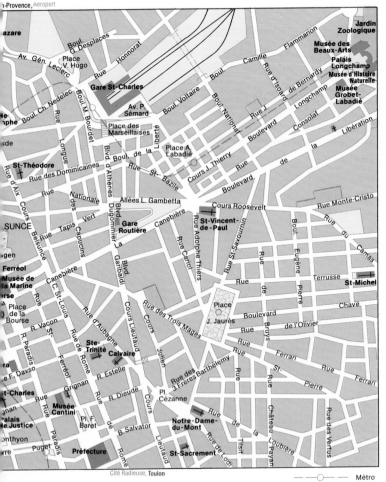

Greek port layout . . .   *and Château d'If*

Basilique St-Victor

To the east of Fort St-Nicolas is the fortress-like Basilique St-Victor, which once belonged to an abbey founded in the 5th c. In its present form, with its turreted towers, it is of 11th and 14th c. date; the foundations go back to Early Christian and Carolingian times (visitors admitted; entrance fee). In the crypt can be seen the original catacomb chapel and the Grotto of St Victor, and in the basilica a 14th c. Black Madonna.

Parc du Pharo

On a hill to the south of the harbour entrance, below which runs a road tunnel, the Tunnel St-Laurent, lies the Parc du Pharo, with the former great castle of the Empress Eugénie (the wife of Napoleon III) and a naval memorial. In summer plays are performed in the open, outside the castle. From the park there is an extensive prospect of the port installations and of the town.

*Notre-Dame-de-la-Garde

Towering up on a 160 m (525 ft) high limestone rock in the south of the town centre, the Basilique Notre-Dame-de-la-Garde is a landmark of Marseilles visible from far around. Occupying the site of a medieval pilgrimage chapel, the church was built between 1853 and 1864 by Espérandieu in neo-Byzantine style of light and dark natural stone. A gilded Madonna crowns the 46 m (151 ft) high belfry.

**View

There is a marvellous panorama from the terrace encircling the church. At the north-west bastion are an orientation table and a telescope; the view embraces the broad Rade de Marseille, the offshore islands of Ratonneau and Pomègues and the Château d'If (see p. 115).

The whole interior of the church is clad in white and dark marble. In the crypt are many votive panels, and model aircraft which have been donated by aviators.

Old Town

The Old Town with its steep crooked streets lies to the north of the Old Harbour. On the north side of the harbour basin is the Quai du Port, with the Hôtel de Ville (Town Hall) built in the second half of the 17th c. on a Genoese model.

A short distance north-west the Maison Diamantée houses the Musée du Vieux Marseille (history of the town, Provençal furniture, 17th–19th c. utensils). Farther west in the Place Vivaux is the Musée des Docks Romains (Musée du Commerce Antique).

Musée du Vieux Marseille

Musée des Docks Romains

Near Fort St-Jean (see p. 111) stands the Romanesque Church of St-Laurent, which was damaged in the Second World War. The side chapels date from the 15th and 16th c., the octagonal tower from the 18th c.

On a terrace in the north-west of the Old Town, above the new port installations, stands the mighty Cathédrale de la Major, with two domed towers and a 16 m (53 ft) high dome over the crossing. It was built between 1852 and 1893 in a mixture of

Cathédrale de la Major

In the Old Port of Marseilles

Notre-Dame-de-la-Garde...

and the Fish Market

Romanesque and Byzantine styles of alternate courses of white and green limestone. With a length of 141 m (463 ft) it is the most spacious ecclesiastical building of the 19th c. The interior is richly decorated with marble and mosaic; in the crypt can be seen the tombs of the Bishops of Marseilles.

A little lower down and to the east stands the Cathédrale St-Lazare (the old cathedral), dating from the 4th to the 12th c. Here in the Chapel of St-Severinus is a reliquary altar; another (of St-Lazarus) is in the left-hand aisle. In the chapel on the left of the fine apse is a Romanesque reliquary of 1122 and an Entombment of the school of della Robbia.

Vieille Charité

Not far north of the cathedral can be found the Vieille Charité, a hospice for the poor. This fine 17th c. building has a chapel by Puget.

South of here is the Cour des Accoules, with a 19th c Calvary chapel, overlooked by the Clocher des Accoules (bell-tower), the remains of one of the oldest churches in Marseilles. In the immediate vicinity in the Place Daviel stands the Hôtel-Dieu, which is reputed to have been founded towards the end of the 12th c. The plans for the construction of the new building were largely the work of the architects Portal and Mansart. In the front courtyard is a monument to the designer Honoré Daumier of Marseilles, with a bronze by A. Bourdelle.

Also in the Place Daviel is the fine Palais de Justice (old lawcourts, 1743–47).

Port Modern

Downhill from the cathedral, about 1 km ($\frac{1}{2}$ mile) from the Old Harbour, the Port Modern (New Harbour; over 200 ha (494 acres); 25 km (16 miles) of quais) was laid out from 1844. Most passenger ships (including ferries for Corsica) tie up in the Bassin de la Grande Joliette which is 20 ha (49 acres) in extent. At the Quai de la Joliette, opposite the end of the Boulevard des Dames, lies the Gare Maritime (Marine Railway Station), immediately above the harbour basin. From the Jetée (breakwater) 5 km (3 miles) long (access only at week-ends), there is a good view of the New Harbour.
Going east along the Boulevard des Dames, one arrives at the Place Jules-Guesde where stands the Arc de Triomphe (Triumphal Arch), erected in 1825–32 to commemorate the capture of Fort Trocadéro at Cadiz.

Location
West and north of the Old Town

See Martigues

Europort Sud

Château Gombert

The Château Gombert, located on the northern edge of the town, is the home of the Musée de l'Art Provençal (open only on Mon., Sat. and Sun. afternoons); this collection of Provençal art is exhibited in the house of a pupil of Mistral.

Location
Place des Héros 5

About 1.5 km (1 mile) farther on in the Massif de l'Etoile, one comes to the Grotte Loubière, a system of caves with impressive karstic phenomena.

Grotte Loubière

Avenue du Prado

The broad Avenue du Prado (called the "Prado" for short), expansively laid out and shaded by plane trees, is the southern continuation of the Rue de Rome and leads to the Rond-Point du Prado. On the left are the Parc Amable Chanot and the exhibition grounds with the Palais des Congrès.

South of the park stretches the Cité Radieuse (Radiant City), or Unité d'Habitation in Boulevard Michelet, a forward-looking housing complex designed by Le Corbusier and built between 1947 and 1952.

*Cité Radieuse

The Avenue du Prado continues in a south-westerly direction from the Rond-Point to the shore. On the left lies the Parc Borély with an 18th c. castle of the same name, in which are housed the Musée de l'Archéologie Méditerranéenne (Egyptian, Greek, Celtic, Roman and Gallic antiquities) and the Musée Lapidaire.

*Parc Borély

*Château d'If

The fortified rock island in the Bay of Marseilles with its Château d'If (Yew Island) is famous on account of the novel "The Count of Monte Cristo" (1844–45) by Alexandre Dumas the Elder. The fortress, built in 1524, was once used as a prison. There is a fine view from the top of the cliff.

Location
2 km (1 mile) south-west of the port

Ferry service

Ratonneau, Pomègues

Le Planier

Not far from the Château d'If lie the two larger islands of Ratonneau and Pomègues, linked by a causeway which encloses the Port de Frioul (yacht harbour; quarantine station). Farther out to sea can be seen the little island of Le Planier (lighthouse).

Allauch   D3

Location
10 km (6 miles) from
Marseilles

The health resort of Allauch is situated amid magnificent hill scenery on the outskirts of Marseilles. In the 17th c. Church of St-Sebastien can be seen a fine painting of the Ascension by Monticelli. The restored mills (also 17th c.) are attractive. In the Place Pierre Bellot is the Musée du Vieil Allauch (local history). Above the village to the east stands the 12th c. Chapel of Notre-Dame-du-Château, from which there is a rewarding view.

Cassis   D3

Location
22 km (14 miles) south-east

The little port of Cassis lies on a semicircular bay, framed by mountains. It was once the haunt of painters, including Vlaminck, Dufy and Matisse; nowadays it is an important recreation centre for the people of nearby Marseilles. White Cassis is a well-known wine.

Of interest are the old settlement centre with remains of 12th and 14th c. fortifications, a castle (1381) and the beautiful Fontaine des Quatre Nations.

The Calanques: excellent natural harbours

South-west of Cassis lie the striking Calanques Port Miou, En Vau and Port Pin; the rock-fringed coves cutting deeply into the land are partly used as natural yacht harbours and are popular with climbers as an ideal place for cliff ascents. During the summer holiday season cars are often broken into and thefts committed; visitors are, therefore, strongly urged to leave no valuables behind in their vehicles.

**Calanques

Warning

La Ciotat   D3

The port and industrial town of La Ciotat, south-east of Marseilles, can be reached via Cassis (see above). Given sufficient time, the visitor should not use the inland route D559 from Cassis but the somewhat narrow and winding Corniche des Crêtes which runs just below the Falaises, the tallest cliff in France, high above the sea to Cap Canaille (362 m (1118 ft)). In the afternoon especially there is a fantastic view of the coast from the Calanques to Cap Croisette. The whole stretch, barely 15 km (9 miles) long, leads via the Grande Tête to La Ciotat.

Location
30 km (19 miles) south-east of Marseilles
**Corniche des Crêtes

La Ciotat lies on the western side of the bay of the same name, dominated by the steep reddish conglomerate cliffs of Cap de l'Aigle (155 m (509 ft)). Offshore is the little Île Verte (Green Island) with a fortress. In the attractive Old Town are many 17th and 18th c. houses; near the Town Hall (1864) is a turreted keep. Notable paintings are to be seen in the parish church at the Old Port. A visit to the Musée d'Histoire Locale (local history) is recommended.

Going northwards along the new harbour, one reaches the district of La Ciotat-Plage, a seaside settlement with hotels and a beach.

Martigues   D3

Région: Provence-Alpes-Côte d'Azur
Département: Bouches-du-Rhône
Altitude: sea-level
Population: 42,000

The picturesque old town of Martigues lies on the Etang de Berre (see entry), about 30 km (19 miles) north-west of Marseilles.

Location

Townscape

The character of the surroundings of Martigues has been strongly influenced by the construction of the motorway and industrial plants; nevertheless the town, which because of its situation on the Canal de Caronte is also called the "Venice of Provence", has still retained to a considerable extent its atmosphere of bygone days. The Canal St-Sébastien and the picturesque corner ‒ the Miroir aux Oiseaux – of the Île Brescon, the central part of the town, are given a particularly attractive apprearance by fishing-boats and hanging nets. The canal is overlooked by the square tower of the 17th c. Church of La Madeleine with its wrought-iron bell-cage.

In Jonquières, in the southern part of the town, near the Church of St-Genest (17th c.), is the Chapelle de l'Annonciade with 17th c. sculpture and paintings.

In Ferrières, in the north of the town, can be found the Musée du Vieux Martigues (local history).

Carry-le-Rouet   D3

Location
16 km (10 miles) south-east
of Martigues

Carry-le-Rouet lying at the foot of the Chaîne de l'Estaque, is a fishing village, yacht harbour and popular seaside resort. The sector of Le-Rouet-Plage at the end of the Charming Vallon de l'Aigle is particularly attractive.

Châteauneuf-les-Martigues   D3

Location
10 km (6 miles) east

The largely agricultural community of Châteauneuf-les-Martigues lies at the foot of the northern flank of the Chaîne de l'Estaque. The bathing beach, the Plage du Jaï, is situated on the spit of land cut off by the Etang de Balmon.

Some 4 km (2½ miles) south in pine-clad uplands is the little village of Ensuès-la-Redonne near the beautiful Calanque des Anthénors; a little to the east lies the modest Bay of Méjean.

Europort Sud   D2/3

Location
5–10 km (3–6 miles) west

Some 5 km (3 miles) west of Martigues begins the most extensive port and industrial complex of southern Europe. It comprises refineries, steelworks, production of man-made materials and oil storage installations. In this coastal zone, known as "Europort Sud", more than 80 million tonnes of oil are handled every year. The 782 km (486 mile) long pipeline to Karlsruhe starts from here.

Marignane   D3

Location
18 km (11 miles) east

The township of Marignane is considerably affected by traffic using the nearby Aéroport Marseille-Marignane, within which lie the installations of Aérospatiale (air and space industry).

Sausset-les-Pins   D3

Location
12 km (7 miles) south-east

On a little bay protected by the southern escarpment of the Chaîne de l'Estaque, lies the fishing port and seaside resort of Sausset-les-Pins. It is popular as a recreation area for the people of Marseilles.

Cap Couronne

The resort of La Couronne is pleasantly situated on a hill above the Anse du Verdon, 6 km (4 miles) west of Sausset-les-Pins. 2 km (1 mile) south rises Cap Couronne, from which there is a good view of the sandy bays to the east.

Maures (Massif des Maures)   D4

Région: Provence-Alpes-Côte d'Azur
Département: Var
Altitude: up to 780 m (2560 ft)

The Massif des Maures is a chain of hills ringing the coast   Location
between Hyères in the west and Fréjus in the east.

Landscape of the Massif des Maures

About 60 km (37 miles) long and up to 30 km (19 miles) wide,
the Massif des Maures is composed of primitive rocks – granite,
gneiss and slate (pink or dark grey in colour, with metallically
glistening mica). It represents the remains of a land mass which
once covered the whole of the western Mediterranean. The
deeply fissured afforested uplands are still relatively isolated.

The Corniche des Maures, the greater part of which is road   Corniche des Maures
D559 along the coast, with its many bays and cliffs, between Le
Lavandou and St-Tropez (see entries), has exceptionally fine
scenery. It passes a considerable number of resorts, just beyond
Cavalaire it skirts Cap Nègre (120 m (394 ft)) and, via Canadel-
sur-Mer and Rayol, reaches the resort and port of Cavalaire
(castle ruin), situated on a sheltered bay.

Reached by road D41 going north from Bormes-les-Mimosas   Collobrières
(see under Le Lavandou) for about 20 km (12 miles),
Collobrières lies in a hollow in the heart of the Massif des
Maures. It is well known for its marrons glacés and Provençal
joinery.

Also inland lies La Garde-Freinet, reached from St-Tropez via   La Garde-Freinet
Grimaud on road D558. Situated on a pass with fine views, the
village was a major strongpoint of the Saracens, but had
already been a Roman military post. Of interest are the ruins of
the former Saracen fortress of Freinet on a hill to the north-east
(about 30 minutes' walk), from which there is an unusually
extensive panorama.

See Port-Grimaud   Grimaud

Menton   D5

Région: Provence-Alpes-Côte d'Azur
Département: Alpes-Maritimes
Altitude: sea-level
Population: 26,000

Menton (Italian Mentone), at the eastern end of the Côte   Location
d'Azur on the border between France and Italy, lies on the Golfe
de la Paix which is divided by a rocky promontory into the Baie
de Garavan on the east and the Baie de l'Ouest on the west. The
favourable situation of Menton makes possible the cultivation
of citrus fruits.

Menton

Menton: the gateway to Italy from Provence

Lower Town

The focus of life is the Casino Municipal (1932) on the west bay, along the shore of which the Promenade George V and its continuation (also called "Promenade du Soleil") extend north to the harbour.

Jardin Biovès

Opposite the harbour to the north-west lies the fine Jardin Biovès (exotic trees), below which flows the Careï. In the park stands the Palais d'Europe (congress centre).

Musée Jean Cocteau

The 17th c. harbour bastion at the beginning of the mole houses the Musée Jean Cocteau, with pictures, drawings, stage designs, etc.

North-east of the casino and parallel to the promenade along the shore runs the Avenue Félix-Faure, the principal shopping street of the western part of the town.

Hotel de Ville

In the next parallel main street, the Rue de la République, stands the Hôtel de Ville (Town Hall). Of particular interest is the Salle des Mariages which was decorated by Cocteau (guided visits).

Musée Municipal

The Musée Municipal north of thè Town Hall, has paintings by Chagall, Dufy, Modigliani, Picasso, Vlaminck and others – the Wakefield-Mori Collection. There is also a comprehensive collection of local and prehistoric exhibits (including the Negroid skull discovered in 1884 in the caves of Baoussé-Roussé (Italian Balzi-Rossi)).

120

Old Town

The Old Town is reached by way of Rue St-Michel, the continuation of the Avenue Félix-Faure (see above). On the east side lies the Plage des Sablettes, the principal beach, which has been artificially improved and is well maintained.

Farther north along the Montée des Logettes and the narrow Rue Longue, the former main street of the Old Town, the atmosphere of which is thoroughly Italian (a tunnel now runs under this area), one passes the remains of the town fortifications. To the left a flight of steps leads up to an observation terrace. To the south stands the Parish Church of St-Michel, with a 17th c. winged altar by Manchello, while to the west and a little higher up is the Église de la Conception; both churches are in the Italian Jesuit style. A short distance to the north the old cemetery lies on the side of the old castle hill (46 m (151 ft); fine view).

* Jardin des Colombières

From the cemetery the Boulevard de Garavan above the eastern bay passes near the Jardin Botanique, the state-run exotic gardens and botanical experimental station surrounding Villa Val Rahmeh, and continues past the Italianate Jardin des Colombières. Then the road reaches the Pont St-Louis on the Franco-Italian border. From here the return to the town centre can be made on the Quai Laurenti along the eastern bay.

* Villa Hanbury

A worthwhile excursion can be taken to the Villa Hanbury, 4 km (2½ miles) on the Italian side of the frontier. More than 10,000 rare plants, which have been acclimatised, thrive in the garden.

Monastère de l'Annonciade

The Monastère de l'Annonciade (Capuchin monastery) lies outside the town to the north-east, high above the road to Sospel. Here there is a marvellous panorama. Continuing under the motorway, a good view on the right of the typical Provençal village of Castellar can be enjoyed.

Castillon Neuf

By following the road up the Valley of the Careï one comes to Castillon Neuf, a village which was exemplarily rebuilt after the Second World War. From the nearby Col de Castillon (707 m (2320 ft)) a fine prospect of the mountains opens up.

Ste-Agnès

A narrow winding mountain road leads north-west to Ste-Agnès, a "village perché" in a most attractive situation with picturesque stepped streets. The hamlet is the starting-point for

Location
11 km (7 miles) north-west

fine walks in the mountains, including the ascent of the Pic de Baudon (2–3 hours), a climb which in parts is very arduous but which rewards the climber with good views.

Mercantour (Massif du Mercantour) C4/5

Région: Provence-Alpes-Côte d'Azur
Départements: Alpes-Maritimes and Alpes-de-Haut-Provence
Altitude: up to 3045 m (9994 ft)

Location

The Massif du Mercantour is situated in the extreme south of the Alpine chain, about 50 km (31 miles) north of Nice as the crow flies. The Franco-Italian frontier runs over its principal crest. A considerable part of this mountainous region forms the Parc National du Mercantour which is continued on the Italian side by the Parco Nazionale Valdieri.

The best route to the National Park from the Mediterranean coast is along the N202 west of Nice, which leads inland up the Valley of the River Var.

*Gorges de la Vésubie (excursion)

After some 20 km (12 miles) the D2565 branches off near Plan-du-Var into the Gorges de la Vésubie, the impressive ravines of the river of the same name. Follow the road through the narrow lower part of the valley for 10 km (6 miles) to the village of St-Jean-la-Rivière. From here a narrow winding little road on the left comes, via the village of Utelle, to the Pilgrimage Church of Notre-Dame-des-Miracles (Madone d'Utelle) which was founded in the 9th c. From the church, which is at a height of 1174 m (3855 ft) the view extends to the Mediterranean.

*Défilé du Chaudan

After the diversion near Plan-du-Var, mentioned above, the main road continues along the river which, not far to the north, rushes through the Défilé du Chaudan, a picturesque gorge framed by vertical cliffs. At the far end of the gorge the national road (Route nationale) crosses the river by the Pont de la Mescla. On the near side of the bridge the D2205 diverges, and it is this road which we now take.

*Gorges de la Mescla

The River Tinée, which is now followed, flows through the Gorges de la Mescla just before its confluence with the Var. The gorges are a scenic highlight of this magnificent stretch. The very narrow twisting road, which in places is fairly steep, continues to climb close to the river.

About 20 km (12 miles) after leaving the national road (Route nationale), the D2565 turns right over the 1500 m (4923 ft) high Col St-Martin into the beautiful upland Valley of the Boréon, the starting-point of many mountain footpaths. The

D2565 continues to follow the main valley to the high mountain region which is popular for winter sports and where are situated the ski centres of Isola 2000, Auron, etc.

**Gorges du Cians

By following the N202 from the Pont de la Mescla (see above), one reaches in some 20 km (12 miles) a junction on the right with the D26 which leads to the Gorges du Cians. The cleft which the River Cians has cut into the rock is up to 30 m (98 ft) deep, but in places only 1 m (3 ft) wide. The road runs alongside the river at the bottom of the gorge.
The road first traverses the Gorges Inférieures, the 5 km (3 mile) long stretch, dominated by 450 m (1477 ft) high chalk pinnacles, to the Moulin de Rigaud. Then the road winds upwards into the more rugged and deeper Gorges Supérieures (7 km (4 miles) long), which are entirely cut into copper-coloured slate. The road continues via Beuil to another popular winter sports area around Valberg.

*Gorges de Daluis

Still fully 20 km (12 miles) farther up the Valley of the Var, beyond the village of Entrevaux, the D902 diverges from the N202 which climbs towards the top of the pass – the Col de Toutes Aures (1124 m (3689 ft)) – 18 km (11 miles) to the west. The D902 follows the upper course of the Var and reveals another rewarding landscape. The Gorges de Daluis are an

In the Upper Valley of the Boréon

impressive 6 km (4 mile) long ravine, with the road up to 200 m (644 ft) above the Var. Curious red slate walls, in places flecked with green, line the road which is led through them in tunnels or around them. This route also goes to Valberg via Guillaume. By driving over the Col de Toutes Aures and via the attractive reservoir of Castillon one can reach Castellane (see entry) and continue into the magnificent gorges of the Verdon (see entry).

Monaco (Principality of Monaco)   D5

Coat of Arms

Flag

International Distinguishing Sign

State: Principauté de Monaco
Administrative Centre: Monaco-Ville
Area: 1.9 sq. km (0.74 sq. mile)
Altitude: 0–65 m (0–213 ft)
Population: 27,000

The independent Principality of Monaco lies in the extreme east of the Côte d'Azur near the Franco-Italian frontier.
Monaco (officially the Principauté de Monaco), with an area of only 1.9 sq. km (0.74 sq. mile), is one of the tiniest States in Europe. The population is predominantly Catholic and consists of native Monégasques (about 17 per cent, with their own colloquial language "Monegasco"), French (about 50 per cent), Italians (about 20 per cent) and the remainder from other countries.
The Principality is within the French customs area, but issues its own postage stamps. Monaco is a hereditary constitutional monarchy, governed, subject to the authority of the Prince, by a Minister of State assisted by three governing councillors. Popular representation is by a national and a municipal council. Two celebrated motor sports events are closely associated with the Principality; the Grand Prix de Monaco, the only Formula One race in Europe held on public roads, and the Monte Carlo Rally, the course of which extends far into French territory.

History

Prehistoric finds on the territory of present-day Monaco-Ville point to the area having been inhabited before the Stone Age. About 900 BC Phoenicians dedicated a rock to the Baal of Tyre (Melkarth cult). After its development into a Greek trading centre, the place became a Roman port called "Herculis Monoeci Portus". Its subsequent history was influenced by the consequences of migration and the rule of the the Saracens. A change took place when the Genoese assumed control in the 8th c. AD. The feudal State of Monaco was given a fortress in 1215, remains of which can still be seen. From 1297 the State has been ruled by the Genoese Grimaldi family which took the princely title in 1614. After temporary Spanish protection, Monaco passed in 1731 to the French line of Goyon de Matignon-Grimaldi and in 1793 was united with France. It was returned in 1814 to Prince Honoré IV. From 1815 to 1860 Monaco was under the protection of the Kingdom of Sardinia which was taken over by France in 1861, when Prince Charles

Roccabruna

III was forced to cede Mentone (Menton) and Roccabruna (Roquebrune). From 1828 the town of Monte Carlo was laid out, and with it the casino, the opera and a luxury hotel. Prince Albert I enacted a constitution in 1911. In 1918 relations with France were put on a new footing. Prince Rainier III took over the government in 1949 from Louis II who had ruled since

1922. In 1956 Rainier married the American film actress Grace
Kelly (Princess Gracia Patricia; died 1982).

Monaco-Ville

Monaco-Ville the oldest district and the seat of the government
and of the Bishop, dominates with its narrow streets a broad
picturesque peninsula jutting out into the sea. Here much
evidence of earlier fortification is to be seen.

In the western part of Monaco-Ville lies the Place du Palais
with the 13th c. Palais du Prince (Palace open 9.30 a.m.–
6 p.m.; changing of the guard 11.55 a.m.). The interior, which
can only be seen when the Prince is absent (usually June to
September; guided tour), contains splendid apartments,
including the throne-room in Empire style, York bedroom
(18th c.) and beautiful 17th c. frescoes (Genoese work).
In the Palace Museum (officially Musée Napoléonien et des
Archives Monégasques) can be seen many mementoes of
Napoleon I, as well as a rock sample from the moon and a stamp
collection. In summer concerts take place in the courtyard.

*Place du Palais

Rue Bellando de Castro leads from the palace to the cathedral,
built between 1875 and 1884 with later additions. Inside can
be seen an altar by Bréa (c. 1500) and tombs of the princes and
bishops.
Opposite stands the Palais de Justice (lawcourts) and near by
the Historial des Princes (historical collection, 9.30 a.m.–
6 p.m.) and the notable Chapelle de la Miséricorde.

Cathedral

View of the Principality of Monaco from the Tête de Chien

Monaco

** Musée Océanographique

The Jardins de St-Martin extend along the coast of the peninsula with a steep cliff on the seaward side, near which stands a statue commemorating Prince Albert I, celebrated as a marine researcher. At the end of the gardens is the Musée Océanographique (marine museum); the façade facing the sea is 87 m (286 ft) high and rests on massive foundations. The museum houses valuable scientific collections (objects from the journeys of exploration of Prince Albert I, finds, submarines and diving equipment of Jacques-Yves Cousteau, slides of marine plants and animals), also an important aquarium, laboratory and library, as well as exhibits of model ships and educational film shows.

On the western slope of the cliff is the interesting Centre d'Acclimatation Zoologique (a centre of animal acclimatisation and a training school).

Fontvieille

To the west below the cliff, which is dominated by the Old Town lies the newly constructed Port de Fontvieille. Also recently completed was the Stade Louis II, an ultra-modern

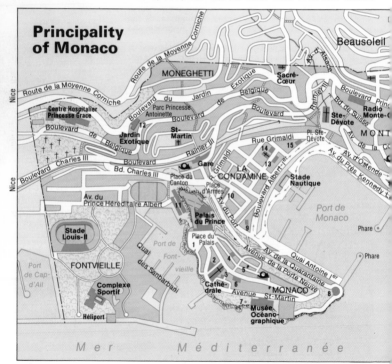

sports stadium with seating for 20,000, all under cover, situated to the rear of the harbour of Fontvieille.

Port

To the north, at the foot of the cliff, lies the almost square-shaped busy port (harbour), which was constructed between 1901 and 1926; large numbers of yachts, including from time to time the Prince's private ship, are to be seen here. On the western side of the port is the modern Stade Nautique Rainier-III, a stadium for water sports.

Near the northern mole of the harbour in the Avenue d'Ostende can be found the Centre de Rencontres Internationales, an international meeting-place with a roof terrace.

Centre de Rencontres

La Condamine

The Boulevard Albert-I is the main street of the district of La Condamine. In this quarter of the town there are a large number of businesses, shops and public buildings (railway station,

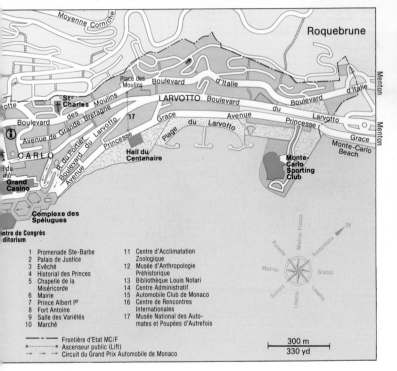

1 Promenade Ste-Barbe
2 Palais de Justice
3 Evêché
4 Historial des Princes
5 Chapelle de la
   Miséricorde
6 Mairie
7 Prince Albert Ier
8 Fort Antoine
9 Salle des Variétés
10 Marché

11 Centre d'Acclimatation
   Zoologique
12 Musée d'Anthropologie
   Préhistorique
13 Bibliothèque Louis Notari
14 Centre Administratif
15 Automobile Club de Monaco
16 Centre de Rencontres
   Internationales
17 Musée National des Automates et Poupées d'Autrefois

——— Frontière d'Etat MC/F
▪▪▪▪▪▪ Ascenseur public (Lift)
→ → → Circuit du Grand Prix Automobile de Monaco

300 m
330 yd

127

Museum of Oceanography

Monaco

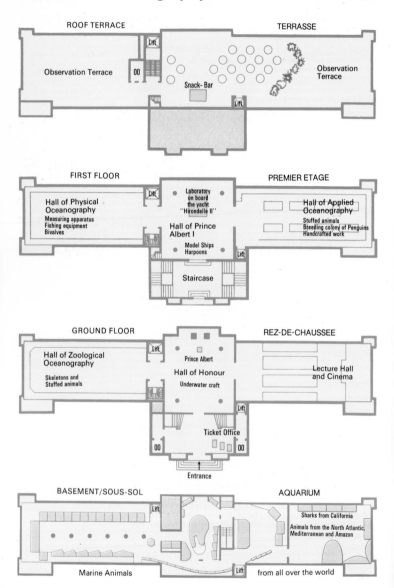

ROOF TERRACE   TERRASSE

Observation Terrace

00

Snack- Bar

Observation Terrace

FIRST FLOOR   PREMIER ETAGE

Hall of Physical Oceanography

Measuring apparatus
Fishing equipment
Bivalves

Laboratory on board the yacht "Hirondelle II"

Hall of Prince Albert I

Model Ships
Harpoons

Hall of Applied Oceanography

Stuffed animals
Breeding colony of Penguins
Handcrafted work

Staircase

GROUND FLOOR   REZ-DE-CHAUSSEE

Hall of Zoological Oceanography

Skeletons and
Stuffed animals

Prince Albert

Hall of Honour

Underwater craft

Lecture Hall and Cinema

Ticket Office

00   00

Entrance

BASEMENT/SOUS-SOL   AQUARIUM

Sharks from California

Animals from the North Atlantic, Mediterranean and Amazon

Marine Animals   from all over the world

The Princely Palace in Monaco-Ville

library, market). In the ravine-like valley cleft on the northern edge of this part of the town, below a road bridge stands the little Church of Ste-Dévote, dedicated to the patron saint of the town; the church has a fine 18th c. marble altar.

Moneghetti

Seemingly endless steps and roads with hairpin bends climb up the eastern slope of the Tête de Chien to the Moyenne Corniche (road N564 on French territory; see Corniche de la Riviera).

These roads give access to the district of Moneghetti in the west of the State, a part of the town which is built in terraces with fine villas and gardens.

The Jardin Exotique (Exotic Garden) is one of the most impressive of its kind. Because of the favourable climate, with little variation in conditions on the constantly warm and damp steep slope, a great variety of the most delicate, and in some cases unique, tropical plants thrive in the Exotic Garden. In the grottoes beautiful fossils can be seen. In the park there is also the interesting Musée d'Anthropologie Préhistorique. The Museum of Prehistory and Anthropology not only exhibits bones discovered in the area but also a collection of coins, ornamental objects, etc. from the pre-Roman and Roman periods in particular. To the north of the museum lies the Parc Princesse Antoinette.

*Jardin Exotique

129

Monte-Carlo

The district of Monte-Carlo occupies a rocky promontory to the north of the Port of Monaco. Its most elevated part is crossed by streets with shops and offices, including the Boulevard Princesse Charlotte (in the west, the head-quarters of Radio/Télévision Monte-Carlo), the Boulevard des Moulins (pavilion of the Office de Tourisme at its south-western end; a short distance to the north is the Church of St-Charles), and the Avenue de la Costa with its many luxury shops.

Casino

The elaborate architecture of the Grand Casino, to the north of the harbour, was the work of Charles Garnier, the architect of the Paris Opéra, and dates from 1878. It houses the legendary gaming-rooms of the Société Anonyme des Bains de Mer (S.B.M.; guided tours).

*Les Spélugues

East of the casino extends the large-scale complex of the Congress Centre (called Les Spélugues), opened in 1978. The Boulevard Louis-II runs under the huge building which has been constructed of elements on a hexagonal plan and includes a 650-room hotel and 100 apartments. On the highest roof-level, of which there is an excellent view from the terrace in front of the casino, there is a striking mosaic composed of coloured tiles. It was designed in 1979 by Victor Vasarely (see Gordes) and has the title "Hexagrace – Le Ciel, la Mer, la Terre"; the Fondation Vasarely in Aix-en-Provence (see entry) was responsible for its execution.

The harbour and city from Monte-Carlo

Larvotto

In the south-west of the district of Larvotto stands the Century Hall (Hall du Centenaire). Near by in the Avenue Princesse Grace can be found the Musée National des Automates et Poupées d'Autrefois (museum of mechanical toys and dolls), housed in a villa of the Belle Époque. On view are a number of dolls, more than 80 automata and over 2000 miniature objects, the purpose of which is to depict life in the 18th and 19th c.

° Musée des Automates

Cap d'Ail   D5

At the foot of the Tête de Chien amid sparse pine woods lies the holiday resort of Cap d'Ail. Of interest are the ruins of the Tour d'Abeglio and the open-air theatre, designed by Jean Cocteau and decorated with mosaics. Several promontories extend out into the sea near Cap d'Ail.

Location
2 km (1 mile) south-west

La Turbie   D5

The picturesque old township of La Turbie is situated on the saddle between a ridge of the Tête de Chien and the Mont de la Bataille. In the Baroque church is a most interesting communion-rail made of agate, a Pietà of the school of Bréa and a fine High Altar. Both town gates are relics of the fortifications begun in the 13th c.

Location
8 km (5 miles) north-west

Mosaic on the roof of the Congress Centre, Les Spélugues

Monaco: Memorial to Prince Albert I   *La Turbie: the Trophée des Alpes*

** Trophée des Alpes
(Trophée d'Auguste)

La Turbie is dominated by a feature visible from afar, the Trophée des Alpes, also called the "Trophée d'Auguste". This is a monument which was erected to the Emperor by the Roman Senate in 6 BC as a memorial to the suppression of the Alpine tribes (14th–13th c. BC). In the 14th c. the monument was converted into a fortress and in 1705 blown up by Louis XV during the War of the Spanish Succession. About 1930 restoration was begun to which the monument owes its present appearance. The funds were provided by an American and his wife. The grounds around the monument have been laid out as a park and from the steep south and south-eastern sides offer a marvellous view of the coast.

Montélimar   C2

Région: Rhône-Alpes
Département: Drôme
Altitude: 81 m (266 ft)
Population: 30,000

Location

Montélimar lies not far to the east of the Rhône, which is dammed in this part, some 150 km (93 miles) south of Lyon. The River Roulion flows past the town centre.

Townscape

Montélimar is known for its traditional nougat, in which

132

almonds grown in the vicinity are an ingredient. Everywhere there are stalls and shops selling nougat.
East above the Old Town rises the castle, dating from the 12th to the 14th c.; from the terraces and tower there is a good panorama (to the north can be seen the cooling towers of the nuclear plant on the bank of the Rhône).

Montmajour   D2

Région: Provence-Alpes-Côte d'Azur
Département: Bouches-du-Rhône
Altitude: 15 m (49 ft)

Visible from a considerable distance, the former Benedictine Abbey of Montmajour, resembling a fortress, is set on a rocky hill 5 km (3 miles) north-east of Arles.

Location

* Monastic Buildings

The Abbey of Montmajour was founded in the 10th c. and throughout the Middle Ages was an important place of pilgrimage. Other monasteries were founded by the monks from this abbey. The plain surrounding the hill was originally marsh and alluvial land and was not drained until the abbey was founded. The monastic buildings, of which some remains are still to be seen, date from the 12th to the 14th and the 18th c. In the lobby of the ticket office two plans are on show which provide a general survey; other explanatory sketches can be found in the parts of the abbey open to the public.
The first part of the monastery to be visited is the huge Romanesque crypt, dating from the 12th c., which forms the load-bearing foundation of the church above, and which is partly built into the rock. The central space is surrounded by a vaulted corridor with apses in a semicircle, to which round-arched openings in the walls provide a connection.
From the crypt one proceeds into the single-aisled church above; this is a short, sturdy, austere space with only two bays in the nave, a semicircular main apse and two subsidiary apses; at the end of the left transept is the square Chapelle Notre-Dame-la-Blanche. In the 18th c. plans were made to extend

Opening times
Wed.–Mon. 9 a.m.–midday and 2–6 p.m.

Former Benedictine Abbey

Montmajour

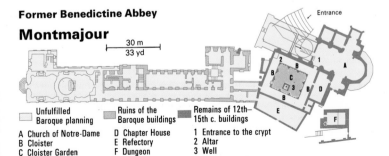

|————| 30 m
|————| 33 yd

Entrance

| Unfulfilled Baroque planning | Ruins of the Baroque buildings | Remains of 12th–15th c. buildings |

A Church of Notre-Dame
B Cloister
C Cloister Garden
D Chapter House
E Refectory
F Dungeon
1 Entrance to the crypt
2 Altar
3 Well

Montmajour

Cloisters of Montmajour . . .

and the Moulin de Daudet

the nave considerably to the west, but the plans were never realised.

Cloister

The Cloister is entered from the second transept and adjoins the church on the south-west. It was probably built at the same time as the church. The rounded arches are divided by double pillars in threes or fours; rich ornamentation can be seen on the corbels which support the ribbed vault. The cloister, in the middle of which stands a well mounted on a pedestal, is overlooked by the battlemented defensive keep.

To the west of the Romanesque buildings large-scale Baroque extensions were undertaken; the ruins of these buildings are, however, normally not open to the public.

On the right of the road about 200 m (220 yd) east of the monastery stands the little Chapelle Ste-Croix (Chapel of the Holy Cross), dating from the 12th c. It was once the cemetery chapel of the monastery as is indicated by the tombs which were hewn into the rock.

Fontvieille   D2

Location
5 km (3 miles) north-east
Moulin de Daudet

North-east of Montmajour, near Fontvieille, stands one of the most popular attractions of Provence for the French – the mill of the writer Alphonse Daudet. It became famous as a result of his "Lettres de mon Moulin" ("Letters from my Mill"), which, however, were not written here but in Paris. Nevertheless it is a fact that Daudet got the inspiration for a great part of his literary output in this region.

In the base of the windmill a little museum has been set up

containing souvenirs of the poet; from the mill there is a good view down the valley as far as the Rhône, with two old watch-towers in the middle distance.

On either side of road D82 about 3 km (2 miles) south of Fontvieille can be seen the remains of two Roman aqueducts which once provided water for Arles, among other places. No attempt has been made at restoration and the ruins are, to a large extent, covered by undergrowth and, therefore, difficult to reach.

°Aqueducs Romains
(Roman Aqueducts)

Montpellier

D1

Région: Languedoc-Roussillon
Département: Hérault
Altitude: 50 m (164 ft)
Population: 202,000

Montpellier, the chief town of the Département of Hérault, is situated some distance west of the Camargue and not far from the coast of the Golfe du Lion. The River Lez flows past the eastern confines of the town.
Although Montpellier is not actually in Provence, it is an attraction for visitors touring the western part of the region and is, therefore, included in this book.

Location

The town came into being after the second destruction of the nearby settlement of Maguelone by Charles Martel (737). In the 13th c. it belonged to the Kings of Aragon, then until 1349 to the Kings of Majorca as vassals of the French. As early as 1289 Montpellier had a university, where Francesco Petrarch studied from 1316 to 1319 and François Rabelais from 1530 to 1532 and from 1537 to 1538. At the end of the 16th c. the town was a headquarters of the Huguenots. In 1622 it was conquered by Louis XIII.

History

Place de la Comédie

The heart of the Inner City is the Place de la Comédie with a fountain of 1776, the Fontaine des Trois Grâces. On the south-west side of the square stands the theatre (opera-house). From here the great boulevards radiate round the area of the Old Town (the greater part a pedestrian precinct), which extends north to the Verdanson, a tributary of the Lez. In the Old Town can be seen evidence of the former prosperity of Montpellier in the form of a few old patrician and merchants' mansions.

*Promenade du Peyrou

From the Place de la Comédie the Boulevard Victor-Hugo leads south-west, and the Boulevard du Jeu de Paume and the Boulevard L.-Rollin north-west to the Promenade du Peyrou, an elevated park on two levels, dating from the 17th and 18th c. It offers a beautiful view as far as the Cevennes and the sea. At the intersection of the promenades stands a 19th c. equestrian statue of Louis XIV; at the western end of the terraces is a water-tower. The water is led through a channel 14 m (46 ft) wide which was constructed between 1753 and 1766 and which terminates in an imposing aqueduct 800 m (875 yd) long and up to 21.5 m (24 yd) high. On both sides of the water-tower steps lead down to the Boulevard des Arceaux where the market is held.

Arc de Triomphe

Forming the gateway to the Old Town, the Arc de Triomphe, a 15 m (49 ft) high triumphal arch in honour of Louis XIV, stands at the east end of the Promenade du Peyrou, on the northern side of which is the stately Palais du Justice (lawcourts). Rue Foch, which goes east from here, is impressive for its fine 19th c. buildings.

Jardin des Plantes

Flanking the Boulevard Henri IV just to the north of the Arc de Triomphe, lies the Jardin des Plantes; laid out in 1593 it was the first botanical garden in France and has a great number of exotic plants.

Musée Atger

Opposite the old Episcopal Palace is the building of the Faculté de Médecine, in which is also housed the Musée Atger. The interesting collection includes drawings by Baroque masters.

St-Pierre

Location
Rue de l'École de Médecine

East of the Faculté de Médecine stands the Gothic Cathedral of St-Pierre, founded in 1364 after the Wars of Religion and restored in 1867. It has a severed façade with twin towers and a high-vaulted canopied portico.

* Musée Fabre

Location
Rue Montpellieret

At the eastern edge of the Old Town, diametrically opposite the Promenade du Peyrou, lies its simple counterpart, the Esplanade. On the west side stands the Musée Fabre which includes a picture gallery with works by old Italian and Dutch painters, as well as paintings by French old masters, modern French pictures and fine 18th c. sculptures.
East of the Esplanade rises the old citadel, where today cultural institutions have their headquarters.

Mont Ventoux   C3

Région: Provence-Alpes-Côte d'Azur
Département: Vaucluse
Altitude: 1909 m (6265 ft)

Location

Mont Ventoux is situated in the north-west of Provence in the latitude of Orange to the east of the Rhône, from which it is separated by the Valley of the Ouvèze.

Landscape

Mont Ventoux (Provençal Mont Ventour=windy mountain) is a long limestone ridge named after the tempest which is

Mont Ventoux, laid bare by storms

frequently experienced in the area. Geologically the western-most peak of the Alps, it is a highly impressive isolated feature of the landscape; the summit is completely bare of vegetation. In 1336 the poet Francesco Petrarca (Petrarch), climbed Mont Ventoux. This first ascent of the mountain for its own sake reflects the increasing feeling for nature of the whole of this age.

From 1902 until the 1960s the present road D974 on the southern slopes of Mont Ventoux was a motor-racing course of international repute.

Above 1500 m (4923 ft), there are extensive ski slopes.

** Drive over Mont Ventoux

The visitor who is following the routes recommended in this guidebook will approach Mont Ventoux from the north-west via the town of Vaison-la-Romaine (see entry). Follow the D938 to Malaucène then turn left on to the D974. This stretch, which traverses exceptionally beautiful scenery with magnificent views on both sides, climbs fairly steeply through coniferous forest. Some 16 km (9 miles) beyond Malaucène at an altitude of about 1400 m (4595 ft) there is a junction where a narrow road leads to the viewpoint of Le Contrat. Beyond the junction the D974 is closed in winter, and even in spring the availability to traffic of this road, which in any case is not particularly wide, may be further restricted by snow on the northern flank of Mont Ventoux. For the last 6 km (4 miles) the road winds upwards, the vegetation becoming increasingly more scanty, until the highest point of the road is reached at the

Col des Tempètes (literally Pass of Storms) where there is an orientation table. From this point there is a magnificent view to the north over the Valley of the Toulourenc and the mountains rising beyond it. At this point the pass is fully exposed to the frequent storms which roar violently over the crest.

On the summit of Mont Ventoux an observatory and a television transmitter have been erected, with a radar station a little lower down. Near the observatory can be found an observation platform facing south, from where the view extends to the Montagne du Lubéron (see Lubéron).

The road downhill on the southern side is less steep, has fewer bends and is also wider than the road on the northern flank. It descends to the valley amid gravel slopes completely bare of vegetation. After 6 km (4 miles) there is a junction; the turning on the right, which is identical to a stretch of the former racing circuit, goes to Bédoin, from where one can drive back to Malaucène (see p. 137), or one can follow the recommended route towards Carpentras (see entry). Road D164 on the left goes via Sault to Apt.

Nice   D5

Région: Provence-Alpes-Côte d'Azur
Département: Alpes-Maritimes
Altitude: sea-level
Population: 339,000

Location

The Départemental capital Nice lies in the east of the Côte d'Azur 30 km (19 miles) from the Franco-Italian frontier.

History

Proof of prehistoric settlement has been found in the caves of the castle hill and of those in Mont Boron farther east. In 4 BC Phocaeans from Marseilles founded the strongpoint Nikaia Polis (Town of Victory) on the castle hill in what is now the Old Town. Later the Romans settled on the Hill of Cimiez on the far side of the River Paillon farther inland in order to protect the Via Julia.

Saxons and Saracens caused great distress in the town, the former in the 6th and the latter in the 9th c. In the Middle Ages Nice belonged to the county of Provence and from 1388 to the Dukedom of Savoy. It was in this period that the harbour and the fortress were built (providing the only access to the sea for Piedmont). In 1792 Nice became part of France, in 1814 it was incorporated in the Kingdom of Sardinia but returned to France in 1860. The sheltered situation and mild climate (average winter temperature 9 °C (48 °F) led to Nice becoming a popular winter health resort in the second half of the 19th c., and one of the first centres of tourism.

Nice is the birthplace of the Italian freedom fighter Giuseppe Garibaldi (1807–82).

Economy

A major factor in the economy of Nice has been its situation in the alluvial cone of the Var Valley, which made possible extraordinary dynamism in its development. The Nice-Côte d'Azur Airport, which was completed only in 1962, is already the second most important in France.

Carnival

The famous carnival, which has existed in Nice since the

Nice: Excavation on the castle hill . . .   *and the famous Promenade des Anglais*

14th c., begins 12 days before Ash Wednesday. During this period various performances and festivities succeed one another on a stretch of about 2 km (1 mile). The focus is near the Place Masséna of the Jardin Albert-I. Processions of floats, cavalcades, masked balls, floral processions, showers of confetti and dancing in the streets are just a few of the highlights. The main Battle of Flowers is on the day after Ash Wednesday. The conclusion of the carnival is marked by a grand firework display on Shrove Tuesday which lights up the whole of the Baie des Anges. At Micarême (mid Lent) a second celebration takes place.

Nice, chief town of the Département Alpes-Maritimes and the seat of a bishop, has a fine situation on the Baie des Anges which is enclosed by foothills of the Maritime Alps. The Old Town is separated from the newer districts by the little River Paillon, the course of which is for the most part covered over. Only in the town itself (for example along the Promenade des Anglais) is there any considerable stretch of sandy beach.

Townscape

Colline du Château (Castle Hill)

The first part of the town to be settled was the Colline du Château (92 m (302 ft) high), which can be reached by lift from the shore promenade (Quai des États-Unis) at the end of the Baie des Anges. The area at the top has been laid out as a park and offers an impressive panorama (orientation table). The citadel which once stood here was destroyed in 1706. The remains of two churches built one above the other in the 11th and 15th c. have been excavated; just to the east of the remains there is a good view of the harbour below.

Tour Bellanda

From the Colline du Château steps lead down to the promenade, passing the Tour Bellanda, a massive round tower built in the 16th c. on the site of the Bastion St-Lambert, and in which Hector Berlioz composed his opera "King Lear". The tower houses the Musée Naval (maritime museum).

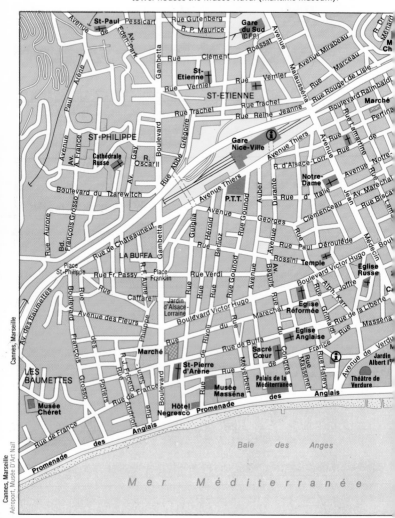

Vieille Ville (Old Town)

The Old Town (popularly also known as "Babazouk"),
with its twisting streets and bustling activity, lies below
the western side of the Colline du Château. In the
north-west it is bounded by spacious boulevards and
parks (Jardin Albert-I, Place Masséna, Promenade du
Paillon).

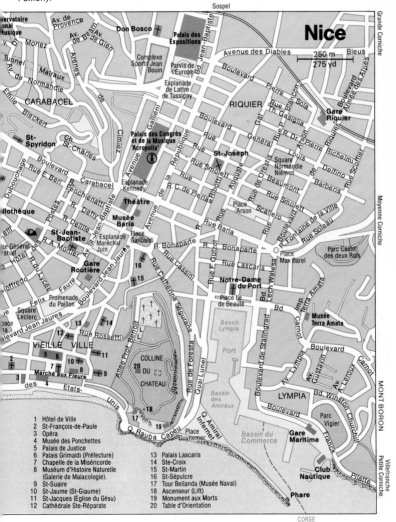

1 Hôtel de Ville
2 St-François-de-Paule
3 Opéra
4 Musée des Ponchettes
5 Palais de Justice
6 Palais Grimaldi (Préfecture)
7 Chapelle de la Miséricorde
8 Muséum d'Histoire Naturelle (Galerie de Malacologie).
9 St-Suaire
10 St-Jaume (St-Giaume)
11 St-Jacques (Eglise du Gésu)
12 Cathédrale Ste-Réparate
13 Palais Lascaris
14 Ste-Croix
15 St-Martin
16 St-Sépulcre
17 Tour Bellanda (Musée Naval)
18 Ascenseur (Lift)
19 Monument aux Morts
20 Table d'Orientation

Nice

Muséum d'Histoire Naturelle (Galerie de Malacologie)	Near the eastern end of the Cours Saleya, a short distance west of the foot of the steps descending from the castle hill, can be found a department of the Muséum d'Histoire Naturelle (Natural History Museum; closed Sunday and Monday) with an aquarium and an interesting collection of molluscs.
*Marché aux Fleurs (flower market)	In the Cours Saleya (temporarily, because of building work, in the Rue St-François-de-Paule, the western prolongation of the Cours Saleya) the very interesting flower market is held daily in the pedestrian zone. It is one of the most important of its kind on the coast.
Chapelle de la Miséricorde	Just north of the flower market stands the Chapelle de la Miséricorde dating from 1736; in the interior are an altar with the "Vierge de la Miséricorde" (Virgin of Mercy) of the early 15th c. by Miralhet and a picture of the Madonna ascribed to Bréa.
Palais Grimaldi	Adjoining the chapel on the north is the former Palais Grimaldi, built 1611–13 and restored in 1907. Today it is the seat of the Préfecture (government administration). Near by stands the Palais de Justice (lawcourts) completed in 1892.
*St-Jacques	The former Jesuit Church of St-Jacques in Rue Droite north of the Préfecture has a richly adorned interior.
Ste-Réparate	At the western end of Rue Rossetti stands the Cathedral of Ste-Réparate, an episcopal church built in the 17th c., with elaborate ornamental plasterwork, fine choir-stalls and wooden panelling in the Sacristy.
*Palais Lascaris	The Palais Lascaris (closed Monday), farther north in the Rue Droite, is also worth seeing. This sumptuous Baroque building was once the palace of the Counts of Castellar. On the ground floor are a fine entrance hall and a 18th c. apothecary's; the rooms on view have rich ornamental plasterwork and painted ceilings of the Italian school.
Musée des Ponchettes	A few steps towards the sea from the west end of the Cours Saleya, on the Quai des États-Unis, can be found the Musée des Ponchettes (once the arsenal of the Sardinian Navy); here temporary exhibitions of modern art are mounted. To the west of the museum stands the Opéra, and behind it the Church of St-Francois-de-Paule (1736; Italian Baroque) with a "Communion of St Benedict", ascribed to Van Loo. In the courtyard of the Hôtel de Ville (Town Hall, farther west) is a representation of Orestes before the statue of Athene.

Ville Moderne (New Town)

	The buildings in the Ville Moderne include those over the covered-in River Paillon.
*Jardin Albert-I	The Jardin Albert-I is the park-like area between the Avenue des Phocéens and the Avenue de Verdun; here is situated the Théâtre de Verdure (open-air theatre). The gardens extend north as far as the busy Place Masséna, where can be seen the Fontaine du Soleil, a fine fountain, and the Casino Municipal (1883). To the north extends the busy Avenue Jean Médecin,

Colourful Mediterranean blooms in the flower market of Nice

one of the principal shopping streets in the town, in which farther north stands the neo-Gothic Church of Notre-Dame.

To the west of the Avenue de Verdun the Quai des États-Unis is continued by the Promenade des Anglais along the shore of the Baie des Anges. Lining this highway, which was constructed between 1822 and 1824 and which has been subsequently extended several times, are many luxury buildings, including the Palais de la Méditerranée (theatre; casino) and the well-known Hotel Negresco.

**Promenade des Anglais

The Musée Masséna (closed Monday) stands in a park to the west of the Palais de la Méditerranée. It houses relics of the Roman era, numerous works of the Nice school of painting (including pictures by Bréa, Durandi, etc.), Impressionist and Post-Impressionist pictures (Degas, Renoir, Boudin, Vuillard, etc.), a large collection of arts and crafts and the weapon collection of Félix Joubert.

*Musée Masséna

Les Baumettes

The university quarter of Les Baumettes lies farther to the east. At Avenue Baumettes 33 is the Musée des Beaux-Arts Jules Chéret (closed Monday). This important collection has works by Charpeaux, Chéret (died 1932 in Nice), Fragonard, Braque, Carrière, Chagall, Dufy, Raffael, etc.; in addition there is pottery by Picasso.

*Musée Chéret

Still farther west one comes to the Musée International d'Art

Musée d'Art Naïf

143

The seashore promenade along the broad Baie des Anges

Naïf (Museum of Primitive Art; closed Tuesday), which originated in a bequest by the art critic Jakovsky. It provides an excellent survey of primitive art from all over the world. Adjoining is a research and information centre.

St-Barthélemy

Prieuré du Vieux Logis

From the eastern side of the university quarter the dead-straight Boulevard Gambetta and its continuation the Boulevard de Cessole lead north to the district of St-Barthélemy. A 16th c. building at 59 Avenue St-Barthélemy houses the extensive collection of religious art of the Prieuré du Vieux Logis (open Wed. Thurs. and Sat). The exhibits date from the 14th to the 16th c. Represented are works of the schools of Avignon and Paris as well as Flemish, Burgundian and German masters.

Cimiez

*Roman Settlement

On a plateau in front of Mont Gros in the district of Cimiez can be seen the considerable remains of the Roman settlement of Cemenelum. The amphitheatre (over 5000 seats) and the baths, the largest complex in Gaul, are poorly preserved. Early Christian churches have also been shown to have existed in this part of Nice.

Musée d'Archéologie

The Musée d'Archéologie (Archaeological Museum; closed Sunday morning and on Monday) is located within the area of the ancient settlement. Exhibited are finds from the excavations

The harbour, dominated by Mont Boron

– coins, jewellery, Greek, Etruscan and Roman pottery –
showing their relationship according to the subject.

The building of the Archaeological Museum also houses the
Musée Matisse (closed Sunday morning and Monday). The
exhibits – paintings, drawings, sculpture and ceramics – were
donated by the family to the town of Nice. Especially
interesting are the sketches for the Chapel in Vence (see
entry).

Musée Matisse

To the east, lying above the Roman ruins, stands the Monastère
Notre-Dame-de-Cimiez, originally a Benedictine foundation
which was taken over by the Franciscans in the 16th c. and
extended in the 17th. Its present appearance is characterised by
the restoration carried out in 1850 according to Gothic models.
Inside the church is a notable Crucifix by Bréa. In the square
outside, from which there is a fine view, stands a marble cross
dating from 1477.

Monastère Notre-Dame-de-
Cimiez

Carabacel

The Avenue de Flirey and the connecting Boulevard de Cimiez
lead south from the amphitheatre and baths. At the crossing
with the Avenue du Docteur-Ménard stands the Musée
National Message Biblique Marc Chagall (closed on Tuesday),
the most important exhibition of Chagall's works (paintings,
etchings, lithographs, sculptures, stained glass, mosaics, wall
tapestries on Biblical themes), especially his 17 large canvases,
the "Biblical Message" (1957–67).

*Musée Chagall

Nîmes

Palais des Congrès et de la Musique

Going farther along the Boulevard de Cimiez and then southwards along the Boulevard Carabacel one comes to the buildings which were erected above the bed of the River Paillon. On the left stands the Palais des Congrès et de la Musique (called the "Acropolis"; congress and function centre). Opposite on the south is the theatre; on the north lies a large car park with the Palais des Expositions (exhibition and fair building) behind it.

Muséum d'Histoire Naturelle (Musée Barla)

In the Boulevard Risso not far south of the congress centre is the Musée Barla (closed on Tuesday), a branch of the Muséum d'Histoire Naturelle. It includes collections dealing with biological evolution, palaeontology, geology and mineralogy.

A short distance south-east lies the Place Garibaldi, with a statue of the Italian freedom fighter who was born in Nice. From this square Rue Cassini leads south-east to the harbour.

The Harbour

Mont Boron (178 m (584 ft)) dominates the town on the east. At its foot lies the harbour area with Port Lympia and the Avant-Port (Outer Harbour). Three- and four-storeyed plain residential buildings in the Italian style characterise the scene.
Adjoining on the north is the district of Riquier, developed in a chequer-board plan after 1780.

Villefranche   D5

Location
6 km (4 miles) east

On the far side of Mont Boron lies Villefranche, a beautiful natural harbour developed in the early 14th c. by Charles II of Anjou. The township is surrounded by olive-clad hills and has such a mild climate that even bananas ripen here.
In the south of the picturesque Old Town stands the Citadel (1580), a fortification on the seashore. In the Church of St-Michel, built in Italian Baroque, is a figure of Christ carved in elm, and another of St Rochus (16th c.).
The remarkable Rue Obscure runs beneath huge shady arches. By the harbour stands the fishermen's Chapel of St-Pierre (often closed) – the interior of which was decorated by Jean Cocteau – and the Palais de la Marine.

Nîmes   D2

Région: Languedoc-Roussillon
Département: Gard
Altitude: 39 m (128 ft)
Population: 130,000

Location

Nîmes lies to the north-west of the Rhône Delta, half-way between Avignon and Montpellier. Strictly speaking, the town is not in Provence, but is included here since the relics of the Roman era make it one of the principal attractions of this region.

History

The old Nemausus was the capital of the Volcae Arecomici; it submitted in 121 BC to the Romans and soon became one of the most important towns in Gaul, on the road from Italy to Spain. The old buildings and extensive town walls bear witness to its

The Arena of Nîmes, a theatre yesterday and today

prosperity. In the Middle Ages until 1185 Nîmes had its own
Viscount and then passed to the Counts of Toulouse. Since
three-quarters of the inhabitants were Calvinist, the town
suffered greatly during the Wars of Religion, especially in 1704
in the time of the uprising in the Cevennes.

There are reduced rate combined entrance tickets for the most
important attractions in the town; these can be obtained at the
appropriate ticket offices.

Note

* * Arènes (amphitheatre)

The chief monument in Nîmes is the Amphitheatre which is to
be found near the town centre. It dates from the 1st century AD
and is 133 m (146 yd) by 101 m (110 yd) in area and up to 21 m
(69 ft) high. With a capacity of 21,000 spectators it was not the
largest of the 70 known Roman amphitheatres, but it is one of
the best preserved, especially in the upper part. The 60
arches of the exterior circuit are embellished in the lower part
with pilasters and in the upper part with Doric half-columns.
Brackets for the wooden masts of the awning can be seen on
the top. The richly decorated main entrance faces north-west.
The crowds thronging the theatre were able to leave by 124
exits in a few minutes.

In the 5th c. the Western Goths turned the arena into a fortress.
In the Middle Ages it served as a knight's castle, then as
dwellings for about 2000 people with their own chapel.
Nowadays theatrical performances and bullfights take place

Location
Place des Arènes

Opening times
daily 9 a.m.–midday and
2–7 p.m.; in winter closed
Tues.

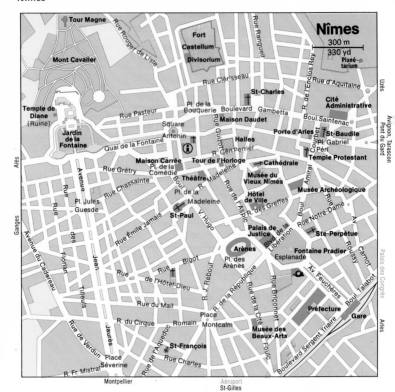

here in summer; the technical additions, however, somewhat detract from the general effect.

East of the amphitheatre extends the Esplanade, a busy traffic zone laid out like a square. Here stands the Fontaine Pradier, a marble fountain of 1848 representing a personification of Nîmes.

**Maison Carrée

Location
Place de la Comédie

Opening times:
daily 9 a.m.–midday and 2–5 p.m.; in winter closed Tues.

The Maison Carrée is situated in the Place de la Comédie, reached by the Boulevard Victor-Hugo going north-west from the amphitheatre. Standing on a podium, it is a splendidly maintained Roman temple which was erected between 20 and 12 BC. In the Middle Ages the building was used on occasions as a convent; in the 18th c. it was thoroughly restored, then during the French Revolution sold to the Département as national property. An art museum which still exists was set up here in 1821.

Tall Corinthian columns bear the richly ornamented entablature with a frieze finely decorated with acanthus. Fifteen steps lead

up to the Pronaos (antechamber) and the Cella on the same level. In the cella are the exhibits of the Musée des Antiques including Roman statues, mosaics and reliefs.
Opposite the Maison Carrée stands the Classical façade of the former theatre.

*Jardin de la Fontaine

West of the Maison Carrée and on the edge of the Inner City lies the beautiful Jardin de la Fontaine (Garden of the Source). It was laid out in the 18th c. in the area of the former fortified ramparts and includes the ruins of an ancient sanctuary of a sacred spring. The garden extends over several levels, the lowest forming the water-basins and the waterways joining them. Groups of life-size Baroque statues give atmosphere to this attractive feature.

Location
Quai de la Fontaine

The Roman Temple of Diana, a partly ruined rectangular building, is to be found on the western edge of the park beneath a number of ancient trees. Presumably it was part of the Roman baths. Since it had been used as a church in the Middle Ages, it was severely damaged during the Wars of Religion, and later the ruins provided building material.

Temple de Diane

Above the Jardin de la Fontaine rises the 114 m (374 ft) high Mont Cavalier, with subtropical plants and shady footpaths. On its summit stands the Tour Magne, a 30 m (98 ft) high Roman monument, dating from the year 15 BC. The tower is the largest feature of the wall which surrounded the town in the Roman era. From the top an extensive view of the city and surroundings may be enjoyed.

Tour Magne

Castellum (Château d'Eau Romain)

In 1884 the remains of an ancient water-tower (Castellum Divisorium) were discovered near the fort, north-east of the Jardin de la Fontaine. Its purpose was to distribute the water-supply for the town which flowed over the Pont du Gard (see entry). The remains consist of a collecting basin, 6 m (20 ft) in diameter, from which a number of supply channels lead off.

Location
Rue de la Lampèze

Notre-Dame et St-Castor

The Cathedral of Notre-Dame et St-Castor stands in the centre of the Old Town, almost due east of the Maison Carrée and reached from the latter along the Rue de l'Horloge with its 14th c. clock-tower. Originally built towards the end of the 11th c., the cathedral has been renewed several times. On the gable of the west front is an interesting Romanesque frieze in relief, with scenes illustrating the story of the Creation.

Location
Place aux Herbs

Musée de Vieux Nîmes

Opposite the cathedral on the south stands the former Bishop's Palace in which is housed the Musée du Vieux Nîmes with its collection of regional history and also the adjoining Musée

Location
Place aux Herbs

149

Taurin (Bullfighting Museum). Of interest in the museum which developed from the private ethnological collection of Henri Beaucquier, are products of local textile manufacture which is no longer carried on, as well as furniture from Provence and Languedoc, arts and crafts, etc.

Opening times
daily 9 a.m.–midday and
3–6 p.m.; in winter 9 a.m.–
midday and 2–5 p.m.

*Musée Archéologique

In the Boulevard Amiral Courbet which borders the Old Town in the east is the Musée Archéologique (officially Musée Lapidaire et Archéologique/Musée d'Histoire Naturelle). Its exhibits include Gallo-Roman finds and inscriptions, sculptures up to the Middle Ages and an exceptional collection of coins, as well as a good collection of glass and pottery; in the former chapel can be seen a beautiful mosaic.

Location
Boulevard Amiral Courbet

Opening times
daily 9 a.m.–midday and
3–6 p.m.; in winter Wed.–
Mon. 9 a.m.–midday and
2–5 p.m.

Porte d'Arles (Porte d'Auguste)

Near the northern end of the Boulevard Amiral Courbet stands the Porte d'Arles also known as the "Porte d'Auguste" after Augustus who had the town surrounded by walls. This town gate dates from 15 BC and in the 14th c. was incorporated into the walls of a fortress. It was not again uncovered until 1752 when the fortress had suffered damage. Today there is a bronze statue of Augustus in the interior. The position of the side wings of the gate, which were destroyed during the French Revolution, are marked on the pavement. The Porte d'Arles was the starting-point of the road to Rome.

Location
Boulevard Amiral Courbet

Musée des Beaux-Arts

The Musée des Beaux-Arts (Museum of Art) can be found in Rue de la Cité Foulc which leads south from the amphitheatre. Its collection of paintings includes primarily works by old masters of the 16th to 18th c., especially of France, Germany and the Netherlands, but also of Italy and Spain. Notable is the ancient mosaic on the ground floor.

Location
Rue de la Cité Foulc

Opening times
daily 9 a.m.–midday and
3–6 p.m.; in winter daily
9 a.m.–midday and 2–5 p.m.

Orange   C2

Région: Provence-Alpes-Côte d'Azur
Département: Vaucluse
Altitude: 46 m (151 ft)
Population: 28,000

Orange lies in the Lower Valley of the Rhône, some distance from the left bank of the river which here receives the waters of the Aigues. The motorway from the north divides near the town, one branch going to Marseilles, the other towards Nîmes.

Location

In Roman days the town was known as "Arausio Secundanorum". Later Orange was the chief place of the little

History

◄ *Maison Carrée, a relic of the Roman era*

Principality of Orange which passed to the Netherlands line of the House of Nassau, and even today the Queen of the Netherlands bears the title of a Princess of Orange-Nassau. In 1713 Orange was ceded to France.

* * Théâtre Romain (Roman Theatre)

Location
Place des Frères-Mounet

Opening times
9 a.m.–midday and
4–6.30 p.m.; in winter
9 a.m.–midday and 2–5 p.m.

Tickets also valid for the
Musée Municipal

The Roman Theatre, in the south of the Inner City, is the best preserved and one of the finest of antiquities. It was set up at the beginning of the Imperial era (1st c. AD), but probably renewed in the next century. It is a magnificent example of the Roman theatre, with its back wall, composed of massive stone blocks, several storeys high, towering over every other building to a height of 38 m (125 ft) and a width of 103 m (338 ft). Its circles and tiers of stepped seats, supported against the hillside, provided seating for 7000. During the summer months festivals take place here, generally with an above average attendance. The exceptional acoustics of the building contribute greatly to the performances.

Inside the theatre, on the right immediately behind the ticket office, is a Plexiglass panel with explanations of the history of the building, and an automatic tape-recorded commentary.

The over-all impression of the auditorium and stage is only marginally affected by the technical installations. On the rear wall of the stage can be seen a marble statue of Augustus.

Temple

Adjoining the theatre on the west are the ruins of a great Roman temple which was situated at the end of a 400 m (438 yd) long stadium. The Musée Municipal immediately opposite contains antique fragments, etc.

Colline St-Eutrope

Above the theatre to the south a beautiful park has been laid out on the Colline St-Eutrope; from its northern side there is a wonderful view of the auditorium and far over the town towards Mont Ventoux.

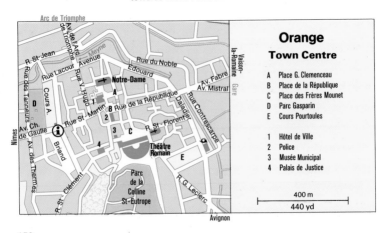

Orange
Town Centre

A   Place G. Clemenceau
B   Place de la République
C   Place des Frères Mounet
D   Parc Gasparin
E   Cours Pourtoules

1   Hôtel de Ville
2   Police
3   Musée Municipal
4   Palais de Justice

400 m
440 yd

Orange: the Roman theatre, still in use today

Old Town

The Old Town lies to the north of the Roman theatre. In the Place Clemenceau stands the Hôtel de Ville (Town Hall), dating from 1671, and near by the Cathedral of Notre-Dame (1083–1126) which was severely damaged during the Wars of Religion.

*Arc de Triomphe

The arterial road N7 which leaves Orange in a northerly direction leads to the Arc de Triomphe (Triumphal Arch) situated outside the town and sited on a circular space framed by plane trees. It was erected during the reign of Augustus to commemorate victories by the Second Legion whose veterans founded Arausio. In spite of severe weathering it is the finest of its kind in France. Three arches with coffered vaulting form the gateways. Once there were a bronze Quadriga (four-horse chariot) and four statues on the top, with a representation of a Gallic battle on the frieze; below on either side are trophies from Gallic vessels.

Location
Avenue de l'Arc de Triomphe

Pont du Gard

D2

Région: Laguedoc-Roussillon
Département: Gard

The Pont du Gard, an exceptionally well-preserved Roman aqueduct is situated about 25 km (16 miles) west of Avignon.

Location

The Pont du Gard: a Roman aqueduct

Note

Cars are often broken into and thefts committed in and around the large car parks near the Pont du Gard.

Pont du Gard (aqueduct)

The Pont du Gard is a 49 m (160 ft) high and 275 m (300 yd) long aqueduct, spanning the deeply incised Valley of the Gard or Gardon. Probably built about 19 BC by Agrippa, the son-in-law and co-regent of the Emperor Augustus, the three-tiered construction is one of the greatest and best-preserved Roman monuments. Visitors are recommended to walk through the covered channel, above the topmost row of arches, in which water was conveyed to Nîmes in a pipeline altogether 41 km (25 miles) long.
The road bridge at the level of the first storey was added in 1747.

Port Grimaud   D4

Région: Provence-Alpes-Côte d'Azur
Département: Var
Altitude: sea-level

Location

Port-Grimaud is situated where the Bay of St-Tropez penetrates farthest inland, at the foot of the Massif des Maures.

Port-Grimaud: view of the town and lagoons

*Townscape

The very attractive modern holiday resort of Port-Grimaud is, with its maze of channels, like a Venetian fishing and lagoon settlement. When the resort was translated from the drawing-board to reality in 1966, great importance was laid on creating a townscape typical of the region.

The resort is free of traffic; there are car parks outside the little town for holiday-makers and visitors. As well as motor-boats on regular routes, there are four-seater electric boats for self-drive on the canals.

By the canals, on which there are many fine sailing-ships and cabin cruisers, there are boutiques, shops and restaurants; the market is held in the main square. Many of the apartment houses have their own mooring-places outside the front door. Facing the sea stands the ecumenical Church of St-François d'Assisi, designed according to Romanesque models; a coin-operated turnstile gives access to the tower from which there is an exceptional panorama of the little town, the lagoons and the mountainous hinterland.

Grimaud   D4

Grimaud is situated inland on the site of a settlement which was used by the Ligurians; it is a "village perché", high above the Plain of Cogolin and with a particularly picturesque town-scape. Of interest are the ruins of the fortress (11th c.; view) and the Church of St-Michel, also dating from the 11th c. Also well

Location
5 km (3 miles) west

155

preserved is the Maison des Templiers (House of the Templars) with its Gothic arcades. Some 2 km (1 mile) east on the road from Port-Grimaud stands the charming Chapel of Notre-Dame-de-la-Queste.

La Garde-Freinet

See Maures (Massif des Maures)

Roquebrune-Cap-Martin

D5

Région: Provence-Alpes-Côte d'Azur
Département: Alpes-Maritimes
Altitude: sea-level to 300 m (985 ft)
Population: 13,000

Location

The municipality of Rocquebrune-Cap-Martin is situated near the Franco-Italian border a little west of Menton.

Roquebrune

The inland old community of Roquebrune is built like an eyrie on a greyish-brown conglomerate hill. Most of the narrow little streets are vaulted and are full of atmosphere; going uphill through these streets one reaches the castle (9 a.m.–midday and 2–6 p.m. daily; entrance fee), which dominates the whole town. The castle dates from the 10th c. and from its fortified tower one has a fine view.

Cap-Martin and the Maritime Alps

A street in Roquebrune

Hotel Vistaëro and Monaco

To the west above Roquebrune on the Grande Corniche (see Corniches de la Riviera) stands the luxury hotel Le Vistaëro, which has a breath-taking situation right on the mountainside and from which there is a marvellous view.

*Le Vistaëro

Cap-Martin

Cap-Martin, stretching like a tongue into the sea, offers beautiful walks; along the west bank runs the Promenade Le Corbusier (the architect was drowned here in 1965). At the foot of the Sémaphore (signal station) lie the ruins of the Church of St-Martin, built by the monks of Lérins in the 11th c. In the midst of olive and pine woods a number of impressive villas have been built.

Route Napoléon

C3/4–D4/5

Length: 325 km (202 miles)
Highest point: Col Bayard 1240 m (4070 ft)

The Route Napoléon, a tourist road opened in 1932, runs north-west from Cannes via Grasse and Digne to Gap, and links the Mediterranean with the Alps. The route approximates that which Napoleon took to Grenoble, after he had landed in Golfe-Juan on 1 March 1815 on his return from Elba; the route is marked by small eagles. With a legacy of Napoleon six

General

157

Church of the Three Marys . . .

and a gipsy pilgrimage

refuges, named after him the "Réfuges Napoléon", were built on the tops of the passes which are particularly exposed in winter, however only three of them are still in existence.

**Drive on the Route Napoléon

In this guidebook not all the Route Napoléon is described but only the section, about 220 km (137 miles) long from Cannes via Grasse and Castellane (a particularly worthwhile excursion into the Gorges of the Verdon; see all these entries), continuing via Digne and Sisteron to Gap (see entries). This corresponds to the last part of the recommended route in the introduction to this guidebook.

The road (picture on p. 29), which is normally passable all the year, opens up the unusually charming diversity of scenery from the Mediterranean coastal regions, over the mountains of Haute Provence to the peaks of the High Alps around Gap.

Saintes-Maries-de-la-Mer   D2

Région: Provence-Alpes-Côte d'Azur
Département: Bouches-du-Rhône
Altitude: sea-level
Population: 2000

Location

Stes-Maries-de-la-Mer is situated in the extreme west of

Provence, in the flat country of lagoons and salt steppes of the Camargue.

The place owes its name to the legend, according to which the three Marys – Mary (sister of the Virgin Mary), Mary Salome (mother of the Apostles James and John) and Mary Magdalene (the penitent), and other saints – landed here in the year 45 and converted Provence to Christianity.

History

In recent years the place has been intensively remodelled into a holiday centre. In general the conversion has been successful, since the erection of tall buildings has been avoided; the harbour is still being extended.

In and around Stes-Maries-de-la-Mer cars are often broken into and thefts committed.

Warning

*Church

The fortress-like church in the heavily commercialised town centre (pedestrian zone) dates from the 10th, 12th and 15th c.; inside is a well for use in case of siege. In a chapel above the apse are the reliquaries of the first two Marys, in the crypt those of their black servant Sarah. Gipsies come from far and wide to worship Sarah (pilgrimages on 24, 25 May and at the weekend after the 22 October). From the roof of the church (fee) there is a fine view.

Musée Baroncelli

The Musée Baroncelli is in the former Town Hall, a few yards south of the church. It has collections dealing with local history and folklore from the Gallo-Roman era up to the beginning of the 20th c.; there are also slides and dioramas of the animal and plant life of the Camargue and archaeological finds from the vicinity.

Location
Rue Espelly

Opening times: daily
9 a.m.–midday and 2–7 p.m.;
in winter Thurs.–Tues.
9 a.m.–midday and 2–5 p.m.

Arènes

In the southern outskirts of the town between the Place du Marquis de Baroncelli and the beach of fine sand, stands the Arena for bullfights and similar events which take place during the season.
A drive through the Camargue (see entry) is to be recommended.

Saint-Gilles

D2

Région: Languedoc-Roussillon
Département: Gard
Altitude: 7 m (23 ft)
Population: 11,000

St-Gilles lies not far beyond the western border of Provence on the edge of the Carmargue.

Location

**Church

In the heart of the Old Town stands the church, erected in the 12th c. and restored on a smaller scale in the 17th c. The west front is especially beautiful (best lighting in the late afternoon) with its three doorways and wealth of reliefs and statues; this is a masterpiece of Romanesque in southern France. The damage to the figures was caused by the iconoclasm of the French Revolution. The entrance to the crypt is on the right of the façade. The interior of this three-aisled church without transepts is characterised by Gothic forms which are surprisingly broad for this epoch.

To the left of the façade a narrow lane leads to the ruins of the old Choir, which was destroyed in the 17th c. Here is the Vis de St-Gilles (Screw of St Gilles), a now free-standing staircase with a circular flight of stairs inside it. Also to be seen here are the remains of the old apse (the base of pillars, etc.).

Maison Romane

From the open space in front of the church (Place de la République) a narrow lane leads to the charming little Place de l'Olme. Here stands the Maison Romane (Romanesque House) where capitals decorated with figures are to be seen on the first and second storeys. Immediately adjoining is the Office de Tourisme (Tourist Office).

St-Gilles is the starting-point for excursions into the Camargue (see entry).

Saint-Maximin-la-Sainte-Baume   D3

Région: Provence-Alpes-Côte d'Azur
Département: Var
Altitude: 303 m (994 ft)
Population: 6000

Location

At the northern edge of the Massif de la Ste-Baume about 50 km (31 miles) north-east of Marseilles lies St-Maximin-la-Ste-Baume.

History

The little basin (formerly the bed of a lake), was already settled at the time of Roman occupation. The town is famous as the place where, it is said, the bones of St Mary Magdalene were discovered.

Ste-Madeleine

The three-aisled Dominican Church of Ste-Madeleine is a magnificently furnished Gothic building of the 13th–15th c. The interior is rather severe and without transepts. On the right in a side chapel can be seen a 15th c. altar with representations of St Laurence, St Antony, St Sebastian and St Thomas Aquinas; in a second chapel is the coat of St Louis of Anjou with rich embroidery (scenes from the life of Christ), a 13th c. work. Also of note are the choir-stalls and the fine High Altar, both dating from the late 17th c.

Crypt

The entrance to the crypt (light switch on the grille) is in the left-hand aisle; the crypt was first constructed in the 4th c. as a burial-place. Here can be seen four sarcophagi (one of which

Saint-Gilles: a perfect example of Romanesque in southern France

is said to have contained the remains of St Mary Magdalene);
they date from late antiquity to Early Christian times, and have
reliefs of Biblical scenes.

Abutting the north wall of the nave is the Early Gothic cloister
(entrance behind the Town Hall which is situated to the left of
the façade of the church). With its old cedars, thujas, yews and
chestnuts it is an extremely evocative place. The Chapter House
and the Sacristy, which form a link with the church, have now
been deconsecrated and serve as conference and lecture
rooms.

Cloister

Nans-les-Pins

D3

The wine village of Nans-les-Pins lies in the northern foothills
of the Chaîne de la Ste-Baume and is dominated by the ruins of
a medieval castle.

Location
12 km (7 miles) south

Beyond Nans-les-Pins road D80 leads up into the mountains.
Some 8 km (5 miles) along this road near the Hostellerie de la
Ste-Baume is the beginning of the footpath which leads to the
Ste-Baume (Holy Grotto), an opening in the calcareous rock
face which has been converted into a chapel. It is said to have
been inhabited by St Mary Magdalene and for a long time has
been used as the goal of a pilgrimage.

*Sainte Baume

A further 30 minutes brings the walker to the top of St-Pilon
(994 m (3262 ft); orientation panel) from which there is a good
view. Even more comprehensive is the view farther east from

the rock called "Joug d'Aigle" (1116 m (3663 ft)) and the Croix des Béguines (1154 m (3787 ft)). From here there is a good impression of the geological structure of the Massif.

Tourves   D3

Location
5 km (3 miles) south-east of
St-Maximin-la-Ste-Baume

Tourves, a road junction in an area of intensive agriculture, has the impressive remains of the uncompleted Château de Valbelle (18th c.).

There are several grottoes with prehistoric paintings in the nearby Caramy valley.

Saint-Raphaël   D4

Région: Provence-Alpes-Côte d'Azur
Département: Var
Altitude: sea-level
Population: 24,000

Location

The port of St-Raphaël, half-way between St-Tropez and Cannes, has a charming situation on the north side of the Gulf of Fréjus at the foot of the Esterel range.

Townscape

In the old heart of the town stands the 12th c. Église des Templiers (a Templar church), with a tower which was built as protection against pirates. Adjoining the church on the north is the Musée d'Archéologie Sous-Marine (Museum of Underwater Archaeology) with a notable collection of amphorae which were mostly rescued from ancient wrecks.

Parallel to the shore runs the Promenade René-Coty, which is beautifully laid out and extremely popular in the season. From here and also from the pleasant Avenue de Gaulle there is a good view of the strange rock formations, the Lion de Terre (Lion of the Land) and Lion de Mer (Lion of the Sea) near Port Santa-Lucia.

Agay   D4

Location
9 km (5 miles) east

The very charming winding road along the red rocky coast leads to the resort of Agay on the bay of the same name, which is enclosed by Cap Drammont and the Pointe de la Baumette. At the latter there is a lighthouse and a memorial to the French airman and author Antoine de Saint-Exupéry (1900–44).

Agay is a good starting-point for tours to the Esterel Massif (see entry).

The Mausoleum and Municipal Arch of Glanum

Saint-Rémy-de-Provence

D2

Région: Provence-Alpes-Côte d'Azur
Département: Bouches-du-Rhône
Altitude: 60 m (197 ft)
Population: 8000

St-Rémy-de-Provence is situated not far east of the lower course of the Rhône, about 20 km (12 miles) south of Avignon in the northern foothills of the Alpilles.

Location

*Glanum (Excavation Site)

South of the little town, on the road into the Alpilles, lie the remains of the Graeco-Roman settlement of Glanum Livii (2nd c. BC and 1st–3rd c. AD) which was destroyed in the year 480 by the Western Goths. On the right, in an open space surrounded by plane trees stands the impressive group of monuments known as "Les Antiques"; here stand the Municipal Arch, a souvenir of the foundation of the town, and the 18 m (59 ft) mausoleum in memory of Julius Caesar's two adopted sons, both dating from the 1st c. BC. The lower part of the square base of the mausoleum is decorated with reliefs of battle scenes; above the base rises a temple-like upper part borne on columns. The reliefs on the frieze of the archway of the Municipal Arch and the coffered internal vaulting are notable but the reliefs on the outside of the walls are dilapidated.

Les Antiques

163

To the left is the road leading to the extensive excavation site (open daily 9 a.m.–midday and 2–6 p.m.; entrance fee).

St-Paul-de-Mausole

Close to the excavation site on the right of the road stands the former Monastery of St-Paul-de-Mausole (now a psychiatric hospital), with a church and a beautiful little cloister dating from Romanesque times. From 1889 to 1890 Vincent van Gogh was accommodated in the mental institution here.

St-Rémy-de-Provence
Les Antiques

Excavation site of the Graeco-Roman town of

Glanum

(2nd c. BC–3rd c. AD)

at St-Rémy-de-Provence

1 Basin of Fountain

GREEK PERISTYLE HOUSES
  2 Maison des Antes
    (House of the Antes)
  3 Market (Shrine of Cybele)
  4 Maison d'Atys (House of Atys)

ROMAN BATHS
  5 Heating chamber
  6 Caldarium (hot water)
  7 Tepidarium (tepid water)
  8 Frigidarium (cold water)
  9 Palaestra (courtyard)
 10 Swimming-pool
    (cold running water)

OTHER EXCAVATIONS
 11 Maison de Capricorne
    (House of the Ibex; mosaics)
 12 Building with apse
 13 House of Sulla (Sylla; mosaics)
 14 Covered water channel
 15 Forum
 16 Wall with apse
 17 Victory monument or altar
 18 Roman Theatre
    (not yet excavated)
19/20 Roman Temple (perhaps
    dedicated to Caius and Lucius,
    grandsons of Augustus)
 21 Well
 22 Buleuterion (Council chamber)
 23 Hall with Doric pillars
 24 Fortified gate
 25 Nympheum (presumably above
    the sacred well of Glanum)
 26 Altars (dedicated to Hercules)
 27 Celtic shrine

50 m
55 yd

Glanum, once a thriving settlement

Saint-Tropez D4

Région: Provence-Alpes-Côtes d'Azur
Département: Var
Altitude: sea-level
Population: 6000

The little port and well-known resort of St-Tropez lies on the southern bank of the gulf of the same name at the foot of the eastern part of the Massif des Maures.

Location

The Greeks called the settlement Athenopolis; by the Romans it was named Heraclea Caccabaria. The present name is said to go back to St Tropez or Torpes, who was beheaded by the Romans and whose remains were discovered here. In the time of the Saracens the little coastal village was hard pressed but was able to recover and in the 15th c. became a republic.
After the Second World War St-Tropez developed into a resort which was extremely popular, especially with prominent people. However it must be said that the gloss, which the wealthy brought with them, has paled somewhat in the wake of mass tourism.

History

Citadel

High over the town towers the Citadel, dating from the year 1592. In the gateway is a large modern relief by Paul Landowski, depicting a ship's cannon being made ready for

Opening times
daily 10 a.m.–6 p.m.

The harbour of St-Tropez, a favourite subject with artists

action. Within the fortress is the Musée de la Marine et de l''Histoire Locale (Museum of Shipping and Local History); from the battlements there is a good view of the gulf and the Massif des Maures.

Old Town

The Old Town of St-Tropez is situated to the west below the citadel and is bordered on the other side by the harbour basin. Part of it has been laid out as a pedestrian zone where shops, boutiques and restaurants abound. Rue de la Citadelle leads down into the centre; on the right in Rue du Portail-Neuf stands the 18th c. church, in Italian Baroque style, in which can be seen a bust of St Tropez and beautiful woodcarving (at Christmas-time there is a fine Provençal crib).

North-west of the church near the harbour and the Hôtel de Ville (Town Hall) stands the former Palais des Bailli de Suffren (1726–88), Bailiff of the Order of Malta and Admiral of the French fleet. From here it is not far to the Mole Jean-Réveille enclosing the harbour on the north, from where there is a good view of the town. Luxury yachts are often to be seen in the harbour.

*Musée de l'Annonciade

Location
Rue de la Nouvelle Poste

At the southern corner of the harbour basin stands the former Chapel of the Annunciation; it now houses the Musée de l'Annonciade with a very notable collection of the works of

166

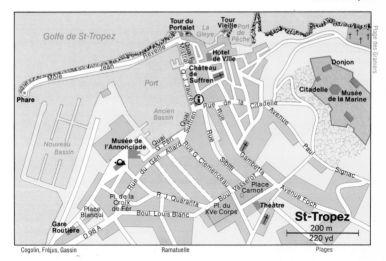

Golfe de St-Tropez · Tour du Portalet · La Gleye · Tour Vieille · Port de Pêche · Plage des Graniers · Réveille · Hôtel de Ville · Château de Suffren · Jean · Môle · Donjon · Citadelle · Musée de la Marine · Phare · Port · Ancien Bassin · Rue de la Citadelle · Avenue · Paul · Nouveau Bassin · Musée de l'Annonciade · Quai du Gén. Allard · Quai G. Péri · Rue Sibilli · Rue G. Clemenceau · Rue Gambetta · Rue Yasseror · Signac · Pl. de la Croix de Fer · R. J. Quaranta · Boul. Vasseror · Place Carnot · Avenue Foch · Place Blanqui · Boul. Louis Blanc · Pl. du XVe Corps · Théâtre · Gare Routière · D 98 A · **St-Tropez** · 200 m · 220 yd

Cogolin, Fréjus, Gassin · Ramatuelle · Plages

artists who have been active in St-Tropez, including Signac, Derain, Van Dongen, Rouault, Braque, Bonnard, Matisse and Maillol.

Opening times
Wed.–Mon. 10 a.m.–midday and 2–6 p.m.

Cogolin   D4

Cogolin, a little inland, is a centre of wood and textile processing both by hand craftsmanship and industrial means. The main products are furniture made of bamboo, reeds, etc., carpets, and brier pipes. In the village is a pleasant 16th c. church, a clock-tower and the remains of the former fortifications.

Location
9 km (6 miles) west

About 5 km (3 miles) east lies the large yacht harbour of Les Marines de Cogolin.

Ramatuelle   D4

On the hilly and for the most part wooded peninsula to the south of St-Tropez lies the picturesque hill village of Ramatuelle with its fortified houses and imposing gates. It is surrounded by vineyards and pine groves. In the little cemetery is buried the actor Gérard Philipe (1922–59); his grave is completely overgrown with ivy.

Location
12 km (7 miles) south

About 4 km (2 miles) east and below Ramatuelle Cap Camarat extends into the sea; there are fine views and good beaches.

Cap Camarat

A scenically very rewarding but winding stretch of road D93 from St-Tropez passes Ramatuelle and crosses the Col de Collebasse before coming to the resort of La Croix-Valmer which lies like an amphitheatre on the Bay of Cavalaire.

Ste-Maxime   D4

Location
14 km (9 miles) north

On the far side of the bay to the north of St-Tropez lies the port of Ste-Maxime, very popular as a holiday and winter health resort. In the church to the west of the harbour is a striking marble altar (18th c.) from the Carthusian Monastery of La Verne near Collobrières in the Maures mountains. In the Musée de la Photographie et de la Musique are over 300 musical instruments and cameras. Above the little town on the north-east is a signal station 127 m (417 ft) above sea-level from which there are fine views.

Salon-de-Provence   D3

Région: Provence-Alpes-Côte d'Azur
Département: Bouches-du-Rhône
Altitude: 82 m (269 ft)
Population: 36,000

Location

Salon-de-Provence is situated on the edge of the Plaine de la Crau, north of the Etang de Berre and north-west of Marseilles.

History

Once on this site, on the Hill of Valdemech, stood the Roman Castrum Salonense. The present-day town had its origins in the time of Charlemagne, after the salt-marshes were drained. Salon was the native town of Adam de Craponne, who set up the drainage and canal system between the Durance, the Rhône and the Etang de Berre in the 16th c., and it is also the last resting-place of Nostradamus who lived here for a long time.

*Château de l'Empéri

Opening times
Wed.–Mon. 9 a.m.–midday
and 2.30–6.30 p.m.

Occupying a dominating position in the centre of the town, the Château de l'Empéri is one of the largest and best-preserved fortifications in Provence. The beautiful 12th c. Chapel of Ste-Cathérine is well worth seeing.

Musée de l'Empéri

The Musée de l'Empéri is housed in the château. It traces the history of French weaponry from the time of Louis XIV to the end of the First World War and includes uniforms, equipment, firearms, swords, etc.

St-Michel

Location
Rue St-Michel

Not far east of the castle stands the 13th c. Church of St-Michel with a Romanesque doorway and an uncommon tympanum decorated with sculpture.
Near by can be seen the attractive 17th c. Town Hall, a fountain with a statue of Craponne and the Porte Bourg-Neuf, part of the Old Town fortifications.

Maison de Nostradamus in Salon-de-Provence

The former house of the cosmologist Nostradamus (Michel

de Nostre-Dame; 1503–66) accommodates the interesting Nostradamus Museum. It includes mementoes, historical editions of his prophecies and a reproduction of his study.

*St-Laurent

In the extreme north of the Inner Town stands the Church of St-Laurent (14th–15th c.), a magnificent example of Provençal Gothic. Inside can be seen a 16th c. alabaster statue of the Madonna, a Romanesque marble relief, a beautiful "Descent from the Cross" (14th c.) and the Tomb of Nostradamus which in its present form is a modern work.

Location
Square St-Laurent

La Barben
D3

Charmingly situated in the Valley of the Touloubre is the little village of La Barben. About 1 km ($\frac{1}{2}$ mile) east of the village stands the Château La Barben on a steep rocky height. It is surrounded by beautiful parkland with an animal compound and an aquarium.

Location
8 km (5 miles) east

Cornillon-Confoux
D3

The picturesque village of Cornillon-Confoux, which is noted for its wine, lies on a spur from which there is a fine view of the Etang de Berre. Of interest are the 17th c. castle and the 12th c. church.

Location
12 km (7 miles) south

The lively little fishing and yachting port of St-Chamas lies some 3 km (2 miles) south-west of the Etang de Berre (see entry). It boasts prehistoric dwelling-caves, the single-arched Pont Flavien (a richly decorated bridge over the Touloubre; 1st c. AD) and a 17th c. church.

St-Chamas

Sénanque (Abbeye de Sénanque)
D3

Région: Provence-Alpes-Côte d'Azur
Département: Vaucluse
Altitude: 480 m (1575 ft)

The Cistercian Abbey of Sénanque lies at the foot of the Plateau de Vaucluse on its southern side, a few kilometres north of Gordes in the Valley of the Sénancole.

Location

The monastery was founded in 1148. The heyday of the Cistercian abbey was during the 14th c., but in the 16th c. decline set in, partly through the Wars of Religion. In the French Revolution the deconsecrated estate was sold but with the return of the Cistercians in 1855 the abbey was once more occupied. In 1969 the last monks left the abbey and joined the Monastery of Lérins.

History

Sénanque

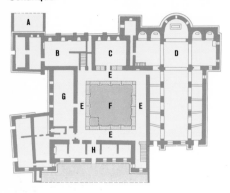

Cistercian Monastery of
Sénanque

A Entrance
B/C On the upper floor sleeping-quarters (Dormitorium)
B Monks' Hall (Scriptorium)
C Chapter House
D Monastic Church
E Cloister
F Cloister garden
G Dining Hall (Refectory)
H Lay brothers' building

|———————————| 30 m
|———————————| 33 yd

* Monastery Buildings

Viewing times
daily 10 a.m.–1 p.m. and
2–7 p.m.

As one approaches the buildings from Gordes (see entry) on a rather narrow road with passing places, there is a good view of the monastery far below in the lavender fields of the valley cleft. The complex of buildings is very well preserved.

The cloister area is entered through the 19th c. wing which was added on the right. The route which is indicated by arrows leads first into the dormitorium (monks' sleeping-quarters) in the upper storey; this is an austere room, the Gothic pointed arches of which are a continuation of the vaulting which covers the transepts of the monastic church. From the dormitorium one goes down into the attractive cloisters which open into the cloister garden through round arches each divided by two pairs of pillars. The capitals of the pillars are decorated with plant designs. Of the well which is situated in the south-west corner there remain only the pillars which supported the vaulting. Adjoining the cloister is the chapter house which later received its ribbed vaulting during the Gothic period.

The refectory was recently restored to its original appearance. Here there is a clear depiction of the development of the Cistercian Order which, especially in France, was one of the most important monastic orders.

The three-aisled monastic church (built in the late 12th c.) gives an impressive sense of space through the absence of additional adornment. The transepts are unusually wide and the choir has a semicircular main apse on each side of which are two other apses. An unusual feature is the cupola above the crossing; most Cistercian churches only have a ridge turret.

The monks' hall, the only room in the monastery which could be heated, and the scriptorium are on the same level as the cloisters.
The exit is via the stairs to the dormitory.

In the cloister buildings exhibitions on various themes are mounted and concerts take place, including church music and Gregorian chant.

The Abbey of Sénanque in the valley of the Sénancole

Silvacane (Abbeye de Silvacane) D3

Région: Provence-Alpes-Côte d'Azur
Département: Vaucluse
Altitude: 230 m (755 ft)

The former Cistercian Abbey of Silvacane lies on the left bank   Location
of the Durance below the Montagne du Lubéron and north of
Marseilles.

The name of the abbey comes from the Latin silva cannorum   History
(forest of reeds) and indicates that the area was formerly
marshland. The monastery was founded in 1144; the first
building to be erected was a church in the late 12th c., the
monastic buildings arose about 50 years later. In the Hundred
Years War the abbey suffered severe damage and about the
middle of the 15th c. it almost completely lost its importance.
Like a great deal of other Church property, Silvacane was sold
during the French Revolution and is said to have been
destroyed to provide building material. In 1846 the State
inherited the property and subsequently considerable restoration work was carried out.

Monastery Buildings of Silvacane

In spite of extensive renovation in the 19th c. the three-aisled   **Opening times:** Wed.–Mon.
monastic church still gives a good impression of the severe   10–11.45 a.m. and
Romanesque style of the Cistercians. As in Sénanque (see   2–6.45 p.m.; closed in winter

171

entry) the nave leads to an unusually wide crossing, which is succeeded by the main choir and two subsidiary choirs (all of which here are based on a rectangular plan). Over the portico on the west front can be seen the arms of the Cathedral Chapter of Aix-en-Provence and this was added in the 15th c. after Silvacane had passed into the possession of the cathedral.

The adjoining monastic buildings are not yet completely restored. The cloisters, shaded by old trees, is a pleasant place and adjoining it is the refectory which was newly built in the 15th c. Of interest here are the rose-window and the beautifully decorated capitals.

Sisteron   C3

Région: Provence-Alpes-Côte d'Azur
Département: Alpes-de-Haute-Provence
Altitude: 482 m (1582 ft)
Population: 7000

Location

Sisteron lies in the extreme north of the area covered in this guidebook on the Route Napoléon and to the north of the Montagne de la Lure; it is not far from the confluence of the Buech with the Durance.

History

It is believed that the caves in the vicinity were lived in from very early times, but there is no actual proof of this. Augustus subdued the tribes of the Avantici and Vocones which were settled here and built Segustero at an important narrow point of the Durance on the Roman Via Domitia. In the 5th c. Sisteron became the seat of the Bishop and remained so until the French Revolution. In the 9th and 10th c. the Saracens held the town; in 1348 half the population died of the plague. About the middle of the 14th c. a beginning was made with the defence works, most of which can still be seen today. In 1481 Sisteron fell to the Kingdom of France, but the Wars of Religion caused great devastation. On his journey from Elba to Paris Napoleon passed through the Defile of Sisteron without much difficulty.

Townscape

Situated high above the place where the Durance breaks through its mountain ridge the Citadel of Sisteron crowns an unusually impressive landscape.

In summer a little tourist railway (starting-point at the Place de la République) runs up to the citadel.

*Citadel in Sisteron

Opening times
daily 8 a.m.–7 p.m.

Above the town to the north on a high rocky hill, through which road N85 runs in a tunnel, stands the Citadel, built in the 12th and extended in the 16th and 19th c. It is a fortified barrier on several levels from which not only the narrows of the river but also the entire north and south hinterlands could be controlled. The greater part of the fortifications was the work of the architect Jean Erard (16th c.). From the highest turrets of the building there is an unusually impressive view to the north over the Alpine region and to the east to the other side of the narrows

Rocher de la Baume in Sisteron: a visual geology lesson ▶

where rises the Rocher de la Baume, a steep rock face on which the almost vertical faulting due to erosion can clearly be seen. On the north side of the citadel an open-air theatre has been constructed.

Notre-Dame-des-Pommiers

Location
Place du Général-de-Gaulle

In the centre of the Lower Town stands the former Cathedral of Notre-Dame-des-Pommiers which was built between 1160 and 1220. Like many churches in this area of the Alps it reveals the influence of Lombardy. Of special interest are the figure decoration on the entrance, the capitals of the half-pillars in the nave and the two Baroque altars.

Town Walls

To the south of the church in the Allée de Verdun can be seen three well-preserved towers of semicircular plan which were once part of the town walls.

Old Town

In the Old Town of Sisteron are a number of fine 16th and 17th c. houses; a walk through the picturesque streets, which in places lead beneath flying buttresses, is marked by arrows.

Tarascon   D2

Région: Provence-Alpes-Côte d'Azur
Département: Bouches-du-Rhône
Altitude: 9 m (30 ft)
Population: 11,000

Location

Tarascon is situated on the left bank of the lower course of the Rhône about half-way between Avignon and Arles. To the north rise the heights of Montagnette.

Legend and Fable

Tarascon gets its name from the Tarasque, a fabulous man-eating creature of wild appearance said to have dwelt here and which was only pacified by St Martha. It has become the heraldic animal of the town celebrated by a festival in June, the Fête de la Tarasque.

No less romantic is the second notability, Tartarin de Tarascon, the hero of the novel by Alphonse Daudet. Short and somewhat stocky with a black beard and quite warlike in his behaviour, he is nevertheless more inclined to dream his adventures than to carry them out in reality; in the long run he values physical well-being more highly than war and deprivation and with his lovable humanity he is, for many, the embodiment of the Provençal character.

Château du Roi René

Location
Boulevard du Château

Immediately north of the road bridge on the banks of the Rhône stands the massive fortress-like castle. Its origins go back to the late 14th c. and it was named after René, Duke of Anjou, called

Tarascon Castle: once a literary centre

"Good King René", who ordered the completion of the castle in the middle of the 15th c. and who provided for artists and scientists a comfortable courtly existence.

Protected on one side by the river and on the other by a deep moat, the solid castle resisted every siege and attack right up to the bombardment by Allied forces in 1944. The building comprises a court of honour, from which entrance can be obtained to a number of rooms, and the chapel; there is a fine view from the battlements.

Opening times
Wed.–Mon. guided tours
hourly from 9 a.m. to 5 p.m.

Ste-Marthe in Tarascon

Obliquely opposite the castle stands the Church of Ste-Marthe, originating in the 10th c. but now predominantly Gothic. The doorway to the south aisle is interesting, in spite of damage to the figures in the decoration. Inside the church is a panel by Pierre Parrocel, a less well-known member of the family of painters; in the crypt can be seen the Sarcophagus of St Martha whose remains were said to have been discovered in Tarascon.

Location
Boulevard du Château

Hôtel de Ville

Not far east of the castle stands the 17th c. Hôtel de Ville (Town Hall); in the Old Town there are a number of fine old buildings.

Location
Rue des Halles

175

Beaucaire   D2

Location
2 km (1 mile) west of
Tarascon

The little town of Beaucaire lies on the right bank of the Rhône opposite Tarascon and is in the Région of Languedoc-Roussillon and the Département of Gard. It was once famous in the whole of the Western World for its market (Foire de Beaucaire), which has existed since 1217 and which takes place from 21 to 28 July. Noteworthy is the beautiful Town Hall (1679–83), built by J. Hardouin-Mansart. Above the town are the ruins of a castle of the 13th–14th c. from which there is a rewarding view.

Toulon   D3

Région: Provence-Alpes-Côte d'Azur
Département: Var
Altitude: sea-level
Population: 182,000

Location

The port of Toulon is situated at almost the most southerly point of the French Riviera on a bay which forms an excellent natural harbour.

History

The settlement, called "Telo Martius" by the Romans, has only acquired military importance in recent times. The fortifications, set up towards the end of the 16th c. and strengthened by Vauban, withstood in 1707 the combined forces of the Netherlands and England under Prince Eugene. In 1793 the town was taken by the English Admiral Hood; a little later after a six-week siege it was recaptured by the Army of the Revolution, under the 23-year-old battalion commander Bonaparte (later Napoleon I).
When German troops entered the town in 1942 the French scuttled their naval fleet, in order to prevent it falling into the hands of the German forces.

Townscape

Situated on the Bay of Toulon the town is the base of the French Mediterranean fleet. The Bay of Toulon is bordered in the south by the Peninsula of St-Mandrier with Cap Cépet. It consists of the inner Petite Rade (inner roads) and the Grande Rade (great roads). The two roadsteads are separated by a causeway 1250 m (1368 yd) long with roads on either side.

Old Town (Vieille Ville)

The Vieille Ville (Old Town), which was severely damaged during the Second World War, lies by the Darse Vieille (Old Harbour) on the north-west of which stands the Préfecture Maritime (daily Cérémonie des Couleurs after sunset). The fronts of the row of houses along the Quai Stalingrad, which leads south-east to the Rond-Point Bonaparte, were rebuilt after the Second World War; the buildings are dominated by the tower of the impressive Ancien Hôtel de Ville (former Town Hall; on the entrance doorway are caryatides by Puget). From here the busy Rue d'Alger runs north and leads to Rue Hoche

Toulon and its harbour, seen from Mont Faron

at the end of which is the Place Puget with the curious Fontaine des Trois Dauphins (1782; by Castel).

To the north of the Préfecture Maritime stands the Musée Naval (also called "Musée de la Marine" (Marine Museum)); the exhibits include old models of ships, etchings and drawings and an exhibition about the development of artillery.

In the centre of the Old Town south-east of the Place Puget is the Cathedral of Ste-Marie-Majeure (11th–12th c.; rebuilt in the 17th c.) with an 18th c. belfry. Near by lies the colourful Marché (Market; vegetables, flowers) and the Musée du Vieux Toulon (local collections, sacred art); there is a library on the broad Cours Lafayette. At the east end of Rue Garibaldi, which branches off here, stands the impressive Porte d'Italie, a 16th c. bridge. Farther on, to the south of the cathedral, is the Place de la Poissonnerie, the fish market.

Leaving the Place Puget, the busy centre of the Old Town, by Rue Muraire (also called "Raimu") one comes to the fine Opera House (1862–64). North-west lies the Place de la Liberté with the Monument de la Fédération by Allard. Farther to the west, on the Boulevard Leclerc, is the Musée d'Art et d'Archéologie (Museum of Art and Archaeology; pictures from the 13th to 20th c., prehistoric and ancient finds). In the same building is the Musée d'Histoire Naturelle (Natural History Museum; geological and palaeontological collections). Adjoining is the attractive Jardin Alexander-I with magnolias, palms, cedars, etc. and to the south of this the large Palais de Justice (lawcourts).

Museums

177

Toulon

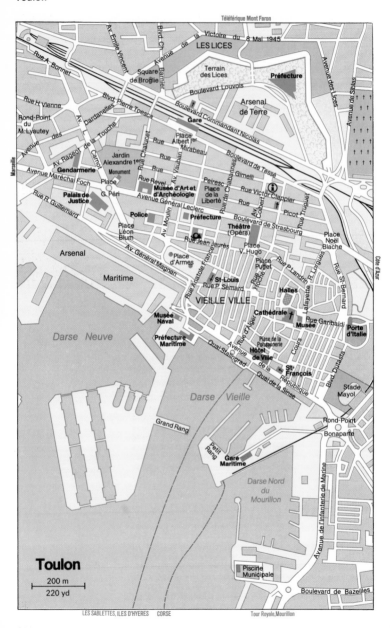

Téléférique Mont Faron

LES LICES

Avenue de la Victoire du 8 Mai 1945

Rue A. Bonnet

Av. Émile Vincent

Blvd. Ay. Ranier

Square de Broglie

Terrain des Lices

Préfecture

Avenue des Lices

Boulevard Louvois

Rue H. Vienne

Blvd. Pierre Toesca

Arsenal de Terre

Av. Dardanelles

Rond-Point du M. Lyautey

Gare

Boulevard Commandant Nicolas

Avenue des

Av. Rageot de la Touche

Place Albert 1er Mirabeau

Rue Chalucet

Boulevard de Tessé

Marseille

Carnot

Jardin Alexandre 1er Monument

Rue

Rue Vauban

Rue Gimelli

Gendarmerie

Avenue Maréchal Foch

Rue Revel

Rue de Chabannes

Peiresc Place de la Liberté

Rue Victor Clappier

Av. Colbert Picot

Av. Huguet

Palais de Justice

Place G. Péri

Avenue Général Leclerc

Rue

Rue St-Bernard

Rue R. Guillemard

Police

Préfecture

Boulevard de Strasbourg

Place Noël Blache

Av. Moulin

Théâtre (Opéra)

Place Léon Blum

Place V. Hugo

Av. Anatole France

Côte d'Azur

Arsenal

Av. Général Magnan

Place d'Armes

Place Jean Jaurès

Place Puget

Rue P. Landrin

Maritime

Rue Hoche

VIEILLE VILLE

St-Louis Rue P. Sémard

Rue Lafayette

Rue Garibaldi

Halles

Rue des Longues

Musée Naval

Cathédrale Musée

Porte d'Italie

Darse Neuve

Préfecture Maritime

Rue d'Alger

Place de la Poissonnerie

Cours Lafayette

Blvd. Dutasta

Quai Stalingrad

Hôtel de Ville

Avenue de la République

St-François

Stade Mayol

Darse Vieille

Quai de la Sinse

Grand Rang

Rond-Point Bonaparte

Petit Rang

Gare Maritime

Darse Nord du Mourillon

Avenue de l'Infanterie de Marine

Toulon

200 m
220 yd

Piscine Municipale

Boulevard de Bazeilles

LES SABLETTES, ILES D'HYERES   CORSE   Tour Royale, Mourillon

A ferry leaves Toulon for Corsica

At the western end of the Quai Stalingrad along the Darse Neuve (New Harbour) begin the workshops, docks and stores of the Arsenal Maritime behind the fine Porte de l'Arsenal (1738).

Mourillon

Beyond the Rond-Point Bonaparte one reaches Mourillon, the quarter in the south-east. From the Tour Royale, an impressive building of the time of Louis XII at the southern end of the roadstead, there is an exceptional panoramic view. To the north-east stands Fort St-Louis (1707) guarding a little harbour.

Probably the finest street is the Corniche Mistral which leads along the Grande Rade de Vignettes of Mourillon past the Jardin d'Acclimatation (botanical garden), to the charming residential district of Cap Brun (103 km (338 ft); fort, view). Below the coastal road runs the Sentier des Douaniers (Customs Officers' Path), a winding footpath along the coast leading to the Batterie Basse du Cap Brun and to the romantic bays of Méjean and Magaud.

*Corniche Mistral

The Corniche du Mont Faron (Corniche Marius Escartefigue), a panoramic road half-way up Mont Faron, borders the district of Ste-Anne (with the spacious Hôpital Maritime) and Super-Toulon. The last named has only been opened up relatively recently and is characterised by fine villas situated on the slope. There are magnificent views early in the morning and shortly before sunset.

179

**Mont Faron

Mont Faron (542 m (1779 ft)) dominates the town in the north; from Super-Toulon a cableway 1437 m (1572 yd) long goes up to the Tour Beaumont, 493 m (1618 ft). From here there is a very rewarding but very narrow, steep and winding road (mostly one-way traffic and certainly not suitable for large motor or towed caravans), which leads up to the fort on the summit of Mont Faron. In this squat building the Musée Mémorial du Débarquement en Provence has been set up, a collection and documentation of the landing of the Allied forces from 15 August 1944. There are weapons, articles of equipment and on the lower floor a diorama. From the flat roof of the fort (orientation table, telescope) there is a superb panorama of the town and the port and mountains rising all round.

On the plateau on the summit, which is charming because of its great variety of flowers, there is also a little zoological garden.

Cuers   D4

Location
22 km (14 miles) north

Cuers, situated inland, is well known as a wine-producing and cork-processing centre. On the south-eastern edge of the Barre de Cuers (696 m (2284 ft)) there are extensive areas of flower cultivation. The centre of the village is picturesque with its fine parish church (great organ of 1669), the medieval gateway and pretty little streets. Above the village stands the ruins of a former castle from which there are good views.

Ollioules   D3

Location
8 km (5 miles) west

Ollioules, on the southern slope of the gorge of the same name, is well known for flower-growing (auctions). There is a ruined castle in the village.

**Gorges d'Ollioules

Not far north of the village one reaches the Gorges d'Ollioules which is well worth a visit. It has been cut by the River Reppe and there are strange rock shapes. Above the gorge on a sheer volcanic rock lies the village of Evenos, a "village perché" which has been all but abandoned. It has the remains of a castle, the keep of which, like the old houses, is built of blocks of basalt.

La Seyne-sur-Mer   D3

Location
4 km (2 miles) west of
Toulon

La Seyne-sur-Mer is an industrial town with several parts; it has important shipyards, mussel-beds and works for the processing of olive-wood. Of interest are the 17th c. Church of Notre-Dame-du-Bon-Voyage, the former Fort de Balaguier, also 17th c., and the Musée de la Seyne (local history). To the east lies the pleasant yacht and fishing harbour with a movable bridge.

Tamaris

Tamaris (the name comes from the tamarisks that grow here) is a popular resort with a harbour for yachts; it is reached along a beautiful coastal road and round two peninsulas. To the west above the resort stands Fort Napoléon, and behind it along the Rade du Lazaret is the district of Les Sablettes which lies on a sandy spit between Cap Sicié and Cap Cépet. From here there is a particularly fine view of the roadsteads of Toulon and the sea.

Signes   D4

To the north, inland from Toulon, in a hollow on the edge of the headwaters of the Gapeau lies the old vine- and fruit-growing village of Signes. It is reached either via Ollioules (west N8 and D2) or via Solliès-Pont (east N97, D554 and D2). Here in the Place St-Jean stands a beautiful chapel which was restored in the 17th c.; inside can be seen pictures, votive tablets and penitents' garments. The square is embellished by an 18th c. fountain. In the Church of St-Pierre, which has also been restored (16th c. belfry), the beautiful wooden altar of the 14th and 17th c. is worthy of note. The Tour de l'Horloge, the medieval clock-tower, is also worth seeing.

Location
30 km (19 miles) north of Toulon

See Bandol – Surroundings.

Six-Fours-la-Plage

Uzès   C2

Région: Languedoc-Roussillon
Département: Gard
Altitude: 138 m (453 ft)
Population: 8000

Uzès is actually situated beyond the boundaries of Provence some 40 km (25 miles) west of Avignon.

Location

Uzès has a picturesque situation on a tree-clad hill above the Valley of the Alzon. With its narrow streets the town centre is surrounded by a ring of boulevards shaded by plane trees. Visitors are recommended to walk; the best facilities for parking are on the broad Esplanade on the western edge of the Old Town.

Townscape

*Place aux Herbes

A few steps east of the Esplanade lies the Place aux Herbes, the beautiful main square of the town, shaded by plane trees and embellished with a fountain. All round the square are houses with vaulted arcades. Here the colourful market takes place.

In Rue de la République farther north stands the Hôtel de Joubert with a pretty staircase and inner courtyard. From here one turns east and on the far side of the Place Dampmartin reaches the equally interesting Hôtel Dampmartin. On the north rises the great complex of buildings of the Château Ducal (Ducal Castle; entrance from the Place du Duché).

Uzès

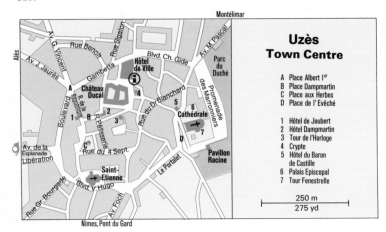

Montélimar

Uzès
Town Centre

A Place Albert Ier
B Place Dampmartin
C Place aux Herbes
D Place de l'Evêché

1 Hôtel de Joubert
2 Hôtel Dampmartin
3 Tour de l'Horloge
4 Crypte
5 Hôtel du Baron
   de Castille
6 Palais Episcopal
7 Tour Fenestrelle

250 m
275 yd

Nîmes, Pont du Gard

Château Ducal

Opening times
daily 9.30 a.m.–midday and
2.30–7 p.m.

The former castle of the Dukes of Uzès dates from the 11th to the 17th c., but was again altered in the 19th c. In the inner courtyard the Renaissance façade between the keep and the chapel tower deserves particular attention; it is divided by groups of pillars and decorated with relief medallions. There is a good panorama from the Tour Bermonde (the tower was certainly built in the 11th c. but did not receive its balustrade until 1839).

Hôtel de Ville

Opposite the castle gateway stands the Hôtel de Ville (Town Hall) which was erected in the year 1773 under Louis XVI. The façade facing the castle still shows the elegance of the time when it was built, while the north front, where the main entrance is situated, was renewed about 1900. The façades of the courtyard with their pillars are interesting; the view of the ducal castle through the wrought-iron grille is a charming one.

Crypte

Opposite the north-east corner of the castle is the entrance to the so-called "crypt", an Early Christian cult chamber hacked out of the rock. On the walls in half-relief are the figures of John the Baptist and an Orans (a figure praying with outstretched arms).

Palais Episcopal

Location
Place de l'Evêché

Opening times
daily 3–6 p.m.;
in winter Sat. and Sun.
2.30–5.30 p.m.

From the castle and the town hall one goes east past the Ancien Hôtel des Monnaies (former Mint) to the Palais Episcopal, the former Bishop's Palace. Today the lawcourts and the library are situated here and in the second storey is the Musée d'Art et de Tradition de l'Uzège (Museum of Art and History of the region of Uzès) with exhibits of art, ethnology, prehistory and natural history, as well as mementoes of the writer André Gide whose family originated from Uzès.

182

Uzès: a hilltop township

To the south by the bishop's palace stands the one-time Cathedral of St-Théodorit dating from the 17th and 19th c.; the previous building was destroyed during the Wars of Religion. The present façade was only built in the 19th c.

Cathédrale

The most interesting part of the cathedral is the round Tour Fenestrelle (Window Tower), a belfry put up in the 12th c. on a Lombardian model. Since at that time it served as a watch-tower, it escaped destruction by the Albigenses.

Tour Fenestrelle

On the far side of the square opposite the bishop's palace is the Hôtel du Baron de Castille, a classic building with an elegant pillared façade (18th c.).

Hôtel du Baron de Castille

St-Etienne in Uzès

On the southern edge of the Old Town stands the Church of St-Etienne a large Baroque building (1765–78). The tower standing near by, with a square plan, dates from the 13th c.

Location
Boulevard Victor-Hugo

Vaison-la-Romaine   C3

Région: Provence-Alpes-Côte d'Azur
Département: Vaucluse
Altitude: 200 m (656 ft)
Population: 6000

Vaison-la-Romaine

Location | Vaison-la-Romaine, at the foot of the north face of Mont Ventoux, is about 30 km (19 miles) north-east of Orange.

History | In the 4th c. BC this was the chief place of the Celtic Vocones. Later the Romans founded Vasio Vocontiorum in the fertile region of the Valley of the Ouvèze and in five peaceful centuries this developed into a flourishing community. As early as the 3rd c. AD Vaison was the seat of a bishop and in 442 and 529 ecclesiastical councils were held here; in the 11th–12th c. it was resolved to build a cathedral. However, a little later Raymond, Count of Toulouse, laid siege and conquered the town, robbed the Bishop of his property and had a castle built on the highest spot of the mountain which rises above the town. The Upper Town was surrounded by a wall and not until the 18th c. was the territory of the former Roman city settled again.

*Roman Excavations

Location north of the centre

Opening times daily 9 a.m.–6 p.m.; closed Sun. and Tues. morning

Tickets valid for all places of interest in the town

Quartier de Puymin | North of the Avenue Jules Ferry can be found the two separate sites of Roman excavations. The eastern part corresponds to the Quartier de Puymin and the western to the Quartier de la Villasse. It has always been known that a Roman settlement existed on the territory of Vaison but it was not until 1907 that the remains were systematically uncovered. The initiator and leader of this work was the priest Joseph Sautel (1880–1955).

The extensive gently sloping Quartier de Puymin is laid out like a park with oaks, cypresses, etc. In the lower part foundations of walls have been uncovered including those of the House of the Messii, the Portico of Pompey (pillared hall), the Nymphaeum, etc. The statues which have been set up on the excavation site are copies of the original ancient ones which can be seen in the museum.

In addition to a large and very well-arranged lapidarium (Roman tombstones, statues, etc.), the museum in the centre of this site includes the model of the theatre. Other specialised groups concern the Roman dwellings and Gallo-Roman pottery. A showcase containing urns for ashes is interesting, among them are some made of glass. Immediately by the entrance there is a historic map on the wall showing the Province of Gallia Narbonensis.

Just above the museum a tunnel leads to the ancient theatre, which has been comprehensively restored and now serves its original purpose once more as an open-air theatre.

Quartier de la Villasse | To the west on the far side of the square (information pavilion of the Office de Tourisme) extends the Quartier de la Villasse, the second large excavation site. It has not been so heavily restored as the one previously mentioned, and provides, as it were, a more original impression. Of interest here are the great arch of the former basilica and the carefully paved Roman street which was provided with gutters. In some places mosaic floors can be seen under a protective covering.

Notre-Dame | On the western outskirts of the Quartier de la Villasse stands the Church of Notre-Dame, the former cathedral. Its origins go back to Merovingian times, but the present building was erected between the 11th and 13th c.; its plan is smaller than

184

that of its predecessor as can be seen from the former foundations which have been uncovered round the church. Adjoining on the north of the church is the cloister dating from the 12th c. but which had to be extensively renovated in the 19th c. Of interest are the beautifully decorated capitals of the pillars of the arcades.

North-west of the excavations, in the Avenue St-Quenin, stands the chapel of the same name dating from the late 12th c. and partly restored in the 17th. Unusual from the architectural point of view is the Romanesque choir which is built on a triangular plan and includes a main apse and two subsidiary apses.

St-Quenin

Upper Town (Haute Ville)

South of the River Ouvèze the Upper Town rises up the castle hill. The river is crossed by a bridge originally built by the Romans and one passes through a medieval gate tower. In the

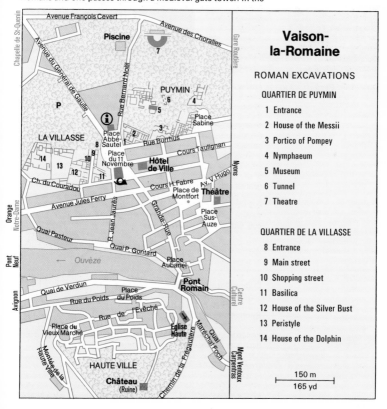

Vaison-la-Romaine

ROMAN EXCAVATIONS

QUARTIER DE PUYMIN

1 Entrance
2 House of the Messii
3 Portico of Pompey
4 Nymphaeum
5 Museum
6 Tunnel
7 Theatre

QUARTIER DE LA VILLASSE

8 Entrance
9 Main street
10 Shopping street
11 Basilica
12 House of the Silver Bust
13 Peristyle
14 House of the Dolphin

150 m
165 yd

Remains of the basilica in the Lower Town　　　*An idyllic corner of the Upper Town*

romantic narrow streets of the Upper Town which, protected by the castle, had developed from the 14th c., artists and craftsmen have settled in recent times, producing pottery, olive-wood carving, etc. At the eastern edge of the Old Town stands the church and, from the open space in front of it, there is a good view of the valley below. The cube-shaped ruin of the castle (the interior is not open to the public) stands right on the top of the Old Town and can be reached on a narrow footpath with few directions. From the rocky plateau which in the south falls vertically and is completely unprotected (caution!) there is a rewarding panorama.

Vaison-la-Romaine is the northern starting-point for the drive over Mont Ventoux (see entry).

Vence

Région: Provence-Alpes-Côte d'Azur
Département: Alpes-Maritimes
Altitude: 325 m (1067 ft)
Population: 14,000

Location

Vence lies in the east of the Côte d'Azur somewhat inland and half-way between Nice and Antibes.

Townscape

In the centre of the Old Town stands the former Cathedral of

An exhibit of the Fondation Maeght . . .   *in the open air*

St-Véran of the 10th–15th c. The interior has fine choir-stalls and a Roman sarcophagus which serves as an altar. The choir and the tower chapel are decorated with Carolingan interlace work. East of the church in the Place Godeau stands an ancient column of the former Vintium; also of interest are the battlemented belfry and the charming Renaissance gate. In the west on the edge of the Old Town lies the attractive Place du Peyra with the fountain of the same name. Also to the west outside the town centre in Avenue Henri Isnard stands the 15th c. Chapelle des Pénitents-Blancs.

On the northern outskirts on the right of road D2210 stands the inconspicuous Chapelle du Rosaire (Rosary Chapel; open only on Tues. and Thurs. 10–11.30 a.m. and 2.30–5.30 p.m.) which belongs to a Dominican nunnery. It can be recognised by the severely linear representation of Mary, Jesus and St Dominic over the doorway. The interior was designed by Henri Matisse with bold black outlines on white tiles on Biblical themes. These include the Birth of Christ, St Dominic and the Passion of Christ (Way of the Cross).

`Chapelle du Rosaire

St-Paul-de-Vence   D5

The little town of St-Paul-de-Vence which has managed to retain its medieval character is attractively situated on a hill. The well-preserved circle of rampart-walls, dating from the 16th c., is provided with sturdy reinforcing supports on the steep slopes; there is a stately defence tower. In the early 13th c.

Location
3 km (1 mile) south

church can be seen a fine treasury with silver-work, reliquaries and a ciborium of 1439. Near by is a watch-tower. In the Place de la Fontaine with a beautiful well-known fountain, is the Musée Provençal.

·· Fondation Maeght

Not far north-west of St-Paul-de-Vence lies the Fondation Maeght (daily 10 a.m.–12.30 p.m. and 3–7 p.m.), named after the couple who sponsored it. It is an uncommonly interesting combination of open-air and art museum, together with a studio colony. As well as mosaics by Braque, Chagall and Tal-Coat, the ceramic sculptures of Miró in the so-called labyrinth are worthy of particular note and so are the bronze figures of Giacometti. The chapel was furnished by Braque and Ubac. The museum includes works by Arp, Bonnard, Chagall, Giacometti, Kandinsky and Miró. The exhibitions are constantly being made topical. Concerts, symposiums, films and comprehensive archives complete the whole.

Tourette-sur-Loup   D5

Location
5 km (3 miles) west of Vence

The charming former defence village of Tourette-sur-Loup with its medieval towers lies on a rocky plateau above the Valley of the Loup, surrounded by olive groves, pine woods and fields of violets. In the 14th c. church is a notable ancient altar and an altar-picture of the school of Bréa. Also of interest is the Musée d'Artisanat Local (Museum of Local Industry).

Verdon (Grand Canyon du Verdon)   D4

Région: Provence-Alpes-Côte d'Azur
Département: Alpes-de-Haute-Provence

Location

The Verdon, 175 km (109 miles) in length, is the most important tributary of the Durance. Between Castellane and the man-made Lac de Ste-Croix it flows through the impressive wild gorges of the Grand Canyon du Verdon.

Landscape

For a length of 21 km (13 miles) the Verdon has cut a mighty ravine in fossil-filled chalk. The depth reaches 700 m (2297 ft), the water of the river falling 153 m (502 ft) over this stretch.

Timetable

The round trip described below is about 120 km (75 miles) long. To have sufficient time to appreciate to the full the numerous scenic beauties, one should allow at least six hours, and if possible a whole day.

·· Drive through the Grand Canyon du Verdon

The most convenient starting-point for a circular tour of the Grand Canyon du Verdon is the little town of Castellane on the Route Napoléon (see these entries).
Take road D952 in a south-westerly direction downstream, through the Defile of Porte St-Jean and Clue du Chastel. At the fork (in about 12 km (7 miles)) bear left on to the D955, cross

Point Sublime: the classic view of the Verdon Gorge ▶

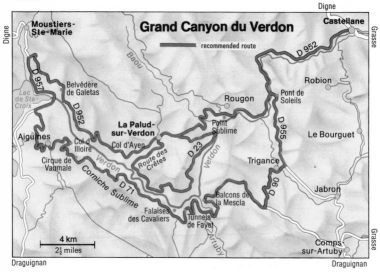

Digne

Grand Canyon du Verdon

Moustiers-Ste-Marie

Castellane

Digne

Grasse

—— recommended route

D 952

Baou

Belvédère de Galetas

Robion

D 952

Pont de Soleils

Lac de Ste-Croix

Rougon

D 957

Point Sublime

Le Bourguet

La Palud-sur-Verdon

D 955

Aiguines

Col d'Ayen

Col d'Illoire

D 23

Verdon

Route des Crêtes

Verdon

Trigance

Cirque de Vaumale

D 71

Corniche Sublime

Jabron

D 90

Falaises des Cavaliers

Balcons de la Mescla

Tunnels de Fayet

4 km

2½ miles

Artuby

Comps-sur-Artuby

Grasse

Draguignan

Draguignan

the river (Pont de Soleils; signposted "Rive Gauche") and continue south over attractive uplands. Some 6 km (4 miles) beyond the fork, near the picturesquely situated village of Trigance with its dominating castle on your right, take road D90 until you reach the D71 which you follow north-west.

Corniche Sublime,
Balcons de la Mescla

The Balcons de la Mescla (mescla=mixing, referring to the nearby confluence of the Artuby with the Verdon) provide the first high spot of the drive. Here there is a fine view into the gorge 250 m (821 ft) below. A little farther on cross a boldly curved bridge over the Artuby, which joins the Verdon at this point.

The road continues its winding course, with breath-taking views high above the Verdon and through the Tunnels de Fayet (views between the tunnels).

Falaises des Cavaliers

There is a viewing platform near the restaurant at the Falaises des Cavaliers; then the road continues, with a stretch up to 400 m (1313 ft) above the river as it rushes along the ravine.

Lac de Ste-Croix

After driving round the impressive cwm of Vaumale and crossing the 964 m (3164 ft) high Col d'Illoire, the road winds its way down to the deep turquoise-green Lac de Ste-Croix (about 2500 ha (6178 acres)), a lake formed by the damming of the Verdon. On the shores of the lake a leisure complex is being developed (sailing, wind surfing, camping, etc.). At the point where the Verdon leaves the gorge and enters the reservoir, cross the river by the bridge (fine view of the gorge on the right).

Some 7 km (4 miles) beyond the junction of the D19 and D957, bear right into the D952 and follow its winding course uphill. This road borders the northern (right) bank of the Verdon. Passing the Bélvédère (viewpoint) de Galetas and crossing the

Col d'Ayen (1032 m (3387 ft)), you reach La Palud-sur-Verdon. Here there are two possibilities; either to continue on the D952, or – considerably more worth while – to take the D23 on the right and drive directly along the gorge.

The 23 km (14 miles) long Route des Crêtes draws close to the edge of the Grand Canyon, and on its course passes several viewpoints – the Bélvédère l'Imbut, the Bélvédère des Glacières, the Bélvédère du Tilleul, the particularly impressive Bélvédère de l'Escalès and finally the Bélvédère de Trescaire – before again joining the D952.

Route des Crêtes

The D952 heads for probably the finest viewpoint of the tour, the Point Sublime. From the car park it is about ten minutes' walk to the viewing platform, from which the visitor can enjoy the classic view of the Gorge of the Verdon. The platform stands 180 m (591 ft) above the confluence of the Baou with the Verdon; there is a magnificent view of the resurgence of the river near the Couloir Samson.

Point Sublime

Farther on, below the romantic ruins of a castle, you traverse the Defile of the Clue Carejuan, and a good 5 km (3 miles) beyond the Point Sublime you reach the road junction near Pont de Soleils, and so back to Castellane.

** Sentier Martel (Martel Footpath)

Loitering in the immediate vicinity of the river is dangerous, since, depending on the operation of the dam and the sluices, the water-level can rise considerably in a very short time and a violent current can result. When walking through the gorge one should not tarry in places where there is no escape path up the cliff.

Warning

The Sentier Martel (Martel Footpath) is named after the great French speleologist Edouard Martel (1859–1938) who was the first in the present century to explore the entire length of the Gorge of the Verdon. The path runs along the bottom of the defile and can be reached from the road at Point Sublime or at the Chalet de la Maline on the Route des Crêtes. A walk along the whole length of this section is not particularly easy and will require from six hours to a whole day. Stout footwear, provisions, drinking-water and suitable clothing, including waterproofs, are essential.

Practical Information

Warning

ATTENTION AU FEU

In urban areas and centres of tourism there has been a considerable increase in the theft of property. It is sensible to carry money, cheques, etc. on one's person and not to leave valuable articles on view in vehicles. Tourists with motor and towed caravans are advised not to spend the night in isolated locations away from camping sites.

Everywhere there is acute danger of forest fires during long periods without rain. It is, therefore, strictly forbidden to light a fire within 200 m (220 yd) inside a security zone, to smoke in forests, to discard the glowing remains of cigarettes, cigars or the tobacco from pipes or any easily ignitable objects. Camping is only permitted in places expressly provided for the purpose.

Access

By car

From the Channel ports to the Riviera is a distance of some 700 miles and even if the motorway (Autoroute du soleil) is used, at least two days, and preferably three, will be required for the journey. The motorway is subject to tolls which are certainly not low. The alternative "Routes nationales" are good but may be crowded during the high season.

By air

The most important airports for the area covered in this guidebook are Marseille-Marignane and Nice, but there are good services to Nîmes and Montpellier which are also served by internal airlines, as are Toulon/Hyères and St-Raphaël–Fréjus.

By rail

The principal route from the north of France to the Riviera is via Lyon and Marseilles to Toulon, Cannes and Nice. Visitors wishing to avoid the long car journey from Paris or the Channel ports can use one of the motorail services to Avignon, Fréjus–St-Raphaël, Toulon and Nice.
Details of services and fares can be obtained from:
French Railways (SNCF)
179 Piccadilly, London W1V 0BA (tel. (01) 493 4451/2)
610 Fifth Avenue, New York, N.Y. 10020 (tel. (212) 582 2110)
1500 Stanley Street, Montreal H3A 1R3, P.Q. (tel. (514) 288 8255/6)

Accommodation

See Hotels, Youth Hostels

Airlines

International routes are flown by Air France, the national airline; inland traffic is handled by Air Inter. Both airlines are represented at all French airports; abroad information for both companies is provided by the offices of Air France.

158 New Bond Street, London W1Y 0AY (tel. (01) 499 9511)   Air France
666 Fifth Avenue, New York, N.Y. 10019
1 Place Ville-Marie, Suite 3321, Montreal H3B 3N4, P.Q.

Bathing

See Water Sports

Bicycle Hire

French Railways (SNCF) have bicycles for hire at 250 stations,   Train + Bicycle
including the following places featured in this guide:
Aix-en-Provence, Antibes, Arles, Avignon, Beaulieu-sur-Mer, La Ciotat, Draguignan, Fréjus, Gap, Grasse, Hyères, Le Lavandou, Marseilles, Menton, Monte-Carlo (Monaco), Montélimar, Montpellier, Nice, Nîmes, Orange.

Boating

See Marinas

Bus Tours

France has a well-developed bus network, complemented by many privately run services. Information can be obtained at any office de tourisme (see Information).

Camping

Camping plays a more prominent role in France than in other European countries. Almost every place of touristic interest has one or often several camp sites (terrains de camping). Sites are classified from one to four stars, according to the facilities provided. During the height of the season sites along the coast and on the major holiday routes are generally full (complet), but as a rule available space can be found inland. The French themselves are very fond of "camping à la ferme" (camping on a farm), where an informal holiday can be spent, usually for an extended period. Visitors from abroad who have a good knowledge of French may well find a farm holiday an enjoyable experience.
As the region has a large number of camp sites, a detailed list here would be superfluous.

In high summer in Provence drinking-water can be in short   Note
supply. Therefore economy in the use of water is necessary, and attention is drawn to this in many places by notices.

193

Car Hire

Avis

4 Avenue des Belges
F-13100 Aix-en-Provence
tel. (42) 27 58 56

32 Boulevard Albert-I
F-06600 Antibes
tel. (93) 34 65 15

12 bis Avenue Victor Hugo
F-13200 Arles
tel. (90) 96 82 42

34 Boulevard St-Roch
F-84000 Avignon
tel. (90) 82 26 33

1 Rue Georges Clemenceau
F-06310 Beaulieu-sur-Mer
tel. (93) 01 00 13

69 Boulevard de la Croisette
F-06400 Cannes
tel. (93) 38 15 86

c/o Garage Volkswagen
F-84200 Carpentras
tel. (90) 63 28 64

Avenue P.-Brossollette
F-83300 Draguignan
tel. (94) 68 27 39

9 Avenue du Commandant Dumont
F-05000 Gap
tel. (92) 51 26 09

Pont de la Villette
F-83400 Hyères
tel. (94) 40 66 65 44

38 Boulevard Charles Nédelec
F-13001 Marseille
tel. (91) 39 55 55
Aéroport Marseille-Marignane
F-13700 Marignane
tel. (91) 89 02 26

11 Boulevard Lucien Degut
F-13500 Martigues
tel. (42) 07 07 96

9 Rue Victor Hugo
F-06500 Menton
tel. (93) 35 50 98

9 Avenue d'Ostende
Monte-Carlo/Principality of Monaco
tel. (93) 30 17 53

84 Boulevard St-James
F-26200 Montélimar
tel. (75) 51 26 20

12 bis Rue Jules Ferry
F-24000 Montpellier
tel. (67) 64 61 84
Aéroport de Montpellier
tel. (67) 65 57 56

2 Rue des Phocéens
F-06000 Nice
tel. (93) 80 63 52
Aéroport Nice–Côte d'Azur
F-06200 Nice
tel. (93) 83 12 73

1 Rue de la République
F-30000 Nîmes
tel. (66) 2100 29

Place de la Gare
F-83700 St-Raphaël
tel. (94) 95 60 42

13 Boulevard Louis Bland
F-83990 St-Tropez
tel. (94) 97 03 10

175 Boulevard du Maréchal Joffre
F-83000 Toulon
tel. (94) 41 30 01
Aéroport de Toulon
tel. (94) 75 03 61

55 Boulevard de la République   EuropCar
F-13100 Aix-en-Provence
tel. (42) 27 41 27

26 Boulevard Foch
F-06600 Antibes
tel. (93) 34 79 79

2 bis Boulevard Victor Hugo
F-13200 Arles
tel. (90) 93 23 24

27–29 Avenue St-Ruf
F-84000 Avignon
tel. (90) 82 49 85

45 Rue du Docteur Margon
F-83150 Bandol
tel. (94) 29 40 40

c/o Garage Total
Port de Beaulieu
F-06310 Beaulieu-sur-Mer
tel. (93) 01 13 78

2 Avenue de Nice
F-06800 Cagnes-sur-Mer
tel. (93) 20 99 66

3 Rue du Commandant Vidal
F-06400 Cannes
tel. (93) 39 75 20

32 Boulevard Albin Durand
F-84200 Carpentras
tel. (90) 63 17 85

35 Avenue Carnot
F-83200 Draguignan
tel. (94) 68 16 94

308 Avenue de Verdun
F-83600 Fréjus
tel. (94) 51 53 88

6 bis Avenue du Commandant Dumont
F-05000 Gap
tel. (92) 51 25 76

4 Boulevard Victor Hugo
F-06130 Grasse
tel. (93) 36 37 36

Aéroport du Palyvestre
F-83400 Hyères
tel. (94) 38 98 07

232 Avenue de l'Europe
F-34280 La Grande-Motte
tel. (67) 58 16 17

Rotonde du Port
F-83980 Le Lavandou
tel. (94) 64 83 41

93 Avenue du Prado
F-13008 Marseille
tel. (91) 79 05 29
Aéroport Marseille-Marignane
F-13728 Marignane
tel. (42) 89 09 72

Résidence La Venise
F-13100 Martigues
tel. (42) 07 36 80

9 Avenue Thiers
F-06500 Menton
tel. (93) 28 21 80

47 Avenue de la Grande-Bretagne
Monte Carlo/Principality of Monaco
tel. (93) 50 74 95

3 Place Max Dormoy
F-26200 Montélimar
tel. (75) 01 52 31

6 Rue Jules Ferry
F-34000 Montpellier
tel. (67) 58 16 17
Aéroport de Fréjorgues
tel. (67) 64 77 33

89 Rue de France
F-06200 Nice
tel. (93) 87 08 53
Aéroport Nice–Côte d'Azur
tel. (93) 72 36 44

17 Rue de la République
F-30000 Nîmes
tel. (66) 21 31 35
Aéroport de Garons
tel. (66) 70 06 88

68 Cours Aristide Briand
F-84100 Orange
tel. (90) 51 67 53

Place de la Gare
F-83700 St-Raphaël
tel. (94) 95 56 87

Place de la Poste
F-83990 St-Tropez
tel. (94) 97 15 41

203 Boulevard Georges Clemenceau
F-13300 Salon-de-Provence
tel. (90) 56 46 41

1 Boulevard Gambetta
F-13150 Tarascon
tel. (90) 91 10 01

Rond-Point Bir-Hakeim
F-83000 Toulon
tel. (94) 41 09 07
Aéroport du Palyvestre
F-83400 Toulon-Palyvestre
tel. (94) 38 98 07

Quai de Verdun
F-84110 Vaison-la-Romaine
tel. (90) 36 18 71

43 Avenue Victor Hugo   Hertz
F-43400 Aix-en-Provence
tel. (42) 27 91 32

6 Route de Lyon
F-84000 Avignon
tel. (90) 86 61 69

6 Avenue du 11 Novembre
F-83150 Bandol
tel. (94) 29 40 24

35 Boulevard du Maréchal Juin
F-06800 Cagnes-sur-Mer
tel. (93) 20 33 57

147 Rue d'Antibes
F-06400 Cannes
tel. (93) 99 04 20

1 Avenue des Alpes
F-05000 Gap
tel. (92) 52 04 22

Le Palyvestre A/P
F-83400 Hyères
tel. (94) 58 06 44

7 Avenue des Commandos d'Afrique
F-83980 Le Lavandou
tel. (94) 71 19 68

16 Boulevard Charles Nédelec
F-13001 Marseille
tel. (91) 90 04 46
Aéroport Marseille-Marignane
F-13700 Marignane
tel. (91) 42 89 90 10

57 Rue Grimaldi
Monte-Carlo/Principality of Monaco
tel. (93) 50 79 60

1 Rue André Ducatez
F-26200 Montélimar
tel. (75) 01 60 61

18 Rue Jules Ferry
F-34000 Montpellier
tel. (67) 58 65 18

12 Avenue de Suède
F-06000 Nice
tel. (93) 81 51 21
Aéroport Nice–Côte d'Azur
tel. (93) 72 36 72

39 Boulevard Gambetta
F-30000 Nîmes
tel. (66) 67 26 70

11/13 Boulevard Edouard
F-84100 Orange
tel. (90) 34 00 34

Place de la Gare
F-83700 St-Raphaël
tel. (94) 95 48 68

Route de la Nouvelle
F-83990 St-Tropez
tel. (94) 97 22 01

18 Avenue François Cuzin
F-83000 Toulon
tel. (94) 41 60 53

1 Rue Lapierre   InterRent
F-13100 Aix-en-Provence
tel. (42) 27 85 44

7 Avenue Champfleury
F-84000 Avignon
tel. (90) 86 06 61

Impasse Florian
F-06400 Cannes
tel. (93) 39 36 95

17 Rue de Cassis
F-13008 Marseille
tel. (91) 79 37 17
Aéroport Marseille-Marignane
F-13700 Marignane
tel. (42) 89 50 00

Route de Fos
F-13500 Martigues
tel. (42) 06 33 25

Gare SNCF (Railway station)
F-06000 Nice
tel. (93) 88 00 18
Aéroport Nice–Côte d'Azur
tel. (93) 72 36 54

2 Rue des 4 Fages
F-30000 Nîmes
tel. (66) 29 47 75

Champ de Mars
F-83100 Toulon
tel. (94) 41 77 21

Consulates

See Diplomatic and Consular Offices

Currency

The unit of currency is the French franc (F) which is made   Currency
up of 100 centimes. There are banknotes for 10, 20, 50, 100
and 500 francs, and coins in denominations of 5, 10 and
20 centimes and $\frac{1}{2}$, 1, 2, 5 and 10 francs.

Practical Information

Exchange rate

The rate of exchange fluctuates; up-to-date rates can be found in most daily papers and at banks and exchange bureaus (bureaux de change).

Currency regulations

There are no restrictions on the import of French or foreign currency. The export of foreign currency in cash is permitted up to a value of 5000 francs, or to any higher amount which has been declared on entry into France. Up to 5000 French francs may be exported.

Visitors are recommended to take travellers' cheques or Eurocheques. Many hotels and shops accept credit cards (Eurocard, American Express, Visa, Diners Club, etc.).

Cashing cheques

Travellers' cheques, etc. can be cashed at exchange offices and banks (with the exception of savings-banks). It should be noted that banks are closed at week-ends, on public holidays and often on Mondays.

Customs Regulations

Visitors to France are allowed the usual duty-free allowances of alcohol and tobacco, etc. For goods bought in ordinary shops in Great Britain or another EEC country (i.e. duty and tax paid), the allowances are 300 cigarettes or 150 cigarillos or 75 cigars or 400 g of tobacco; 1½ litres of alcoholic drinks over 38.8 proof or 3 litres of alcoholic drinks not over 38.8 proof or 3 litres of fortified or sparkling wine, plus 4 litres of still table wine; 75 g of perfume and 375 cc of toilet-water. For goods bought in a duty-free shop or on a ship or on an aircraft, the allowances are two-thirds of these amounts (250 g of tobacco); the allowance of tobacco goods is doubled for visitors from outside Europe. The duty-free allowances on return to Great Britain are the same as those for British visitors to France.

Diplomatic and Consular Offices

United Kingdom

Embassy
35 Rue de Faubourg St-Honoré
F-75008 Paris; tel. (1) 2 66 91 42
Consular section: tel. 2 60 33 06

Consulate-General
24 Avenue du Prado
F-13006 Marseille
tel. (91) 53 43 32
There is also a consulate at Nice

United States of America

Embassy
2 Avenue Gabriel
F-75008 Paris
tel. (1) 2 96 12 02 and 2 61 80 75

Consulate-General
9 Rue Armeny
F-13006 Marseille
tel. (91) 54 92 00
There is also a consulate at Nice

Canada

Embassy
35 Avenue Montaigne
F-75008 Paris
tel. (1) 2 25 99 55
Consular section
4 Rue Ventadour
F-75001 Paris
tel. (1) 0 73 15 83

Consulate-General
24 Avenue du Prado
F-13006 Marseille
tel. (91) 37 19 37 and 37 19 40

Emergencies

There are emergency telephones on all motorways and on some national roads.
In the larger towns the police may be contacted by dialling 19; in country districts the gendarmerie should be contacted.
In the case of an accident without personal injury, it is sufficient to contact a notary (huissier) for an assessment of the damage.

AA Continental Emergency Centre

The AA (in association with G. A. Gregson & Sons) operates an emergency centre at Boulogne. This is open day and night from 1 April until 30 September, and during other months from 9 a.m. until 6 p.m. The address is:
F-62201 Boulogne-sur-Mer
Tour Damremont (18ième)
Boulevard Chanzy
tel. (21) 30 22 22

Events

January

Monte-Carlo: International Motor Rally

February

In many places (especially in Nice): Carnival
Menton: "Golden Fruit" Parade
Monte-Carlo: Television Festival
St-Raphaël: Mimosa Festival

March

Cagnes: Flower Show
Hyères: Flower Parade; horse-racing
Monte-Carlo: International tennis tournament; Art Festival
Toulon: Spring Festival

March–April

International Cat Show

April

Antibes: Antique Fair; "Old Timer" Rally
Le Lavandou: Flower Parade
Marseilles: International Boating Week
Roquebrune-Cap-Martin: Good Friday Procession
St-Tropez: Water sports
Toulon: Flower Parade

Practical Information

April–May	Cannes: International Film Festival
May	Antibes: Festival of young solo musicians; International Bridge Tournament Cavaillon: Grand Parade Grasse: Rose Festival Nice: May Fair Stes-Maries-de-la-Mer: Gipsies' pilgrimage (24–25 May) St-Tropez: Second-hand Fair Sisteron: Patronal Festival Toulon: Cartoon Film Festival; Veteran Car Rally
May–June	Monaco: Grand Prix (motor-racing)
June	Antibes: Flower Festival; International Motor Rally Cavalaire-sur-Mer: St Peter's Festival La Ciotat: Midsummer's Eve Bonfire Le Lavandou: Midsummer's Eve Bonfire; Venetian Festival Menton: Festival Parade Nice: Fishermen's Festival; St Peter's Fair Nîmes: Bullfights Sanary-sur-Mer: Fishermen's Festival Stes-Maries-de-la-Mer: Votive Festival Tarascon: Festival of the Tarasque (heraldic animal of the town) Toulon: Festival of the Sea
July	Everywhere: Events for the National Holiday (14 July) Antibes: "Golden Rose" Song Festival; Jazz Festival Arles: Dance and Folklore Festival Cannes: International Folklore Festival Hyères: Festival of St Mary Magdalene, Gardeners' Festival Martigues: Folk Festival with Fishermen's Festival Menton: Torchlight Procession Nîmes: Jazz Festival St-Tropez: Fishermen's Festival Toulon: Music Festival; St Peter's Festival
July–August	Aix-en-Provence: International Music Festival Avignon: Festival (drama, music) Cagnes-sur-Mer: Horse-racing Cannes: Theatre and Music Festival Nice: Flower Festival; International Summer Academy Orange: Performances in Roman Theatre St-Rémy: Music Festival Sénanque: Medieval music
August	Antibes: Concerts in the Château Bandol: Fishermen's Festival Beaulieu-sur-Mer: Torchlight Procession Cagnes-sur-Mer: Antiques Fair Digne: Lavender Festival Fréjus: Feria; Wine Festival; bullfights Gap: Summer Festival; Flower Parade Grasse: Jasmine Festival Menton: Procession of Lanterns Monaco: Firework Festival Roquebrune-Cap-Martin: Votive Procession St-Jean-Cap-Ferrat: Venetian Festival St-Raphaël: Sea Procession St-Rémy-de-Provence: Provençal Costume Festival

Digne: Lavender Market	August–September
Cannes: International Amateur Film Festival Le Lavandou: Arts and Craft Fair Nîmes: Wine Festival	September
Le Ciotat: Michaelmas Fair; Fishermen's Festival Nîmes: Vintage Festival; bullfights	September–October
Antibes: International Motor Rally Montpellier: Wine Festival	October
Cannes: International Amateur Golf Championship	October–November
Marseilles: Nativity Market Monaco: Monegasque National Festival Toulon: Nativity Market	November
Les Baux: Christmas Midnight Mass	December

Food and Drink

French cuisine is world famous, both for its quality and for its variety. Great importance is paid to a varied menu. Undue haste in serving and eating is unknown, and at least one hour should be allowed for a meal. Even modest, unpretentious country inns often have a remarkable culinary standard in which regional dishes play an important role.

French Cuisine

At first glance prices may appear to be quite high, but when one considers the quality and variety of the fare one will quickly revise this judgement.

When the price of a menu states "service compris", no additional tip is called for, unless an unsolicited additional service is to be rewarded. When the menu states "service non-compris" or "service en sus", a service charge of 10–15 per cent will be added to the bill. In cafés or bars it is customary to leave a few coins (pourboire) from the change brought by the waiter.

Places providing food and/or drink are called restaurants, rôtisseries, bistros (usually simple hostelries, but can also be places offering high-class service), brasseries (originally the retail bars of breweries, but now more generally restaurants). Snacks (sandwiches, etc.) are also served in cafés, tea-shops and bars. In larger towns there are reasonable self-service restaurants ("self"), and at railway stations and airports quick-service restaurants.

Eating places

White bread, cut from long crusty baguettes, is always served with meals.

The various meals are as follows: petit déjeuner – a simple breakfast of coffee, bread, butter and jam and/or the popular croissants; déjeuner (lunch, from about midday to 2.30 p.m.) – in most restaurants this consists of a fixed menu, with a starter, a main course and dessert; the lunch can also be chosen à la carte by the customer; dîner (or souper, served between 7 and

Meals

9 p.m.) – similar to lunch, except that soup sometimes replaces the starter (hors d'œuvre) as the first course.

Provençal Cuisine

Provençal cuisine makes use of the wide range of local produce and seafood and is particularly varied and appetising. Among the most common ingredients are olive oil, tomatoes, garlic, and herbs such as rosemary, thyme, sage, basil, etc., called "herbes de Provence".

Among soups, fish soup occupies a special place. One of the best known is bouillabaisse, prepared from various sea-fishes, often mussels and crustaceans, olive oil, garlic and various flavourings. This is served with slices of white bread and is sometimes fortified with a dash of brandy. Similar, and often preferred by connoisseurs, is bourride, which as well as fish contains green beans, carrots and potatoes, and is enriched with "aïoli" (a mayonnaise prepared from garlic and olive oil). Aigo-saou is a soup made of white fish and rouille sauce of garlic, hot peppers and saffron.

Other soups which should be mentioned are the "soupe au pistou", prepared from beans, potatoes and a seasoning mixture of garlic, olive oil, bacon and basil.

Meat is generally enriched with a sauce, for instance braised beef or poultry prepared with tomatoes.

Vegetables and salads (légumes et salades) also occur in great variety. Salade Niçoise consists of radishes, peppers, beans, olives, anchovies and tuna fish. Tomates à la Provençal are tomatoes stuffed with olive oil, a lot of garlic and parsley, and cooked in the oven or under the grill; aubergines and courgettes are similarly braised. Ratatouille consists of onions, courgettes, aubergines, tomatoes, peppers, garlic and herbs, stewed in olive oil. Also popular are artichokes, fennel and beet, sometimes grilled or fried.

Fish and crustaceans (poissons et crustacés): in addition to the soups already mentioned, popular fish dishes are the "brandade", a mousse of salt cod, olive oil, cream, garlic and lemon, as well as grilled barbel, sole, bream and other sea-fish. The visitor should also try cuttlefish or squid (calmar, seiche), which are prepared in various ways, mussels (moules, coquillages), oysters (huîtres), crayfish (langoustes), shrimps (crevettes) or crabs (tourteaux).

Pasta (pâtes): As well as the different varieties of pizza and "pan bagnat" (a kind of bread filled with olives, tomatoes and anchovies and baked in oil), there is pissaladière, a popular spicy flan of onions, olives and sardine fillets. In Nice in particular Italian pasta, such as ravioli, cannelloni and lasagne, is frequently served.

The numerous different kinds of cheese (fromage) are for the most part made from sheep's or goat's milk. They bear such names as Annot, Banon (prepared from sheep's milk in winter and from goat's milk in spring), Brousse, Claqueret (a soft cheese served with diced onions), Poivre d'Ane (with Provençal herbs), Sospel, etc.

Desserts: There is a great variety of fruit. Cakes, pastries and sweetmeats are equally available in many kinds, for example the "torta bléa" (a cake with raisins and pine seeds), the "beignets de fleurs d'acacia" (pancakes with acacia blossoms), "calissons" (biscuits made of almond paste with melon and honey), as well as nougat (especially around Montélimar) and candied fruits.

Drinks (boisssons): The national drink of France is wine (see entry). There is also good beer, mostly from breweries in Alsace, and various kinds of mineral water (eaux minérales). In the area of Nice a popular grape brandy called "branda" is produced. Lérinade is a liqueur formerly prepared by monks. The aniseed-flavoured "pastis" is generally diluted with iced water.

Drinks

Guided Tours

Most secular historic buildings and certain parts of churches (crypt, treasury) can only be visited with a guide. As the majority of tourists are French, commentary in English is the exception. However, explanatory texts in English are sometimes available. The guide expects a tip at the end of the visit.

Coin-operated tape recorders (guides parlants) are frequently encountered at places of interest. These provide a commentary in French and sometimes in other languages as well.

Tape-recorded commentary

Hotels

The hotels in France are generally good and within their categories will satisfy every requirement. Apart from in the larger towns rooms are often furnished with the "grand lit", the French double bed, and the charge for occupancy of such rooms by two people is only slightly more than for single occupancy. Most recommended hotels are recognised by the Commissariat Général au Tourisme as Hôtels de Tourisme and are classified by an appropriate sign. Further information is contained in the official hotel guide, republished annually, and in regional accommodation lists which are available free of charge from Offices de Tourisme and Syndicats d'Initiative (see Information).
A considerable number of hotels of various categories, especially in areas in which tourism is encouraged, have been modernised with help from the Fédération Nationale des Logis de France and are associated in the hotel group "Logis de France"; they offer up-to-date amenities at reasonable cost. Even more reasonable terms are offered by the "Auberges Rurales" which are characterised by a family atmosphere and wholesome food. Both groups are featured in a booklet which appears annually.
Many hotels, especially on the roadside outside built-up areas, are designated as "Relais" (the word actually means a posting house where horses were changed). They are mostly good independently run places and include the "Relais de Campagne et Château-Hotels" and "Relais du Silence".
The "Relais Routiers" are principally used by long-distance drivers and are, therefore, situated on main roads. They are generally more simple but nevertheless good.

French hotels are divided into official categories which are designated by one star (the lowest) up to four stars (the highest), with the addition of the suffix "L" for the luxury class.

Hotel Categories

Practical Information

Aigues-Mortes	***Saint-Louis, 10 Rue Amiral Courbet, 23 r. ***Hostellerie du Rempart, 20 r. **Bourse, Place Anatole-France, 15 r. **Les Quatre Vents, Route de Nîmes, 15 r. **Victoria, Place Anatole-France, 15 r. *Provence, Avenue de la Gare, 28 r. *Tour de Constance, Boulevard Diderot, 17 r.
Aix-en-Provence	****Roi René, 14 Boulevard du Roi René, 65 r. ****Pigonnet, Avenue du Pigonnet, 50 r. ****Cézanne, 40 Avenue Victor-Hugo, 44 r. ****Mas d'Entremont, Montée d'Avignon, 14 r. ***Novotel Aix Beaumanoir, Autoroute A8, 97 r. ***Novotel Aix Sud, Arc de Meyran, 80 r. ***Thermes Sextius, 55 Cours Sextius, 65 r. ***Le Manoir, 8 Rue d'Entrecasteaux, 43 r. ***Résidence Rotonde, 15 Avenue des Belges, 42 r. ***Grand Hôtel Nègre Coste, 33 Cours Mirabeau, 37 r. ***Super Aix, Quartier Celony, on the N7, 36 r. ***Ibis, Chemin des Infirmeries, 83 r. **Saint-Christophe, 2 Avenue Victor-Hugo, 54 r. **Gril Campanile, Jas de Bouffan, 50 r. **Globe, 74 Cours Sextius, 40 r. **Concorde, 68 Boulevard du Roi René, 39 r. **Climat de France, Rue Ampère, 38 r. **Moulin, 1 Avenue Robert-Schumann, 37 r. **Europe, 3 Rue de la Masse, 30 r. **Le Prieuré, Route des Alpes, 30 r. *Casino, 38 Rue Leydet, 26 r. *Paul, 10 Avenue Pasteur, 24 r. *Croix de Malte, 2 Rue Van-Loo, 23 r.

Antibes	L****Baie Dorée – La Maison du Gouverneur,
	  Boulevard de la Garoupe, 12 r.
	***Tananarive, Route de Nice, 50 r.
	***Royal, Boulevard Maréchal-Leclerc, 43 r.
	***Josse, 8 Boulevard James Wyllie, 30 r.
	***Motel Mercator, Chemin des Groules, 18 r.
	***First Hotel, 21 Avenue des Chênes, 16 r.
	***Mas Djouliba, 29 Avenue de Provence, 13 r.
	**Bleu Marine, Les Quatre Chemins, 18 r.
	**Postillon, 8 Rue Championnet, 14 r.
	**El Brazero, Chemin des Ames-du-Purgatoire, 12 r.
	**Belle Epoque, 10 Avenue du 24-Août, 10 r.
	**Caméo, Place Nationale, 10 r.
	*Toulouse, 4 Rue E.-Macé, 30 r.
	*Terminus et Suisse, 54 Avenue Soleau, 26 r.
	*Modern Hôtel, 1 Rue Fourmilliert, 24 r.
	*Méditerranée, Avenue Reille, 20 r.
	*Nouvel Hôtel, Avenue du 24-Août, 18 r.
	
	In Cap d'Antibes:
	L****Du Cap – Eden Roc, Boulevard Kennedy, 100 r.
	***Du Levant, Chemin de la Plage la Garoupe, 26 r.
	***Garoupe et Réserve du Cap, Boulevard Francis Meilland,
	  26 r.
	***Résidence Beau Site, 141 Boulevard Kennedy, 26 r.
	***Castel Garoupe – Motel Axa, Boulevard de la Garoupe, 20 r.
	***Gardiole, Chemin de la Garoupe, 20 r.
	***Miramar, Chemin de la Plage la Garoupe, 14 r.

In Juan-les-Pins:
L****Hélios, 3 Avenue Dautheville, 70 r.
L****Belles Rives, Boulevard du Littoral, 42 r.
L****Juana, Avenue Gallice la Pinède, 42 r.
****Beauséjour, Avenue Saramartel, 30 r.
****Parc, Avenue Guy de Maupassant, 27 r.
***Astoria, 15 Avenue du Maréchal Joffre, 45 r.
***Beachotel, Avenue Alexandre-III, 43 r.
***Le Passy, 15 Avenue Galiet, 36 r.

****Jules César, Boulevard des Lices, 61 r.   **Arles**
***Primotel, near Palais des Congrès, 102 r.
***Forum, 10 Place du Forum, 45 r.
***D'Arlatan, 26 Rue du Sauvage, 41 r.
***Cantarelles, Quartier Villevieille, 35 r.
***Nord – Pinus, 14 Place du Forum, 35 r.
***Mireille, 2 Place St-Pierre, 30 r.
***Mapotel Les Cabanettes en Camargue,
    572 Hameau de Saliers, 29 r.
***Motel le Rodin, 20 Rue Rodin, 26 r.
***Auberge La Fenière, on the N453, 24 r.
***Select, 35 Boulevard Georges Clemenceau, 24 r.
**Ibis, Quartier Fourchon Tertiaire, 64 r.
**Le Cloître, 18 Rue du Cloître, 33 r.
**Le Calendal, 22 Place Pomme, 22 r.
**Saint-Trophime, 16 Rue de la Calade, 22 r.
**Lou Gardianoun, 15 Rue Noguier, 20 r.
**Montmajour, 84 Avenue de Stalingrad, 20 r.
*Lamartine, 1 Rue M-Jouveau, 32 r.
*Poste, 2 Rue Molière, 24 r.

****Sofitel, Pont d'Avignon, Rue Ferruce, 85 r.   **Avignon**
****Europe, 12 Place Crillon, 65 r.
***Mercure Avignon Sud, Route de Marseille, 105 r.
***Bristol Terminus, 44 Cours Jean-Jaurès, 85 r.
***Novotel Avignon Sud, Route de Marseille, 79 r.
***Cité des Papes, 1 Rue Jean Vilar, 63 r.
***Du Midi, 53 Rue de la République, 54 r.
***Régina, 6 Rue de la République, 39 r.
**Savoy, 17 Rue de la République, 43 r.
**Constantin, 46 Rue Carnot, 40 r.
**D'Angleterre, 29 Boulevard Raspail, 34 r.
**Central Hôtel, 31 Rue de la République, 29 r.
**Les Glycines, Pont de Bonpas, 24 r.
**Palais des Papes, 1 Rue Gérard Philipe, 23 r.
**Auberge de France, 28 Place de l'Horloge, 22 r.
*Le Magnan, 63 Portail Magnanen, 30 r.
*Aïgarden, 7–9 Rue de l'Aïgarden, 26 r.
*Excelsior, 2 Rue de la Petite-Calade, 24 r.
*Le Médiéval, 15 Rue de la Petite Saumerie, 23 r.
*Croix Blanche, 2 Place des Carmes, 22 r.
*Saint-Georges, 10 Rue de l'Etoile, 21 r.
*Jacquemart, 3 Rue Félicien David, 20 r.

L****Ile Rousse, Boulevard Lumière, 55 r.   **Bandol**
****Soukana, on Bendor, 50 r.
***Résidence Beau-Rivage, Boulevard Lumière, 23 r.
***Le Provençal, Rue des Ecoles, 22 r.
***La Réserve, Avenue de la Libération, 16 r.
***De la Baie, 62 Rue Marçon, 14 r.

**Les Galets, Route de Toulon, 27 r.
**Le Goëland, Avenue Albert-Premier, 26 r.
**Ermitage, Résidence du Château, 24 r.
**Golf, Plage de Renécros, 22 r.
**Splendid, 83 Avenue Foch, 22 r.
**Ker Mocotte, Rue Raimu, 18 r.
**La Brunière, Avenue du Château, 16 r.
**Triton, 9 Rue du Docteur Mançon, 16 r.
*Coin d'Azur, Plage de Renécros, 21 r.
*Bel Ombra, Rue la Fontaine, 18 r.

Les Baux

L****Oustau de Baumanière, 26 r.
****Cabro d'Or, 20 r.
***La Benvengudo, 18 r.
***Le Mas d'Aigret, 17 r.
***Bautezar, 10 r.
**Hostellerie de la Reine Jeanne, 12 r.

Beaulieu-sur-Mer

L****Métropole, 15 Boulevard du Général Leclerc, 50 r.
L****La Réserve de Beaulieu, 5 Boulevard du Général Leclerc, 42 r.
****Carlton, Avenue E. Cavell, 33 r.
***Don Gregorio, 3 Avenue du Maréchal Joffre, 72 r.
***Frisia Hôtel, 2 Boulevard du Général Leclerc, 36 r.
***Comte de Nice, 25 Boulevard Marinoni, 33 r.
***La Résidence, Boulevard Albert-Premier, 21 r.
**Victoria, 47 Boulevard Marinoni, 80 r.
**Havre Bleu, 29 Boulevard du Maréchal Joffre, 17 r.
*Flora, 6 Avenue Edith Cavell, 23 r.

Cagnes-sur-Mer

***Motel Ascot Studios, 16 Boulevard de la Plage, 25 r.
***Tiercé Hôtel, Boulevard de la Plage, 23 r.
***Le Cagnard, Rue Pontis Long, 19 r.
**Savournin, 17 Avenue Auguste Renoir, 32 r.
*Golf, Avenue de la Gare, 24 r.

Cannes

L****Martinez, 73 Boulevard de la Croisette, 399 r.
L****Carlton, 58 Boulevard de la Croisette, 335 r.
L****Majestic, Boulevard de la Croisette, 248 r.
L****Montfleury, 25 Avenue Beauséjour, 235 r.
L****Gray d'Albion, 38 Rue des Serbes, 189 r.
L****Sofitel – Méditerranée, 2 Boulevard Jean-Hibert, 150 r.
L****Frantel Beach, 13 Rue du Canada, 95 r.
L****Grand Hôtel, 45 Boulevard de la Croisette, 76 r.
****Cannes Palace Hôtel, 14 Avenue de Madrid, 100 r.
****Gonnet et de la Reine, 42–43 Boulevard de la Croisette, 52 r.
***Solhotel Cannes, 65 Avenue du Docteur-Picaud, 100 r.
***Univers Hôtel, 2 Rue du Maréchal Foch, 68 r.
***Mondial, 77 Rue d'Antibes, 65 r.
***Splendid, 4/6 Rue Félix Faure, 65 r.
***Canberra, 120/122 Rue d'Antibes, 62 r.
***Embassy, 6 Rue de Bone, 60 r.
***Acapulco, 16 Boulevard d'Alsace, 59 r.
***Palma, 77 Boulevard de la Croisette, 52 r.
***De Paris, 34 Boulevard d'Alsace, 49 r.
***Abrial, 24–26 Boulevard de Lorraine, 48 r.
***Beau Séjour, 100 Rue Georges Clemenceau, 46 r.
***Licorn Hôtel, 23 Avenue Francis Tonner, 45 r.
***Les Orangers, 1 Rue des Orangers, 45 r.

***Château de la Tour, 10 Avenue Font de Veyre la Bocca, 42 r.
***Belle Plage, 6 Rue Dolfus, 36 r.
***Ligure, 5 Rue Jean-Jaurès, 36 r.
***Century, 133 Rue d'Antibes, 35 r.
***Ruc Hôtel Cannes, 13–15 Boulevard de Strasbourg, 31 r.
***Provence, 9 Rue Molière, 30 r.
**Atlas, 5 Place de la Gare, 52 r.
**Campanile, Aéroport La Bocca, 49 r.
**Des Etrangers, 6 Place Sémard, 45 r.
**Amirauté, 17 Rue du Maréchal Foch, 44 r.
**Cavendish, 11 Boulevard Carnot, 40 r.
**Atlantis, 4 Rue du 24-Août, 37 r.
**Motelia, 285 Avenue de Grasse, 35 r.
**De France, 85 Rue d'Antibes, 34 r.
**Molière, 5–7 Rue Molière, 33 r.
**P.L.M., 3 Rue Hoche, 32 r.
**Select, 16 Rue Hélène Vagliano, 30 r.
**Touring Hôtel, 11 Rue Hoche, 30 r.
*Régence, 13 Rue St-Honoré, 32 r.

***Univers, Place Aristide Briand, 25 r. Carpentras
**Safari Hôtel, Avenue Fabre, 42 r.
**Du Fiacre, 153 Rue Vigne, 16 r.

***Nouvel Hôtel du Commerce, Place Sauvaire, 44 r. Castellane
**Levant, Place Sauvaire, 33 r.
**Verdon, 14 Boulevard de la République, 22 r.

****Logis d'Arnavel, 15 r. Châteauneuf-du-Pape
****Hostellerie du Château des Fines Roches, 7 r.

***Ermitage Napoléon, Route de Nice, 59 r. Digne
***Grand Paris, 5 Boulevard Thiers, 35 r.
**Thermal, 3 km outside, 80 r.
**Mistre, 65 Boulevard Gassendi, 37 r.
**Hostellerie de l'Aiglon, 1 Rue de Provence, 23 r.
**Central Hôtel, 26 Boulevard Gassendi, 22 r.
**Saint Michel, Route des Alpilles, 21 r.
**Bourgogne, Avenue de Verdun, 20 r.
*Julia, 1 Place Pied de Ville, 23 r.

***Grand Hôtel Bertin, 13 Boulevard Foch, 46 r. Draguignan
***Col de l'Ange, Route de Lorgnes, 29 r.
**Postillon, 27 Rue Gisson, 35 r.
**Semeria, 12 Avenue Carnot, 23 r.
**Du Parc, 21 Boulevard de la Liberté, 20 r.
*Moreau, 14 Rue du Cros, 14 r.

**Grand Hôtel des Sources, 14 r. Fontaine-de-Vaucluse
**Du Parc, 12 r.
**Ermitage Vallis Clausa, 11 r.

****Mapotel Résidences du Colombier, Route de Bagnois, 60 r. Fréjus
***Le Ligure, 1074 Avenue de Lattre de Tassigny, 64 r.
***Catalogne, Avenue de la Corniche d'Azur, 33 r.
**Les Palmiers, Boulevard de la Libération, 54 r.
**Azur, St-Aygulf, 43 r.
**L'Oasis, Rue Fabre, 27 r.
**Il était une fois, Rue Frédéric Mistral, 20 r.
*Esterel Terminus, 7 Rue du Général de Gaulle, 30 r.
*La Pérouse, St-Aygulf, 26 r.

Practical Information

Gap
***Grille, 2 Place Frédéric Euzière, 29 r.
**Le Clos, 20 Avenue du Commandant Dumont, 41 r.
**Carina, Chabanas, 30 r.
**Ferme Blanche, Rue de Villarobert, 30 r.
**Mokotel, Route de Marseille, 28 r.
**Paix, 1 Place Euzuère, 24 r.
**Fons Regina, Château de Font-Reyne, 22 r.
*Le Pavillon, Chabanas, Route de Veynes, 35 r.
*Verdun, 20 Boulevard de la Libération, 28 r.
*Méridional, 1 Avenue Jean-Jaurès, 26 r.

Gordes
***Gordos, Route de Cavaillon, 15 r.
***La Gacholle, Route de Murs, 10 r.
***Mayanelle, 6 Rue de la Combe, 10 r.
**Auberge de Carcarille, 9 r.

La Grande-Motte
***Frantel, 140 Rue du Port, 135 r.
***Quetzal, Allée des Jardins, 52 r.
***Méditerranée, 277 Allée du Vaccarès, 42 r.
***Alexandre, Esplanade de la Capitainerie, 16 r.
**Europe, Avenue Navigarde, 34 r.
**Saint-Clair, Avenue de l'Europe, 27 r.
**Acropolis Hôtel, la Motte du Couchant, 22 r.
*Copacabana, 21 r.

Grasse
***Le Régent, Route de Nice, 40 r.
**Bellevue, 14 Avenue Riou-Blanquet, 30 r.
**Aigle, 33 Boulevard du Jeu de Ballon, 20 r.
**La Bellaudière, Route de Nice, 16 r.
**Oasis, Place de la Varanderie, 13 r.

Grignan
**Sévigné, Place de Castellane, 20 r.

Hyères
***Plein Sud, Boulevard du Front de Mer, 189 r.
***Paris, 20 Avenue de Belgique, 32 r.
***Le Manoir, on Port-Cros, 28 r.
***Vieille Auberge St-Nicholas, on the N98, 11 r.
***Pins d'Argent, Plage d'Hyères, 10 r.
**Du Parc, 7 Boulevard Pasteur, 39 r.
**Relais de la Poste, Place d'Armes, 28 r.
**Le Suisse, 1 Avenue Aristide Briand, 25 r.

Le Lavandou
L****Le Club de Cavalière, Plage de Cavalière, 32 r.
****Résidence Beach, Front de Mer, 55 r.
****Les Roches Fleuries, 1 Avenue des Trois Dauphins, 48 r.
****Le 83 Hôtel, La Fossette, 28 r.
***Cap Nègre Hôtel, 45 Avenue du Cap Nègre, 30 r.
***Auberge de la Calanque, 26 Avenue du Général de Gaulle,
    29 r.
***La Lune, 10 Avenue du Général de Gaulle, 24 r.
***L'Espadon, 2 Place Reyer, 22 r.
***Le Roc, St-Clair, 21 r.
***L'Orangeraie, Plage de St-Clair, 20 r.
***Belle Vue, St-Clair, 19 r.
**La Galaxie, 45 r.
**Neptune, 26 Avenue du Général de Gaulle, 35 r.
**Flots Bleus, St-Clair, 26 r.
**L'Ilot Fleuri, Avenue Charles Cazin, 26 r.
**Beau Rivage, Boulevard Front de Mer, 23 r.
*California, Route de St-Tropez, 27 r.

*Terminus, Place Vieille, 25 r.
*Mandariniers, St-Clair, 24 r.

L****Sofitel Vieux-Port, 36 Boulevard Charles Divon, 222 r.   **Marseilles**
L****Petit Nice, Anse de Maldormé, 20 r.
****Frantel Marseille, Rue Neuve St-Martin, 200 r.
****L'Arbois, 47 Boulevard Charles Nédélec, 120 r.
****Concorde – Prado, 11 Avenue Mazargues, 104 r.
****P.L.M. Beauvau, 4 Rue Beauvau, 72 r.
****Grand Hôtel Noailles, 64–66 Canebière, 60 r.
***Concorde Palm Beach, 2 Promenade de la Plage, 161 r.
***Novotel Marseille Est, St-Menet, 131 r.
***Select Hôtel, 4 Allées Gambetta, 68 r.
***Rome et Saint-Pierre, 7 Cours St-Louis, 65 r.
***P.L.M. Astoria, 10 Boulevard Garibaldi, 56 r.
***Résidence du Vieux Port, 18–24 Quai du Vieux Port, 53 r.
***Genève, 3 bis Rue Reine Elisabeth, 48 r.
***Grand Modern'Hôtel, 5 Canebière, 48 r.
***Castellane, 31 Rue du Rouet, 47 r.
***Résidence Bompard, 2 Rue des Flots Bleus, 46 r.
***Manhattan, 3 Place de Rome, 41 r.
***Bristol, 18 Canebière, 35 r.
***Petit Louvre, 19 Canebière, 35 r.
***Paris – Nice, 23/25 Boulevard d'Athènes, 33 r.
***Saint-Georges, 10 Rue du Capitaine Dessemond, 27 r.
**Ibis, 6 Rue de Cassis, 119 r.
**Grand Hôtel de Paris, 11–15 Rue Colbert, 90 r.
**Touring Hôtel, 42 Cours Belsunce, 85 r.
**Grand Hôtel Californie, 60 Cours Belsunce, 67 r.
**Normandie, 28 Boulevard d'Athènes, 58 r.
**Des Deux Mondes, 46 Cours Belsunce, 50 r.
**Lafayette, 9 Allées Gambetta, 50 r.
**Porte de l'Orient, 6 Rue Bonneterie, 50 r.
**Breton, 52 Rue de Mazenod, 49 r.
**Inter Hotel du Globe, 26 Rue Colbert, 49 r.
**Continental, 6 Rue Beauvau, 46 r.
**Méditerranée, 13–15 Place des Belges, 45 r.
**Corona, 12 Rue des Feuillants, 43 r.
**Européen, 115–117 Rue Paradis, 43 r.
**Préfecture, 9 Boulevard Louis-Salvator, 41 r.
**Martini, 5 Boulevard Gustave Desplaces, 40 r.

***Saint-Roch, Le Moulin de Paradis, 39 r.   **Martigues**
***Eden, Boulevard Emile Zola, 38 r.
**Gril Campanile, Boulevard de Thonon, 42 r.
**Lido, Cours du 4-Septembre, 19 r.
*Clair Hôtel, Boulevard Marcel Cachin, 39 r.

***Méditerranée, 5 Rue de la République, 90 r.   **Menton**
***Du Parc, 11 Avenue de Verdun, 74 r.
***Napoléon, 29 Porte de France, 40 r.
***Beau Rivage, 1 Avenue Blasco Ibanez, 40 r.
***Chambord, 6 Avenue Boyer, 40 r.
***Viking, 2 Avenue du Général de Gaulle, 34 r.
***Europ Hôtel, 36 Boulevard de Verdun, 33 r.
**Prince de Galles, 4 Avenue du Général de Gaulle, 68 r.
**Floréal, Cours du Centenaire, 60 r.
**France, 3 Rue St-Michel, 44 r.
**Magali, 10 Rue Villarey, 43 r.
**Princess et Richmond, 32 Avenue du Général de Gaulle, 43 r.

Practical Information

	**Bristol, 24 Avenue Carnot, 40 r.
	**El Paradiso, 71 Porte de France, 40 r.
	**Carlton, 6 Avenue du Général de Gaulle, 37 r.
	**Arcades, 41 Avenue Félix Faure, 36 r.
	**Pin Doré, 16 Avenue Félix Faure, 36 r.
	**Celine Rose, 57 Avenue de Sospel, 35 r.
	**Saint-Georges, 24 bis Avenue Cochrane, 35 r.
	*Mondial – Grimaldi, 12 Rue Partouneaux, 41 r.
	*Claridge, 39 Avenue de Verdun, 30 r.
Monaco	L****Loews Monte Carlo, Avenue des Spélugues, 680 r.
	L****Beach Plaza, 22 Avenue Princesse Grace, 313 r.
	L****Hôtel de Paris, Place du Casino, 240 r.
	L****Hermitage, Square Beaumarchais, 215 r.
	L****Mirabeau, 1/3 Avenue Princesse Grace, 100 r.
	L****Monte-Carlo Beach, Avenue du Bord de Mer, 46 r.
	***Balmoral, 12 Avenue de la Costa, 67 r.
	***Splendid, 4 Avenue de Roqueville, 57 r.
	***Alexandra, 35 Boulevard Princesse Charlotte, 55 r.
	***Louvre, 16 Boulevard des Moulins, 33 r.
	***Miramar, 1 bis Avenue Kennedy, 14 r.
	***Versailles, 4–6 Avenue Prince Pierre, 15 r.
	**Terminus, 9 Avenue Prince Pierre, 54 r.
	**Le Siècle, 10 Avenue Prince Pierre, 39 r.
	**Résidence des Moulins, 27 Boulevard des Moulins, 12 r.
	*Helvetia, 1 bis Rue Grimaldi, 28 r.
	*Cosmopolite, 4 Rue de la Turbie, 24 r.
	*De la Poste, 5 Rue des Oliviers, 24 r.
	*France, 6 Rue de la Turbie, 24 r.
	*De l'Etoile, 4 Rue des Oliviers, 12 r.
Montélimar	****Parc Chabaud, 16 Avenue d'Aygu, 22 r.
	***Motel Vallée du Rhône, Route de Marseille, 51 r.
	***Relais de l'Empereur, Place Marx-Dormoy, 40 r.
	***Auberge de la Cremaillère, Route de Marseille, 22 r.
	**Dauphiné – Provence, 41 Avenue de Gaulle, 26 r.
	**Sphinx, 19 Boulevard Desmarais, 20 r.
	*International Hôtel, on the N7, 146 r.
Montpellier	L****Sofitel, Le Triangle, 125 r.
	L****Metropole, 3 Rue Clos-René, 92 r.
	***Mercure Montpellier Est, 662 Avenue de la Pompignane, 122 r.
	***Frantel, 218 Rue du Bastion Ventadour, 116 r.
	***Grand Hôtel Midi, 22 Boulevard Victor Hugo, 48 r.
	***Royal Hôtel, 8 Rue Maguelone, 46 r.
	***Ponant, 130 Avenue Palavas, 45 r.
	***George V, 42 Avenue St-Lazare, 39 r.
	***Noailles, 2 Rue des Ecoles-Centrales, 30 r.
	**Ibis, 164 Route de Palavas, 102 r.
	**Novotel, 125 bis Avenue de Palavas, 97 r.
	**L'Hôtel, 6/8 Rue Jules Ferry, 55 r.
	**Edouard-VII, Rue Olivier, 47 r.
	**Climat de France, Rue du Caducée, 43 r.
	**Grand Hôtel P.L.M., Place Auguste Gibert, 41 r.
	**France et Lutétia, 3–4 Rue de la République, 40 r.
	*Imperator, 20 Rue Boussairolles, 48 r.
Nice	L****Negresco, 37 Promenade des Anglais, 150 r.
	L****Beach Regency, 223 Promenade des Anglais, 335 r.

L****Méridien, 1 Promenade des Anglais, 315 r.
****Plaza, 12 Avenue de Verdun, 186 r.
****Aston, 12 Avenue Félix Faure, 160 r.
****Sofitel – Splendid, 50 Boulevard Victor Hugo, 150 r.
****Park-Hotel, 6 Avenue de Suède, 145 r.
****Mercure, 2 Rue Halevy, 124 r.
****Westminster – Concorde, 27 Promenade des Anglais,
110 r.
****La Pérouse, 11 Quai Rauba Capeu, 65 r.
***Frantel, 28 Avenue Notre-Dame, 200 r.
***Atlantic, 12 Boulevard Victor Hugo, 123 r.
***Continental Masséna, 58 Rue Gioffredo, 116 r.
***West-End, 31 Promenade des Anglais, 96 r.
***Napoléon, 6 Rue Grimaldi, 80 r.
***Busby, 36–38 Rue du Maréchal Joffre, 76 r.
***Albert-Premier, 4 Avenue des Phocéens, 74 r.
***Grand Hôtel de Noailles, 70 Avenue Jean Médecin, 73 r.
***Brice, 44 Rue du Maréchal Joffre, 60 r.
***Vendôme, 26 Rue Pastorelli, 60 r.
***Windsor, 12 Rue Dalpozzo, 59 r.
***Florence, 3 Rue Paul Déroulède, 53 r.
***New-York, 44 Avenue Maréchal Foch, 52 r.
***Bedford, 45 Rue du Maréchal Joffre, 50 r.
***Chatham, 9 Rue Karr, 50 r.
**Albion, 25 Boulevard Dubouchage, 85 r.
**Frank – Zurich, 31 Rue Paganini, 76 r.
**Univers, 9 Avenue Jean Médecin, 75 r.
**Bruxelles, 17 Rue de Belgique, 73 r.
**Rivoli, 47 Rue Pastorelli, 70 r.
**Roosevelt, 16 Rue du Maréchal Joffre, 66 r.
**Saint-Gothard, 20 Rue Paganini, 63 r.
**National, 64 Avenue Jean Médecin, 61 r.
**Berne, 1 Avenue Thiers, 59 r.
**Des Nations, 25 Avenue Durante, 57 r.
**Sibill's, 25 Rue Assalit, 56 r.
**Mulhouse, 9 Rue Chauvain, 54 r.
**Nouvel Hôtel, 10 bis Boulevard Victor Hugo, 54 r.
**Harvey, 18 Avenue de Suède, 51 r.
**Midland, 41 Rue Lamartine, 50 r.
*P.L.M., 60 Avenue Jean Médecin, 74 r.
*Calais, 2 Rue Chauvain, 50 r.
*France, 24 Boulevard Raimbaldi, 45 r.

L****Sofitel, Chemin de l'Hostellerie, 100 r.   **Nîmes**
****Imperator, Quai de la Fontaine, 61 r.
***Grand Hôtel du Midi, Square de la Couronne, 115 r.
***Novotel Nîmes, 124 Chemin de l'Hostellerie, 96 r.
***Mercure, 113 Chemin de l'Hostellerie, 95 r.
***Du Cheval Blanc et des Arènes, 1 Place des Arènes, 48 r.
**Ibis, Chemin de l'Hostellerie, 108 r.
**Nîmotel, Chemin de l'Hostellerie, 100 r.
**Carrière, 6 Rue Grizot, 55 r.
**Empire, 1 Boulevard Santenac, 45 r.
**Provence, 5/7 Square de la Couronne, 38 r.
**Louvre, 2 Square de la Couronne, 35 r.
**Terminus, 23 Avenue Feuchères, 34 r.
**Milan, 17 Avenue Feuchères, 32 r.
**Royal Hôtel, 3 Boulevard Alphonse Daudet, 32 r.
**Univers, 16 Place des Arènes, 30 r.

Practical Information

Orange	***Euromotel, Route de Caderousse, 99 r.
	***Louvre et Terminus, 89 Avenue Frédéric Mistral, 40 r.
	***Arène, Place de Langes, 30 r.
	**Boscotel, Route de Caderousse, 57 r.
	**Princes, 7 Avenue de l'Arc de Triomphe, 52 r.
	**Glacier, 46 Cours Aristide Briand, 29 r.
Port-Grimaud	****Giraglia, Grande Rue, 48 r.
	***Port, Place du Marché, 20 r.
Roquebrune – Cap-Martin	L****Vistaëro, Grande Corniche, 40 r.
	***Alexandra, Promenade Cap-Martin, 40 r.
	***Victoria et de la Plage, Promenade du Cap, 31 r.
	**Princessias, 15 Avenue Georges Drin, 13 r.
	**Regency, 98 Avenue Jean-Jaurès, 12 r.
	*Westminster, 14 Avenue Louis Laurens, 30 r.
	*Europe-Village, Avenue Hériot, 26 r.
Stes-Maries-de-la-Mer	***Auberge Cavalière, Route d'Arles, 48 r.
	****Pont des Bannes, Route d'Arles, 20 r.
	****Mas de la Fouques, Route d'Aigues-Mortes, 10 r.
	***La Cabane du Boumian, 28 r.
	***Hostellerie du Mas de Calabrun, on the D85A, 27 r.
	***L'Etrier Camarguais, 25 r.
	***Clamador, Route d'Aigues-Mortes, 22 r.
	***Galoubet, Route de Cacharel, 20 r.
	**Le Camargue, 1 Rue Baptiste Bonnet, 32 r.
	**Camille, 29 r.
	**Le Mirage, 27 r.
	**Le Grill, 25 r.
	**Le Mas des Lys, Route d'Arles, 24 r.
St-Gilles	**Cours, 10 Avenue François Brifeuille, 25 r.
	*Globe, Place Gambetta, 23 r.
St-Maximin-la-Ste-Baume	*France, 1–3 Avenue Albert-Premier, 22 r.
	*Relais, Route d'Aix, 12 r.
St-Raphaël	***Etape Cap Boulouris, on the N98, 50 r.
	***Continental, 25 Promenade du Président Coty, 49 r.
	***Beauséjour, Promenade du Président Coty, 39 r.
	***San Pedro, Avenue Colonel Brooke, 25 r.
	**Excelsior, Boulevard Félix Martin, 40 r.
	**Europe et Gare, 9 Rue Amiral Baux, 32 r.
	**Pastorel, 16 Rue de la Liberté, 29 r.
	**France, Place Galliéni, 28 r.
	**Provençal, 197 Rue de la Garonne, 28 r.
	**Moderne, 331 Avenue du Général Leclerc, 25 r.
	**Arènes, 31 Avenue du Général Leclerc, 24 r.
	**Touring, 1 Quai Albert-Premier, 24 r.
	*Genève, 92 Boulevard Félix Martin, 29 r.
St-Rémy-de-Provence	****Château des Alpilles, on the D31, 18 r.
	***Hostellerie du Vallon de Valrugues, Chemin de Canto Cigalo, 34 r.
	***Les Antiques, 15 Avenue Pasteur, 27 r.
	***Castelet des Alpilles, 6 Place Mireille, 19 r.
	**Canto Cigalo, Chemin de Canto Cigalo, 20 r.
	**Cheval Blanc, Avenue Fangonnet, 20 r.
	**Van Gogh, 1 Avenue Jean Moulin, 18 r.
	*Provence, 36 Boulevard Victor Hugo, 27 r.

L****Residence de la Pinède, Plage de la Bouillabaisse, 40 r.   **St-Tropez**
****Byblos, Avenue Paul Signac, 59 r.
****Mandarine, Route Tahiti-Plage, 41 r.
***de Paris, Place Croix-de-Fer, 63 r.
***Lou Troupelen, Chemin des Vendanges, 42 r.
***Résidence des Lices, Avenue Augustin Grangeon, 34 r.
***Ermitage, Avenue Paul Signac, 29 r.
***Levant, Route des Salins, 28 r.
***La Ponche, Place du Revelin, 23 r.
***Les Capucines, Domaine du Treizain, 22 r.
***Yaca, 1–3 Boulevard Aumale, 20 r.
**Coste, Port du Pilon, 30 r.
**Sube et Continental, 15 Quai Suffren, 26 r.
**Citadelle, 24 r.
**Les Palmiers, 26 Boulevard Vasserot, 22 r.
**Mas Bellevue, Route de Tahiti, 20 r.
**Tramontane, Plage de la Bouillabaisse, 20 r.

****Abbaye de Sainte-Croix, Val de Cuech, 22 r.   **Salon-de-Provence**
**Le Roi René, 561 Allées de Craponne, 60 r.
**Grand Hôtel d'Angleterre, 98 Cours Carnot, 26 r.
**Vendôme, 34 Rue du Maréchal Joffre, 22 r.
**Select, 35 Rue du Bailli de Suffren, 19 r.
*Grand Hôtel de la Poste, 2 Cours Carnot, 29 r.
*Régina, 245 Rue Kennedy, 19 r.

***Grand Hôtel du Cours, Place de l'Eglise, 50 r.   **Sisteron**
**Touring Napoléon, 85 Avenue de la Libération, 29 r.
**La Citadelle, Rue Saumerie, 24 r.
**Tivoli, Place du Tivoli, 19 r.
*Rocher, La Baume, 31 r.

***Provençal Bis, 7 Boulevard Victor Hugo, 11 r.   **Tarascon**
**Terminus, Place Berrurier, 25 r.
**Le Provençal, 12 Cours Aristide Briand, 22 r.
*Moderne, Boulevard Itam, 28 r.

****Grand Hôtel, 4 Place de la Liberté, 81 r.   **Toulon**
***Frantel La Tour Blanche, Boulevard Amiral Vence, 96 r.
***La Corniche, 1 Littoral Frédéric Mistral, 22 r.
***Residence du Cap Brun, 20 r.
**Amirauté, 4 Rue Guiol, 64 r.
**Du Dauphine, Rue Berthelot, 57 r.
**Continental et Métropole, 1 Rue Racine, 54 r.
**Maritima, 9 Rue Gimelli, 50 r.
**Louvre, 9 Rue Corneille, 44 r.
**Napoléon, 49 Rue Jean-Jaurès, 43 r.
**Terminus, 7 Boulevard de Tessé, 40 r.
**Moderne, 21 Avenue Colbert, 39 r.
*Rex Hôtel, 51 Rue Jean-Jaurès, 31 r.
*Lutétia, 69 Rue Jean-Jaurès, 30 r.

Entraygues, 8 Rue de la Calade, 19 r.   **Uzès
*Taverne, 4 Rue Sigalon, 12 r.
*Hostellerie Provençale, 3 Rue Grande-Bourgade, 10 r.

***Hostellerie L'Oustau, 11 r.   **Vaison-la-Romaine**
**Logis du Château, 40 r.
**Le Beffroi, 20 r.
*Théâtre Romain, 21 r.

Practical Information

Vence
    L****Château du Domaine St-Martin, Route de Coursegoules, 27 r.
    **Le Floréal, 440 Avenue Rhin et Danube, 43 r.
    ***Diana, Avenue des Poilus, 25 r.
    ***Miramar, Plateau St-Michel, 17 r.
    **Regina, Avenue des Alliés, 26 r.
    **Le Provence, 9 Avenue Marcellin Maurel, 20 r.

Information

Aigues-Mortes
Office Municipal de Tourisme
Place St-Louis
F-30220 Aigues-Mortes
tel. (66) 51 95 00

Aix-en-Provence
Office Municipal de Tourisme
Place du Général-de-Gaulle
F-13100 Aix-en-Provence
tel. (42) 26 02 93

Antibes
Maison du Tourisme
11 Place du Général-de-Gaulle
F-06600 Antibes
tel. (93) 33 95 64

Arles
Office de Tourisme
Boulevard des Lices
F-13637 Arles
tel. (90) 96 29 35

Avignon
Office de Tourisme
41 Cours Jean-Jaurès
F-84000 Avignon
tel. (90) 82 65 11

Bandol
Office de Tourisme
Allées Alfred-Vivien
F-83150 Bandol
tel. (94) 29 41 35

Les Baux
Office de Tourisme
Impasse du Château
F-13520 Les Baux
tel. (90) 97 34 39

Beaulieu-sur-Mer
Syndicat d'Initiative
Place de la Gare
F-06310 Beaulieu-sur-Mer

Cagnes-sur-Mer
Office de Tourisme
26 Avenue A. Renoir
F-06801 Cagnes-sur-Mer
tel. (93) 20 61 64

Cannes
Services de Tourisme
1 La Croisette
F-06400 Cannes
tel. (93) 39 01 01
Information bureaux also at railway station
and in the Palais Croisette

Office de Tourisme
170 Allées Jean-Jaurès
F-84200 Carpentras
tel. (90) 63 57 88 and 63 00 78

Carpentras

Office de Tourisme
Rue Nationale
F-04120 Castellane
tel. (92) 83 61 14

Castellane

Office de Tourisme
Place du Portail
F-84230 Châteauneuf-du-Pape
tel. (90) 39 71 08

Châteauneuf-du-Pape

Office de Tourisme
Rond-Point
F-04002 Digne
tel. (92) 31 42 73

Digne

Office de Tourisme
9 Boulevard Clemenceau
F-83300 Draguignan
tel. (94) 68 63 30

Draguignan

Syndicat d'Initiative
Place de l'Eglise
F-84800 Fontaine-de-Vaucluse
tel. (90) 20 32 22

Fontaine-de-Vaucluse

Office de Tourisme
Place Calvini
F-83600 Fréjus
tel. (94) 51 53 87

Fréjus

Syndicat d'Initiative
5 Rue Carnot
F-05000 Gap
tel. (92) 51 57 03

Gap

Office de Tourisme
Place du Château
F-84220 Gordes
tel. (90) 72 02 75

Gordes

Office de Tourisme
Place du Premier Octobre
F-34280 La Grande-Motte
tel. (67) 56 62 62

La Grande-Motte

Office de Tourisme
Place de la Foux
F-06130 Grasse
tel. (93) 36 03 56

Grasse

Practical Information

Grignan
Syndicat d'Initiative
Grande Rue
F-26230 Grignan
tel. (75) 46 56 75

Hyères
Office de Tourisme
Avenue de Belgique
F-83400 Hyères
tel. (94) 65 18 55

Le Lavandou
Office de Tourisme
Quai Gabriel Péri
F-83980 Le Lavandou
tel. (94) 71 00 61

Marseilles
Office Municipal de Tourisme
4 La Canebière
F-13001 Marseille
tel. (91) 54 91 11

Martigues
Office de Tourisme
Quai Paul Doumer
F-13500 Martigues
tel. (42) 80 30 72

Menton
Office Municipal de Tourisme
Palais de l'Europe, Avenue Boyer
F-06503 Menton
tel. (93) 57 57 00

Monaco
Direction du Tourisme et des Congrès
de la Principauté de Monaco
2a Boulevard des Moulins
Monte-Carlo/Principality of Monaco
tel. (93) 30 87 01

Montélimar
Office de Tourisme
Champ de Mars
F-26200 Montélimar
tel. (75) 01 00 20

Montpellier
Bureau Municipal de Tourisme
6 Rue Maguelone
F-34000 Montpellier
tel. (67) 58 26 04

Nice
Office de Tourisme
32 Rue de l'Hôtel des Postes
F-06047 Nice
tel. (93) 62 06 06

Nîmes
Office de Tourisme
6 Rue Auguste
F-30000 Nîmes
tel. (66) 67 29 11

Orange
Office de Tourisme
Cours A. Briand
F-84100 Orange
tel. (90) 34 70 88

Office de Tourisme
20 Avenue P. Doumer
F-06190 Roquebrune-Cap-Martin
tel. (93) 35 62 87

Syndicat d'Initiative
Avenue Van-Gogh
F-13460 Saintes-Maries-de-la-Mer
tel. (90) 97 82 55

Office de Tourisme
Maison Romane, Place de l'Olme
F-30800 St-Gilles
tel. (66) 87 33 75

Office de Tourisme
Place de la Gare
F-83700 St-Raphaël
tel. (94) 95 16 87

Office de Tourisme
Place Jean-Jaurès
F-13210 St-Rémy-de-Provence
tel. (90) 92 05 22

Office de Tourisme
23 Avenue Général Leclerc
F-83990 St-Tropez
tel. (94) 97 41 21

Office de Tourisme
56 Cours Gimon
F-13300 Salon-de-Provence
tel. (90) 56 27 60

Office de Tourisme
Avenue Paul-Arène
F-04200 Sisteron
tel. (92) 61 12 03

Office de Tourisme
59 Rue Halles
F-13150 Tarascon
tel. (90) 91 03 52

Office Régional de Tourisme
8 Avenue Colbert
F-83000 Toulon
tel. (94) 22 08 22

Office de Tourisme
Hôtel de Ville
F-30700 Uzès
tel. (66) 22 68 88

Office de Tourisme
Avenue du Général-de-Gaulle
F-84110 Vaison-la-Romaine
tel. (90) 36 02 11

Practical Information

Vence
        Office de Tourisme
        Place du Grand-Jardin
        F-06140 Vence
        tel. (93) 58 06 38

Maps and plans

Visitors who are travelling away from the major holiday routes should take a map or maps in addition to the general map provided with this guide. Below is a selection:

1:1,500,000	Shell Motoring Map of France
1:1,000,000	Michelin France, sheet 989
1:750,000	Shell Large Motoring Map of France
1:200,000	Michelin detailed maps of France; for the area covered in this guidebook sheets 80, 81, 83 and 84
1:100,000	IGN maps 60, 61, 66, 67, 68

Marinas

On the Mediterranean coast of France there are a great number of marinas, some of which have developed from fishing ports, others which have been planned and built from new. Marinas with varying facilities are situated at the following places:

Antibes/Port Vauban, Bandol, Beaulieu-sur-Mer, Bendor, Bormes-les-Mimosas, Cannes, Cannes-Marina, Cap d'Ail/Fontvieille, Carry-le-Rouet, Cassis, Cavalaire, Cros-de-Cagnes, Golfe-Juan, Iles des Embiez, La Ciotat, La Coudourière, La Galère, La Grande-Motte, La Madrague, Le Lavandou, Les Lecques, Les Salettes, Mandelieu-La Napoule, Marina-Baie-des-Anges, Marines-de-Cogolin, Marseille (Vieux Port), Méjean, Menton, Menton-Garavan, Miramar-Trayas, Monaco, Niolon, Nice, Port d'Hyères, Port de la Rague, Port de Miramar, Port de Porquerolles, Port de Santa-Lucia, Port de St-Mandrier, Port du Croton, Port du Niel, Port Gallice, Port Pierre Canto, Port Pothuau, Port-Camargue, Port-Grimaud, Sanary-sur-Mer, Sausset-les-Pins, St-Jean-Cap Ferrat, St-Raphaël, St-Tropez, Ste-Maxime, Théoule-sur-Mer, Toulon, Villefranche.

Mementoes

See Shopping

Opening Times

Shopping Centres
        Shopping centres (centres commerciaux) in the catchment area of large towns are normally open from 9 a.m. until 7 (often 9) p.m., even on Saturdays.

Retail trade
        The opening times for middle-sized and small shops are less

regular. Food shops and bakers open very early in the morning and even on Sundays and public holidays are generally open for part of the day. However, almost all shops close at midday for two or three hours (midday–2 or 3 p.m.).

Food shops

Mon.–Fri. 8 a.m.–7 p.m.; Sat. 8 a.m.–midday (sometimes closed for lunch).

Post Offices

Many places of interest (museums, castles, archaeological sites and some churches) are closed during lunchtime, there are a very few exceptions during the main holiday season.

Places of Interest

It goes without saying that visitors should not look round a church while services are in progress.

Parking

At the principal places of interest there are generally adequate parking facilities (a charge is usually made and sometimes the park is guarded).

In inner urban areas there are so-called "zones bleues" (blue zones) which are appropriately signed. In these zones the motorist must display a disc (disque) which is obtainable from the police or from automobile clubs.
Incidentally, in France parking is permitted on both sides of the road. In roads where parking is permitted on one side only, this may alternate daily or twice a month (stationnement alterné). Yellow lines on the edge of the road indicate that parking is prohibited.

Blue Zone

In addition to conventional parking meters, there have existed for some time in towns the so-called "horodateurs". These are automatic ticket-issuing machines, situated centrally on public car parks. On payment of an appropriate sum, depending on the period of parking required, a ticket is issued and this must be clearly displayed behind the windscreen.

Parking ticket machines

Many public car parks, particularly in inner city areas, are not available for motor or towed caravans. In practice this is ensured by horizontal barriers fixed at a height of 1.9–2 m (6–7 ft) at the entrances.

Note for drivers of motor and towed caravans

On large car parks at important places of interest in particular, but also more generally in popular holiday centres, cases of breaking into and theft from cars are on the increase. If possible no articles of value should be left in a vehicle.

Warning

Post and Telephone

Post offices are open from 8 a.m. until 7 p.m. from Monday to Friday (some close for lunch), and from 8 a.m. until midday on Saturday.

For long-distance and even international calls the coin-boxes are the most convenient.

Telephone

221

Practical Information

From the United Kingdom to France	010 33
From the United States to France	011 33
From Canada to France	011 33
From France to the United Kingdom	19 44
From France to the United States	19 1
From France to Canada	19 1

When dialling from France the zero prefixed to the local dialling code must be omitted.

Public Holidays

1 January (New Year)
Easter Monday
1 May (Labour Day)
Ascension Day
Whit Monday
14 July (National holiday; Storming of the Bastille 1789)
15 August (Assumption of the Virgin Mary)
1 November (All Saints)
25 December

Railways

The most important railway route to Provence is the line from Paris and the Channel ports via Lyon to Avignon, Arles, Marseilles, Toulon, Nice and Monaco into Italy. This route is served by many TEE and express (rapide) trains. Among the expresses with such evocative names as "Mistral", "Ligure", "Phocéen", "Rhodanien", etc., the historic "Train Bleu" is particularly well known.

Since 1981 the "Train à Grande Vitesse" (TEV) has run between Paris and Lyon (with continuation to Montpellier and Marseilles). At present this is the fastest train in the world, reaching speeds of up to 260 km (162 miles) per hour.

In the area of the French Riviera rail connections are good. In addition to the route mentioned above, there are lines from Avignon via Salon, Fos-sur-Mer, Marseilles, Tende to Nice (with connection to Turin) and a branch from the main line between Marseilles and Nice which serves Hyères and Draguignan. Haute Provence, the mountainous hinterland, is served by a line from Marseilles to Gap via Aix-en-Provence and Sisteron, with a branch to Digne.

Excursions

Partly in conjunction with local undertakings the French National Railways organise sightseeing and excursion trips by rail, boat and bus under the title of "Excursions, Services de Tourisme SNCF". Starting-points include Aix-en-Provence, Arles, Aubenas, Avignon, Cannes, Cap d'Agde, Gap, La Grande-Motte, Grasse, Hyères, Marseilles, Menton, Montpellier, Nice, Nîmes, St-Raphaël, St-Tropez, Toulon. Further information may be obtained from local Offices de Tourisme and Syndicats d'Initiative (see Information) or from railway stations.

Access

See entry

Detailed information and particulars of fares, etc. can be obtained from French Railways:
179 Piccadilly, London W1V 0AB (tel. (01) 493 4451/2)
610 Fifth Avenue, New York, N.Y. 10020 (tel. (212) 582 2110)
1500 Stanley Street, Montreal H3A 1R3 P.Q. (tel. (514) 288 8255/6)

Information

Restaurants

Les Arcades, Boulevard Gambetta
Camargue, Rue de la République

Aigues-Mortes

Les Caves Henri IV, 32 Rue Espariat
Vendôme, 2 bis Avenue Napoléon
La Bourguignonne, 10 Rue de la Masse
Le Clam's, 22 Cours Sextius
Les Semailles, 15 Rue Brueys
Abbaye des Cordeliers, 21 Rue Lieutaud

Aix-en-Provence

La Bonne Auberge, on the N7
L'Ecurie Royale, 33 Rue Vauban
La Marguerite, 11 Rue Carnot
Auberge Provençale, Place Nationale
Les Vieux Murs, Avenue Amiral de Grasse
Le Caméo, Place Nationale
La Calèche, 25 Rue Vauban

Antibes

Le Vaccarès, Rue Favorin
Lou Marquès, Boulevard des Lices
Mas de la Chapelle, 5 km to the north
La Provence, Place St-Pierre

Arles

Hiely, 5 Rue de la République
Brunel, 46 Rue de la Balance
Les Trois Clefs, 26 Rue des Trois Faucons
La Vieille Fontaine, 12 Place Crillon
Saint-Didier, 41 Rue de la Saraillerie
Au Pied de Bœuf, 49 Route de Marseille
Le Petit Bedon, 70 Rue Joseph Vernet

Avignon

Auberge du Port, 9 Allées J.-Moulin

Bandol

La Riboto de Taven

Les Baux

Josy-Jo, 2 Rue Planastel
Restaurant des Peintres, Haut-de-Cagnes

Cagnes-sur-Mer

Le Royal Grey, 2 Rue des Etats-Unis
L'Orangeraie, 73 Boulevard de la Croisette
Le Bistingo, Palais des Festivals
Le Croquant, 18 Boulevard Jean Hibert
Félix, 63 Boulevard de la Croisette
Le Festival, 52 Boulevard de la Croisette
La Mirabelle, 24 Rue St-Antoine
Poêle d'Or, 23 Rue des Etats-Unis
Villa Fredante, 14 Rue Bateguier
L'Oriental, 286 Avenue Jourdan

Cannes

Practical Information

| | Rescator, 7 Rue du Maréchal Joffre
Caveau Provençal, 45 Rue Félix Faure |

Carpentras
Le Marijo, 73 Rue Raspail
Le Capucin, 3 bis Avenue du Mont Ventoux
Le Vert Galant, Rue Clapies

Fontaine-de-Vaucluse
Hostellerie du Château Philip

Fréjus
Auberge du Vieux Four, 5–7 Rue Grisolle
Auberge de la Colombe d'Or, on the Bagnols road
Les Potiers, 135 Rue des Potiers

Gap
Manoir de Malcombe, Route des Veynes
Le Patalain, 7 Avenue des Alpes
La Petite Marmite, 79 Rue Carnot

Gordes
Les Bories, on the Sénanque road
Le Mas Tourteron, Les Imberts

Grasse
L'Amphitryon, 16 Boulevard Victor-Hugo
Le Richelieu, Traverse Sidi-Brahim
Chez Pierre, 3 Avenue Thiers

Hyères
Le Roy Gourmet, 11 Rue Ribier
Le Tison d'Or, 1 Rue Galiéni
Taverne Royale, 23 Rue de Limans
Le Delfin's, 7 Rue du Docteur Roux-Seignoret

Le Lavandou
Vieux Port, Quai Gabriel Péri
Le Grill, 22 Rue Patron Ravello

Marseilles
L'Oursinade, Centre de la Bourse
Jambon de Parme, 67 Rue La Palud
Georges Mavro, 2 Canebière
Au Pescadou, 19 Place de Castellane
Max Caizergues, 11 Rue Gustave Ricard
Calypso, 3 Rue des Catalans
Maurice Brun, 18 Quai Rive-Neuve
Cousin-Cousine, 102 Cours Julien
Michel, 6 Rue des Catalans
La Ferme, 23 Rue Sainte
Le Bellecour, 26 Cours Julien
Caruso, 158 Quai du Port
La Maison du Beaujolais, 2 Place Sébastopol
Miramar, 12 Quai du Port

Martigues
Auberge Mirabeau, Place Mirabeau
Gousse d'Ail, 42 Quai du Général Leclerc

Menton
Chez Mireille – L'Ermitage, Promenade du Soleil
La Calanque, 13 Square Victoria

Monaco
Dominique Le Stanc, 18 Boulevard des Moulins
Le Bec Rouge, 11 Avenue Grande-Bretagne
Toula, 20 Boulevard de Suisse
Rampoldi, 3 Avenue des Spélugues
La Calanque, 33 Avenue St-Charles

Le Grillon, 40 Rue Cuiraterie   **Montélimar**
L'Auberge Provençale, Boulevard Marre-Desmarais
Le Vendôme, Place d'Armes
Réserve Rimbaud, 820 Avenue de St-Maur
Le Chandelier, 3 Rue Leenhardt
Menestrel, 2 Impasse Perrier
L'Olivier, 12 Rue Aristide Olivier

L'Ane Rouge, 7 Quai des Deux Emmanuel   **Nice**
L'Esquinade, 5 Quai des Deux Emmanuel
La Girelle Royale, 41 Quai des Etats-Unis
Los Caracoles, 5 Rue St-François-de-Paule
Le Madrigal, 7 Avenue Georges Clemenceau
Le Petit Brouant, 4 bis Rue Gustave Deloye
L'Academia, 15 Rue Alexandre Mari
Le Bistrot de la Promenade, 7 Promenade des Anglais
Boccaccio, 7 Rue Masséna
Le Chalutier, 13 Quai des Deux Emmanuel
Le Grillon, 14 Rue Halevy
Chez les Pêcheurs, 18 Quai des Docks
Auberge du Mas Fleuri, 19 Route d'Aspremont
Aux Gourmets, 12 Rue Dante

A la Louve, 1 Rue de la République   **Nîmes**
Le Lisita, 2 Boulevard des Arènes
Le Niçois, 10 Rue Grizot
Au Chapon Fin, 3 Rue Château Fadaise
La Pergola, 11 Rue Enclos Rey
La Grillade, 44 Rue Nationale

Le Pigraillet, Colline St-Eutrope   **Orange**
Le Forum, 3 Rue Mazeau
L'Arausio, 15 Place St-Martin

La Tartane   **Port-Grimaud**
L'Amphitrite
La Marine

L'Hippocampe, Avenue Winston Churchill   **Roquebrune–Cap-Martin**
Le Grand Inquisiteur, Rue du Château
Les Lucioles, 12 Place de la République

Brûleur de Loups, Avenue G. Leroy   **Stes-Maries-de-la-Mer**
Chanta-Grill, 37 Avenue Frédéric Mistral
Chalut, 39 Avenue Frédéric Mistral
L'Impérial, 1 Place des Impériaux

La Rascasse   **St-Gilles**

Le Scirocco, Quai Albert-Premier   **St-Raphaël**
La Mer, Square de Gand
La Voile d'Or, Boulevard Général de Gaulle
L'Etoile de Mer, Avenue du Comandant Guilbaud
La Bouillabaisse, Place Victor Hugo

Le Jardin de Frédéric, 8 Boulevard Gambetta   **St-Rémy**
Le France, 2 Avenue Fauconnet
La Belle Emilie, 18 Boulevard Victor Hugo
Le Mirabeau, 26 Boulevard Mirabeau
Villa Glanum, on the Les Baux road

Practical Information

St-Tropez	Leï Mouscardins, on the port La Ramade, Rue du Temple L'Escale, Quai Jean Jaurès Le Girelier, on the port
Salon-de-Provence	Francis Robin, 1 Boulevard Georges Clemenceau Craponne, 146 Allées Craponne Le Touring, 20 Place Crousillat
Tarascon	Le Trident, Place Colonel Berrurier Restaurant du Midi, 1 Boulevard Victor Hugo
Toulon	Le Dauphin, 21 bis Rue Jean Jaurès Le Melodia, Place du Théâtre La Calanque, 25 Rue Denfert Rochereau Les Bartavelles, 28 Rue Gimelli L'Hippocampe, Place Louis Blanc
Uzès	L'Abbaye, 23 Place aux Herbes L'Alexandry, 6 Boulevard Gambetta
Vaison-la-Romaine	Domaine de la Cabasse, 10 km outside Le Bateleur, 1 Place Aubanel
Vence	Auberge des Seigneurs, Place Frêne Auberge des Templiers, 39 Avenue du Maréchal Joffre
Food and drink	See entry

Roads

The French road network is close meshed and even minor roads are generally in good condition.

Motorways

The motorways (autoroutes) which have been constructed comparatively recently, now have a total length of 4000 km (2486 miles). Apart from short stretches near large towns their use is subject to tolls (péage).
As far as the area covered in this book is concerned, the motorways (Autoroute du Soleil and Autoroute Provencale) function only as access routes; the tolls and the fact that points at which they can be joined and left are relatively widely spaced, make it advisable to use the national roads for exploring the area.

National Roads

Long-distance traffic still makes great use of the excellently engineered national roads (routes nationales) which correspond approximately to A roads in Great Britain. They are designated by red and white stone kilometre posts which bear the road number (e.g. N555) and frequently have three lanes, the centre lane being used for overtaking. Since the network of roads is so dense, the volume of traffic is generally small; long delays, however, can be caused at holiday times on the principal access roads.

Provincial Roads

Provincial roads (routes départementales) are marked with yellow and white kilometre posts (e.g. D555); important stretches are of similar quality to the national roads.

Shopping, Souvenirs

A speciality of Provence is perfume (especially in Grasse) and toilet waters (lavender water, etc.). Also popular are the "herbes de Provence", aromatic herbs which are on sale everywhere.
Articles of daily use and handcrafted objects made from olive-wood can be found in great variety catering for every taste; the same is true of pottery (especially from the world-famous potteries of Vallauris). Unusual souvenirs are the so-called "santons" – Provençal crib figures.
Lovers of music will also be attracted by records and cassettes of Provençal songs.

Son et Lumière

At places of touristic interest the spectacle Son et Lumière (sound and light) takes place after sunset during the summer. Accompanied by lighting effects, often of theatrical quality, historical or legendary episodes are presented to the audience in a kind of radio play; sometimes scenic effects are also introduced.

Souvenirs

See Shopping, Souvenirs

Speed Restrictions

See Traffic Regulations

Summer Time

See Time

Telephone

See Post

Time

From October to March France observes Central European Time, one hour ahead of Greenwich Mean Time; from the end of March to the end of September Summer Time (two hours ahead of GMT) is in force.

Tipping

Tips (pourboire) are normally given in similar circumstances and in similar amounts to those in the United Kingdom.
In addition, guides at castles, museums, etc. and usherettes in theatres and cinemas expect a tip.

Tourist Information

See Information

Traffic Regulations

Driving on the Right

As in other continental countries, vehicles in France travel on the right.

Seat Belts

Seat belts must be worn while the vehicle is in motion.

Right of Way

In general a vehicle approaching from the right has priority (priorité à droite signs are often displayed); at a roundabout, however, vehicles actually negotiating the roundabout have priority. Roads on which traffic has the right of way are marked "passage protégé" at the approach of a junction.

Lighting

In built-up areas where street lighting is adequate side lights are prescribed; at night warning signals may only be given by flashing one's headlights, car horns should not be used.
Adapting headlights to produce the amber-coloured beam customary in France is not mandatory for foreign vehicles, but British vehicles should fit beam-deflectors.

Speed Restrictions

Maximum speeds for vehicles in France:
on motorways 130 km (81 miles) per hour
on twin-track main roads 110 km (68 miles) per hour
on other main roads (routes nationales and routes départe-mentales) 90 km (56 miles) per hour
in built-up areas 60 km (37 miles) per hour
During rain the maximum permitted speeds are reduced from 130 km to 100 km (62 miles) per hour and from 100 km and 90 km to 80 km (50 miles) per hour.
A driver who has not held a driving licence for more than one year may not drive faster than 90 km (56 miles) per hour.

Parking Regulations

See Parking

Travel Documents

Personal Documents

For citizens of the United Kingdom, the United States of America and Canada a passport only is required for entry into France.

Vehicle Documents

A national driving licence and vehicle licence are recognised and must be taken. A "green card" (international insurance

certificate) is advisable. All foreign cars visiting France must display an international distinguishing sign of the approved pattern and design. Failure to do so can result in a fine.
It is advisable to take out personal insurance cover before departure.

Health insurance is available to nationals of EEC countries on the same basis as for French citizens. British citizens should obtain form E111 from the DHSS in good time and return it to obtain a certificate of entitlement.

Health Insurance

Walking

The hinterland and increasingly the coastal region are both popular with walkers and climbers.

A few long-distance footpaths (Sentiers de Grande Randon-née; short form GR plus the number of the footpath) in Provence should be mentioned.
GR9 goes from the Montagne du Lubéron, via Vauvenargues, the Montagne Ste-Victoire and the Chaîne de la Ste-Baume, thence through the Massif des Maures to the Gulf of St-Tropez.
GR4 crosses the eastern summit of the Montagne du Lubéron near Montfuron, crosses the Durance at Manosque, follows the Verdon as far as Castellane, then continues east into the region of the Maritime Alps, climbs over the Montagne du Cheiron and reaches Grasse across the Plaine des Roches.
GR5 leads from Nice over Mont Chauvre d'Aspremont to the Gorges de la Vésubie and then goes northwards into the region of the High Alps.

Long-distance Footpaths

Comité National des Sentiers de Grande Randonnée
92 Rue de Clignancourt
F-75883 Paris

Information

Water Sports

The varied nature of the coast is favourable for many kinds of water sports. As well as stretches of sand and pebbles, which are especially suitable for families and wind surfers, there are, in the more rocky parts, for example along the Corniche de l'Esterel and the Corniche des Maures, many charming bays and good places for diving. However, the density and variety of marine life have considerably declined in recent years through overfishing, underwater hunting and pollution.

Bathing Prohibited

Bathing Dangerous

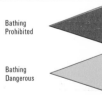

Since conditions of wind and current can change very quickly, most of the larger beaches have a warning system which should be strictly observed in one's own interests. Coloured pennants indicate the prevailing conditions.

Bathing without restriction

Beach Warning System

See entry

Marinas

When to Go

Because of the relatively mild climate, blossom appears early (mimosa blossom from the end of January). This and the pleasant water temperature early in the year make spring an ideal time for a visit to the Côte d'Azur. It must be added, however, that at this time of the year there is quite a lot of welcome rain (many fossils washed out of the rocks on the hillsides can be found). For places at a higher altitude in the hinterland, late spring and early summer are more suitable for a visit.

In the very dry summer season, the heat of which is often interrupted by the cold air currents of the Mistral, the real character of Provence comes into its own, especially when the lavender is in flower. At this season the gorges and clues of Haute Provence, which at other times are accessible only with difficulty, can be explored, or the calanques to the east of Marseilles can be visited without undue risk. A visit to the coast in July and August, however – that is in the high season – can on the other hand suffer from the effects of overcrowding. Thanks to the warm sea-water, bathing is sometimes possible until well into the somewhat rainy season in autumn.

Mild winters made the coast of Provence attractive from the earliest days of tourism. Well-known and well-equipped winter sports resorts are to be found chiefly in the Alpine parts of Haute Provence, east of a line from Cannes through Sisteron to Gap.

Wine

Viticulture

Wine has always been the national drink of France, even though the consumption of beer has gone up in recent times. In addition to good local wines, superior quality wines are also produced. Vineyards are concentrated in the Départements of Bouches-sur-Rhône, Var, Vaucluse and Alpes-Maritimes. Wine production in this area goes back to the Greek colonisation in the 7th–6th c. BC, and is thus the oldest in the whole of France.

Language of the wine-label

Appellation contrôlée: An indication of the place of origin (the right to which is strictly controlled)
Cépage: Type of vine
Clos (before a personal name): vineyard, district
Cuvée: Blending
Vendage tardive: Late-gathered grapes
Vin délimité de qualité supérieure (VDQS): A wine of high quality from a particular area
Grand vin, grand cru, grande réserve or réserve exceptionelle indicate wine with more than 11 Vol-% alcohol content.

Wines of Provence

In Provence there are four wines classified as appellation contrôlée: Palette, from the area of Aix-en-Provence, red, white and rosé, generally light and fruity; Cassis, from the area to the east of Marseilles, predominantly fresh, very dry white wine and full-bodied red wine; Bandol, from the area around La Ciotat and Toulon, pleasant red wines, often with a slight bouquet of violets; also full-bodied fresh dry white wine; Bellet, from the area of Nice, light, elegant red wines and fresh white wines.

The best-known centre of viticulture in this region is Châteauneuf-du-Pape, where production is almost exclusively devoted to red wine. It is pressed from various sorts of grape and with increasing age acquires a rich bouquet. The vintners of Châteauneuf-du-Pape were among the initiators of legislation which has laid down exact standards for the classification according to quality and for the labelling of wines.

Châteauneuf-du-Pape

Youth Hostels

There are about 300 youth hostels (auberges de jeunesse) in France; these can be used by young people in possession of an international identity card, obtainable from the headquarters of their national organisation. In July and August advance booking is necessary; generally a stay in any one youth hostel is limited to three nights.

Auberges de la Jeunesse

Fédération Unie des Auberges de Jeunesse
6 Rue Mesnil
F-75116 Paris
tel. (1) 2 61 84 03

Information

Index

232

Notes

Notes

Notes

The Principal Sights at a Glance